Too Many Women

GERALD HANBURY, BACHELOR.

TOO MANY
WOMEN

A BACHELOR'S
STORY

SECOND EDITION

NEW YORK
FREDERICK A. STOKES COMPANY
PUBLISHERS

TOO MANY
WOMEN

A BACHELOR'S
STORY

SECOND EDITION

NEW YORK
FREDERICK A. STOKES COMPANY
PUBLISHERS

CONTENTS

CONTENTS

"Why do I keep single? Perhaps I love too many women too well,—or, possibly, too many too little!"—JOHN OLIVER HOBBES, "The Ambassador," Act I.

TOO MANY WOMEN

Too Many Women

JANUARY

*The Complete Bachelors—An Unconventional Friend-
ship—The House Party at the Bellews'—Clive
Massey, Englishman*

"MARRIAGE is a mug's game."
George Burn screwed his eyeglass in with a
grimace, and crossed his feet on the mantelpiece, as
though he had said something clever. Archie Haines
and myself exclaimed "Hear, hear!" We are both
in the thirties, so we ought to have known better. At
that moment the maid entered with a letter.

"Another check from one of your Fleet Street pals,
Hanbury?" asked Haines idly. I double the rôles
of barrister and "free lance" indifferently, yet Haines
always talks as though I had found a gold mine.

"No such luck," I replied, scrutinizing the envelope.
"It's from my fond parent. Excuse me!" and drawing out the contents I read the following:

"MY DEAR GERALD:
"We were glad to have news of you and your doings the other day, and to hear that you are making
progress in that combination of law and literature
which you call 'your profession.' But your mother
and I are getting a little anxious about your future.
You show no signs of settling down, although you are
now at an age when most young men have undertaken

the responsibilities of marriage, and all that marriage means. Nothing would give us greater pleasure than to hear you had concentrated your wandering affections upon a particular object. I don't mean that you ought to propose to the first girl you meet, but I do think you should seriously contemplate matrimony. I offer you this intimate advice in your own interest. The middle-aged bachelor is a constant source of anxiety to himself and his friends, and I should be sorry to see you playing that unsatisfactory rôle. Moreover, the wider interests of life are not entered upon until one is married.

"Your mother is the more concerned about you, as she thinks she notices a growing inclination on your part to frivolous self-indulgence. Let me say that I don't quite share her view, which is colored by her maternal anxiety, but I do think you want a little more ballast if your career is to be the successful one we have every reason to anticipate it will be. There is no better ballast than a wife.

"Your affectionate Father."

"George! Archie," I said, as I finished my private perusal of the document, "what do you think of this?" And I proceeded to repeat the contents aloud for my companions' benefit. George's only comment on my father's effusion was to whistle through his teeth, an objectionable habit which does not endear him to his friends.

"A very proper letter," remarked Haines. He is a stockbroker and enjoys his little joke. "It's a scandal, Hanbury, that you haven't long since recognized your responsibilities in the matter. You'll be getting gray-haired before you've found a wife."

"I shall be gray-haired precious soon after I've found one," I retorted. "What about George, though? Isn't he to be included in your indictment?"

"Oh, George!" And Haines shrugged his shoulders. "George's heart is licensed to carry twelve inside. If Lady Lucy and the rest of them like to strap hang in his affections, it's no concern of ours. You're a respectable and responsible member of Society. George isn't!"

George smiled fatuously. He positively reveled in his infamy. But if once the conversation gets on to George Burn and his escapades, it has a knack of staying there. This time I was determined it shouldn't.

"Seriously," I said, "must I give up all this?"— and I waved my arm round the comfortable Jermyn Street room in which we sat, littered with the trophies of the bachelor from gun cases to pipe cleaners,— "because my father thinks I want more ballast?— Ballast!"

"You needn't swear, Hanbury!" interrupted Haines. "Think what you get in return!"

"Five foot four of chiffon and lace, and a yard of milliner's bills every quarter," put in George, roused by the controversy from his reverie. "The fault I find with the whole system," he went on, "is that one never knows what one's getting. Put a wedding ring on a woman's finger, and you change her whole nature. The simple little girl from the vicarage, who ought to be a model of domesticity, makes a bee line for the Smart Set, while the fashionable young woman, who is to found a salon, and win her husband a place in the Cabinet, throws her curling tongs into the area, and becomes a District Visitor. Look at Basil!"

"Poor old Basil!" Haines' voice had a reflective note of melancholy. "But then, what could you expect from a fellow who thought all beautiful women were good, and whose idea of marriage was holding his wife's hand in the spare time he wasn't showing her off to an admiring world at the Carlton? Besides, Basil found his taste at twenty-eight wasn't quite the same as it had been three years earlier, and that he had nothing in common with his wife save selfishness and ignorance of life. He wanted to dine at home sometimes, but she didn't. He wanted to ask his own friends to shoot, but she had always filled the house with hers. Her notion of economy was to cut short her husband's cigars, and dock his wine bill. He thought he could retrench on his wife's dress allowance. As a consequence Basil lives at his club, and Mrs. B—— in her electric brougham."

"And the best place for them," I said, as I got up from my chair by the fire, and crossing over to the American roll-top desk with its tangle of proofsheets and manuscripts, that are the heritage of the literary man, proceeded to seat myself in front of the necessary writing materials.

"What shall I reply to my father?"

George squirted some soda water into a glass. "Say his idea is all rot, and that you aren't 'taking any.'"

"Do put your suggestions in English, and not dialect!"

George made a fresh start. "My dear Dad," he dictated.

I laid my pen down. "If you can't do better than that, you must leave it to Archie. Archie?" And I turned to where Haines lay stretched at ease.

"What line do you want me to take?" that individual asked. "Tentative or abrupt, a gentle toying with the proposal, or a stern rejection?"

"Please yourself," I said. "Only don't be too dramatic!"

Haines cleared his throat and began:

"Your letter has come as a great surprise to me, but a wholesome one. I realize how little I have done to deserve your affection, and how ill I have requited it by my indolence and selfishness. I see things in their true light at last, and am prepared to meet your wishes in every way. Please put up my banns as soon as possible with any lady you like, and your choice in the matter shall be that of your repentant son, Gerald."

"There's a model of filial obedience for you," and Haines looked at me for approval. "Why, you haven't taken a word of it down, Hanbury!"

"I could have done better for you than that," exclaimed George.

"My dear Archie," I said, "if you knew my father's taste in the fair sex you wouldn't leave the choice to him. Also you magnify my sense of duty. I may be thoughtless, but I'm not qualifying for an asylum just yet. Try again on the other tack."

Haines assumed an expression of pained solicitude, but he obeyed.

"Nothing could give me greater pleasure than to fall in with your and mother's idea. I know I have been an unsatisfactory son to you both——"

"Haines!" I spoke sharply. "Not so much stress on the 'unsatisfactory,' if you please! I don't want lessons from you in how to behave to my people."

Haines, however, was wound up, and my admonition passed unheeded.

"—and that I have caused you much anxiety in the past. For the future, it shall be my task to do all I can for you, to live within my allowance, to consort only with good companions, and generally to live a blameless life. But I regret I cannot obey you where marriage is concerned. I was born a bachelor——"

"Who ever heard of any one being born anything else?" interrupted George, with an emphasis of scorn.

"—and a bachelor I shall remain, holding that with Woman 'distance lends enchantment to the view.' Your devoted son, Gerald."

I rose and held out my hand to Haines. "Archie, there's a fortune awaiting you in the East as a professional letter writer, but you're of no use to me. I'll do the job for myself when you and George have gone."

"Answer the confounded thing in any way you like, Hanbury," growled Haines, as the pair made a consorted raid on my whisky and cigarettes preparatory to departure. "You might display a little gratitude, anyhow."

I held the door open.

"I'm full of gratitude to you for showing me how not to do it. If I sent your precious letter I should be either married to a female who would have no thoughts above following the beagles, or find myself cut off with a shilling as a hypocrite."

"You know nothing about diplomacy," retorted the retreating Haines.

"You know less about my father." And the door closed on him.

Then I sat down again and wrote this:

"DEAR FATHER:

"It's awfully good of you and mother to be so concerned about my prospects, professional and matrimonial. I'm not doing much in the way of bar work yet, as I don't possess the influence or ability which make for success on the part of the briefless barrister. If I do happen to meet the daughter of a leading solicitor at a dance or elsewhere she's always so plain that I can't persuade myself to advance my legal prospects at the expense of my reputation as a man of taste.

"As regards your advice that I should 'seriously contemplate matrimony,' I do contemplate it seriously, so seriously that I can't undertake it for the present. I've not got the qualities to make a woman happy. I am too particular about my meals, and I should insist upon smoking in the drawing-room. I should hate to shatter any young girl's ideals of my sex. If I married an unselfish woman, I'd make her miserable, if a selfish one, she'd make me miserable. Perhaps some day I may come across a good and beautiful girl who will look after me as a labor of love. I want too much supervision to marry any one who doesn't fully realize the responsibilities she is undertaking.

"You say I show no signs of settling down. I should be false to my ambitions and ideals if I underwent the process of settling down that most married men undergo, the settling down that one sees in a pudding, into a solid and indigestible mass. I don't want my horizon limited by the four walls of a suburban villa. I am confident I can be successful on my own lines, but they are not the narrow gauge of married life. Of course, I am prepared to admit that my views may undergo a change. At present I am heart-whole, and likely to remain so. When I am mortally wounded in the duel of sex, my outcry will summon the only physician able to effect a cure, namely the rector of a fashionable church.

"Please impress upon mother that what she thinks is self-indulgence is merely the necessary manifestation of the artistic life. You might add that I am always on the look-out for a cheaper cigar than a shilling Upman that is fit to smoke, but so far I haven't been able to find one.

"Your affectionate son,
"GERALD."

After all, there are some things a man does best for himself. Whatever Haines may be able to do in the way of "bulling the market" and "selling a bear," he can't write letters.

.   .   .   .   .

I am beginning to think that I haven't handled my acquaintance with Cynthia Cochrane with quite the sure touch I am accustomed to show. This morning I got the following note from her, written with a spluttering nib in her dressing-room at the "Alcazar" Theater:

"DEAR OLD BOY:

"I'm beginning to get a wee bit angry with you for not coming to look me up once last week. I don't like being neglected by my friends, and especially such an old one as you are. Do be a pal, Gerald, and come and see me! I've had the 'blues' lately, and you're the best person I know to chase them away.

"Yours with love (if you want it),
"CYNTHIA."

Cynthia was with a touring company at a Devonshire seaside place when I first met her some nine years ago now. I was a member of what was, in Oxford language, called a " reading party," but which really proved an association of five undergraduates for golfing, fishing—anything, in fact, rather than for the acquisition of sufficient legal knowledge to pass the examiners in the Honor School of Law. It was a windy morning on the Esplanade, and Miss Cochrane's hat blew off just as she came abreast of George Burn and myself, who were sitting on the sea wall discussing her points. The hat was in a particularly frisky mood, and it gamboled and skipped down the stone causeway as if it were in training for the sprint at the 'Varsity sports. George and I gave it twenty yards start, and then raced after it like two grayhounds slipped for the Waterloo Cup. George possessed a better turn of speed than I did, but just as he reached the quarry it gave a swerve, and I pounced on it with such vigor that my fist went through the straw crown. What with George's language and Miss Cochrane's laughter when I brought the wreckage back, I lost my head and asked her to come to tea with us as a sign that I had her forgiveness. With a friend she came, and conquered, and the reading party took five stalls for the remaining nights of the *Golden Belle*.

The climax of our hospitality was reached by a supper-party after the last performance on the Saturday, and for which the local cellars and provision merchants' were ransacked for appropriate delicacies. To the hosts, whose hearts glowed with a delightful sense of Bohemian abandon, the festivity was a triumph, unclouded by the landlady's hair-net falling into the soup tureen, or the hired waiter's partiality for " bubbly water," indulged in behind the screen. As for our guests, we thought them peerless, although one of the ladies was old enough to be our mother, another's complexion ran into crimson streaks during the feast, and a third's conversational resources were limited to an explanation why she ought to have been the leading lady, from which position apparently some " envious cat " had ousted her. I was finally aroused, by her eternal iteration of this fact, to the point of telling her that any one with half an eye could see why she wasn't playing the " lead." Thereupon she relapsed into silence for the rest of the proceedings. We speeded the company away at midday on Sunday, and I was left with a signed photograph, and a scented lace handkerchief, to mark the episode.

The mental stress of my " Schools," and the excitements of autumn sport, drove recollection of the affair from my thoughts. Following my golden rule, I made no attempt to correspond with Cynthia. I discourage casual correspondence between the sexes on the ground that the sentiments on the paper are never interpreted in the sense in which they were written. I don't like a girl reading between the lines, and then getting annoyed because one's actions don't come up to her imaginary standard. If I have anything to tell a woman, I'll unburden myself in speech. When I write, " I'm so sorry I shan't see you till Tuesday, as I am going out of town," it means what it says, and not " O my darling, how the hours will drag till I gaze into your eyes once more." And yet nine women out of ten would put the second construction on the simple sentence if one had paid them any attentions. I repeat that I had forgotten about Cynthia

till a postcard suddenly announced the end of the tour
and Cynthia's arrival in London.

Since then my acquaintance has run the normal
course of such friendships—a Covent Garden ball
together, motor drives to the Metropole at Brighton,
and the Star and Garter at Richmond, lunches at the
Trocadero and Pagani's, a never-to-be-forgotten dinner at Kettner's and suppers galore. Cynthia would be
away for months at a time on a tour, undergoing the
nerve-destroying experiences of Sunday train jour-
neys from one end of England and Scotland to the
other, of incessant shiftings of wardrobes and paraphernalia from theater to theater, of the discomforts
of theatrical lodgings—but so soon as ever she came
back I would always hear from her, and we picked up
our friendship where it had dropped, the threads un-
raveled by time.

Cynthia's touring days ended eighteen months ago
with the securing of a pantomime engagement at the
Paddington "Grand," where the sale of her picture
postcards representing her as Little Boy Blue broke
all records. Her performance in the character was so
superior to the general standard of "principal boys"
that Mason of the "Alcazar" secured her on a three
years' contract, and immediately cast her for an important part in his "new and original musical play."
I expected that, with the rise in her fortunes and consequent demand for her company on the part of the
numerous section of society which regards supper
with stage favorites as a form of tonic, I should see
less and less of Cynthia, but with a constancy that it
is unusual to find across the footlights, she continued
to accept my invitations, even at the expense of other
folks'. The great bond between the actress and myself

is that we take each other's friendship as a matter of course, our intimacy needing none of those forced displays of affection to keep it going which so many theatrical acquaintanceships require.

I have begun of late, however, to notice a subtle change in Cynthia's outlook on the world. She is beginning to wonder whether the stage does not unfit its votaries for family life. Usually so independent, she now proclaims the fact that she is tired of wandering about on her own; ordinarily so ambitious, she hesitated for a long time before she decided to sign her contract with Mason, and gain the advertisement of the " Alcazar." I don't like those symptoms, nor the firm belief she professes in platonic friendship. Now, if I am certain of one thing it is that such a state of suspended animation in the affections is impossible for men and women. There can be no standing still in friendship between the sexes. Sooner or later one of the pair will cross the frontier dividing friendship from love.

It was at the dinner at Kettner's, served in one of the *cabinets particuliers* for which that famous Bohemian restaurant is justly renowned, where the soft-tinted hangings on the walls, the antique, gold-embossed furniture, and the general atmosphere of mellow peace and seclusion brooding over the old-world surroundings fill the guests with a sense of curious expectation, as though of some cherished secret of existence about to be revealed,—it was at Kettner's that Cynthia caused me serious embarrassment by bursting into floods of tears and sobbing out how unhappy she was. I look upon the emotions of theatrical ladies as part of the business—so much stage thunder—but a man's vanity is inclined to take the individual feelings he arouses as unique and lasting. Were a woman to say that she liked me, I should believe she was my devoted admirer, but should another of my sex be the object of her avowal, I should unhesitatingly call him conceited, if he treated the matter as anything more than the lightest badinage. Therefore I took the display as a personal compliment, dropped the air of amused and tolerant cynicism I adopt, as a rule, for my own protection, and did my best to console Cynthia, my sympathy taking the extremely ineffective form of stroking her hand and telling her that the waiter must not see her with red eyes, that a becoming hat was not improved by being crushed against a dress coat, and that the darkest clouds have a silver lining—an irritating aphorism bearing, by the way, no relation to the facts of life. Amidst the storm of weeping, I gathered that nobody cared for her, that I was very unkind, and she wished we had never met. I pointed out that there was no logical connection between her premises and conclusion, also that it was absurd to say that nobody cared for her, because I did. I meant neither more nor less than that. I *am* quite fond of Cynthia—in a way; she is amusing and lively, with a point of view of her own, her life of independent exertion having given her a broader outlook than that possessed by the insipid damsels of society, who relapse into silence as soon as they have exhausted the topics of the ballroom floor and the latest engagement. I *am* fond of Cynthia in a way, but not a marrying way, merely one of good fellowship. Woman-like, Cynthia read a good deal more into my sympathetic efforts, for she took an unfair advantage of me by turning up her face to be kissed. I believe I possess

self-control in no slight degree, but it doesn't survive
a test such as Cynthia submitted to it. I give a pair
of blue eyes, a rosebud mouth and a dimpled chin anything they ask. I kissed Cynthia—and more than
once. After that it was no good protesting that I only
took a fatherly interest in the welfare of a charming
young actress, so I threw myself with zest into the
rôle of an ardent lover, but it wasn't till next morning,
with a damp fog showing white against my window-
panes, that I realized I had, perhaps, overacted the
part.

Since that night I have taken to seeing Cynthia not
more than once a week, on the theory that " absence
does *not* make the heart grow fonder," although in
her case the system can't be said to have yielded satisfactory results. I object to district messenger boys
coming round before I am out of my bath with frantic
notes ordering me to be at the Marble Arch in a
" taxi " at three, " third tree from the left." I don't
like to be told to " hurry up with the earrings you
promised me, because Cissy is making all the girls
green with jealousy over her pearl necklace."
What's Hecuba to me, or I to Hecuba?

All the same I must settle up something, and
quickly. The worst is that, while I can exercise common sense over the affair here in my rooms, that
quality is conspicuous by its absence when I meet the
fair enemy face to face. Anyhow, in my sober moments I agree with Steward, my old colleague on the
Evening Star, who once said to me in a moment of
confidence, " Half the crimes and all the follies of the
world are due to women. The chief advantage of
Fleet Street is that they are there kept at arm's length
—generally behind a typewriter. The only editor I

knew who tolerated them compounded with his creditors for seven shillings and sixpence in the pound, but he was mentally bankrupt years before he filed his petition." George Burn holds similar views, but more coarsely expressed: "Women are all right as ornaments in a drawing-room, or for driving in a hansom with, but they are infernal nuisances as a permanency." As George has three unmarried sisters I discount his opinion.

The problem of my relations with Cynthia must wait. I can't be bothered to do anything just yet until I've decided once and for all whether I shall change my tailor for the fellow in Seville Row whom Haines recommended. My last tail coat was nothing less than an outrage. Still, I might as well run round this afternoon and take the little girl out for a drive to cheer her up. After the good times we've had together, I mustn't be too abrupt in my behavior to her. Besides, her eyes have just the shade of blue I can't resist.

. . . . .

What a pity it is that there aren't more hostesses like Mrs. Bellew! If there were, I should never suffer the agonies of doubt and hesitation that rack me whenever I receive country-house invitations, doubts as to whether the discomfort of packing, traveling, and the cancelling of other engagements by excuses more or less ingenious will be compensated for by pleasures equal to those I am leaving behind in my flat, and the dwellings of hospitable cockneys. But about Southlands there can be no misgivings. From the tea at one's bedside at 8 A. M. till the last "nightcap" before turning in any time after midnight, everything is done that can make the bachelor rejoice. The valeting is perfection, the bath is laid on exactly right, the hot dishes and fresh toast at breakfast outlast the appetite of the most voracious, and the appearance of the most belated guest. There is none of the dragooning of visitors in the choice of the day's programme, too often indulged in from a mistaken sense of hospitality, so one can shoot, fish, ride, play bezique, or "kiss-in-the-ring" with equal freedom. Old Bellew doesn't keep his best wine and cigars for the Lord-Lieutenant and the county bigwigs, but puts '92 Pommery, and Havanas of a crop which never knew the Yankee and his manures, before briefless barristers and newly gazetted subalterns. His wife exercises equal generosity and taste in the matter of the girls she has staying with her. When she marched into the Hunt ball the other night at the head of her forces, she was followed by the acknowledged belles of the evening. Dolly Thurston and Faith Bellew would hold their own in Belgrave Square, or at the Ritz. Down in Loamshire they made all the other women look guys.

But the favors I have received from Mrs. Bellew, and the favors I hope to receive, cannot blind me to the fact that there is a serious flaw in her character, which, in many of my friends' eyes, would outweigh everything in her favor. She is a matrimonial harpy, and lives for little else than to find husbands for Faith and Sybil. Now, matchmaking ought to require a license from the State, just as much as the carrying of fire arms, for I fail to see why a person may, with impunity, wreck two lives, when, in the latter case, carelessness only involves injury to an individual. Mrs. Bellew finds an intrinsic merit in matrimony which justifies her in attacking the celibacy of every bachelor crossing her threshold, on behalf of her two "olive branches," who might be suitably left to grow alone for a few years before being grafted elsewhere. We owe more to the gardening propensities of Adam and Eve than is usually reckoned.

Faith, the eldest of Mrs. Bellew's girls, has the sweet and unselfish temperament which so often goes with brown eyes and a black bow in the hair. A model daughter, she is prepared to fall in with any of her masterful mother's plans, and take a spouse with the same unquestioning belief in her parent's competency and goodness of heart as in nursery days she received a box of bricks. Sybil, on the other hand, is one of those big, healthy girls, with a complexion that defies the arts of the toilet table, a manner that her friends describe as "bright," and her critics as "boisterous," and not an ounce of sentiment in her.

Knowing Mrs. Bellew's methods I kept wide awake the first night at Southlands, and soon discovered from the way in which his hostess drew him to her side throughout the evening, smiled sweetly when he upset the mint sauce over her flowered silk at dinner, and sent him into the hall with Faith while the rest of us thought of something, "animal, vegetable, or mineral," that Major Griffiths was her prospective victim. The Major gave the impression that he had been born with a grape in his mouth and vine leaves in his hair; not so much from what he said, though that was worth listening to after the ladies had left the room, but from what he did with the various vintages that appeared in generous sequence. He had reached that age when every mother thought he was bound to succumb to the charms of her own child, and he was what a Socialist orator would have called "one

of the idle rich." His fellow clubmen were divided
on the point as to whether Griffiths was single from
choice, or from the disillusionment of an unsuccessful
affaire du cœur in his more active and romantic days,
but whatever the cause which had made shipwreck
of his domestic ideals, leaving him at forty-five a derelict, to the casual observer his mental outlook was
twofold. When he was not engaged in thinking of
his next meal, he was wondering how soon he could
get a bridge four going. But Mrs. Bellew must have
looked upon such a diagnosis as superficial, or else had
had the benefit of a moment's unguarded confidence
from the Major on one of those occasions, such as tea
and hot scones after a wet day's shooting, or supper-
time at a dance, when the soul of man is expansive
and communicative. She, at all events, had no doubts
about her and Faith's capacity to capture that much-
assaulted citadel, the Major's heart.

Once, in the long ago, Mrs. Bellew cherished the
notion of a hopeless affection on my part for Sybil,
a delusion founded largely, I am convinced, on my
outspoken admiration for the latter's prowess at center-
half in a mixed hockey match against a neighboring
house party. Sybil, still in the school-room, and with
her hair flying wild, performed prodigies of skill on
that particular occasion, and was largely instrumental
for her side's success, but earnest concentration has
failed to recall any remembrance that I incriminated
myself very deeply, or uttered sentiments which could
have been construed into a pledge in a court of law,
even with a jury of susceptible tradesmen ready to
stretch every point of the evidence in order to show
their sympathy with the fair plaintiff. A long course
of flippancy on my part, however, has saved me from

having Mrs. Bellew take the field in force against my inaction, because nothing is so effective in counter-acting the schemes of matchmaking chaperones as the assumption of an air of irresponsibility. The toils that would capture a lion are harmless to a mouse, and the social jester forms one of the congregation at the wedding of the man who takes himself seriously. But on the occasion of my visit last week to Southlands for two balls, and a third shoot through the covers, I was compelled to see a good deal of Sybil, even at the risk of "reviving old desires," as Omar Khayyam says, in certain quarters, for the simple reason that there was no other young woman disengaged to re-ceive my attentions. Griffiths was forced by the un-obtrusive yet effectual surveillance of Mrs. Bellew to dance attendance on Faith at a time of life when the last thing he wanted to do was to dance at all.

Dolly Thurston, who, with her mother, Lady Susan, was also staying in the house, had already found a kindred soul in Clive Massey, still up at the 'Varsity and unable to resist the appeal which her soft fluffi-ness and gentle ways made to his young manhood, while he had roused the girl's sympathetic interest by his recital of episodes from his unhappy and murky past, a pastime in which youths of such a blameless type as Massey usually excel. Dolly shared each stand of Massey's during the cover shooting, played his accompaniments after tea, and challenged him to post-prandial picquet in the quietest corner of the back drawing-room. When Lady Susan took it into her head to unburden herself of the hopes and fears con-nected with the social future of her daughter, I was thoroughly competent to reassure her on that score. As Lady Susan was short-sighted, I didn't feel justi-

fied in spoiling Dolly's week by supporting my
general proposition as to the girl's ability to take care
of herself, with a particular instance.   Lady Susan,
for all she talks about Dolly, knows very little concerning her, an ignorance she shares with several
worldly matrons of my acquaintance.

I did my best under the circumstances to please
everybody.   Sybil had supper and three dances with
me at the Hunt Ball, I took her twice into dinner
without a murmur, and read the *Field* from cover to
cover so as to be more fully equipped with topics of
conversation congenial to her cast of mind.   In defiance of all my natural instincts, Massey was left in
undisputed possession of Miss Thurston's society.
Moreover, I turned a deaf ear to the Major's appeals
that I should come to his assistance and take upon my
shoulders a share of those obligations which the
hostess had laid on his.

"Hanbury," he said once, when he had outstayed
the others in the smoking-room, "you'd enjoy a talk
with Miss Bellew; she's no end of a clever little thing."

"That's why you are such pals," I replied.   "Opposite drawn to opposite."

Griffiths, who had buried his nose in his tumbler,
turned a doleful face upon me at the conclusion of the
draught.

"I'm not a lady's man," he remarked.   "Don't
understand 'em, or want to, but I can't quite tell Mrs.
Bellew that.   I'd take it as very friendly, Hanbury,
if you'd play up to the girl a bit, and knock any ideas
out of the mother's head"; and Griffiths mopped
his fiery face with a fiery bandanna.

I refused to undertake such a task, not out of
an unfriendly spirit to Griffiths—for I had the same

feeling for him that I have for a newly born infant, genuine pity that such helpless innocence has been cast on a rough world—but because I was on my good behavior while under Mr. Bellew's roof. His high pheasants are not to be lightly cast away out of quixotic sympathy for one of his wife's victims.

As the week dragged on—I use the word "dragged" advisedly, for "duty," in spite of the many laudatory attributes the evangelists and poets endow it with, is essentially its own reward, no "purse of fifty sovs." being added where it is concerned—I wished myself back in London—London, which held Cynthia Cochrane, George Burn, the Club, and all the unhallowed delights of bachelorhood, and away from Southlands with its managing mother, and its managed daughters, Griffiths, who drew the best stand of the best drive of the best day, and then missed the rocketing birds because he felt so down on his luck, as he explained to me later, Massey, who monopolized the really nice girl of the party without any regard for his seniors' points of view. An English country house, "replete with every modern convenience," as the advertisements describe it, and surrounded by well-stocked covers, is less than nothing if the company assembled in it is composed of inharmonious elements, and inharmonious they certainly were at Southlands last week. I might have left without a single pleasant memory other than the wine and cigars, had I not on the fifth day, while sitting with the rest in the hall after lunch—that meal having been partaken of indoors, owing to rain making outside sport impossible—taken occasion to draw attention to the gloom on Major Griffiths' face.

"Did you see a ghost last night?" demanded

Clive Massey. The Major had—the ghost of his dead peace of mind—but no one thought of that.

Lady Susan surveyed the shrinking soldier through her lorgnon. Griffiths is a modest man, and the interest he was arousing effectually sealed his lips. I was minded to offer some plausible explanation of his silence.

I turned to Lady Susan.

"The Major has a guilty conscience. As you make your bed, so must you lie upon it."

"I regard that remark as extremely indelicate," replied the lady so addressed, with hauteur. "I am not accustomed, Mr. Hanbury, to make beds."

"You mistake me," I rejoined hastily, and stumbled from bad to worse, "I was referring to the Major's bed."

"That will do!" Lady Susan drew herself up with all the frigid dignity at her command. "I am not concerned in the slightest with Major Griffiths' preparations for the night. You have forgotten yourself, Mr. Hanbury."

After which, of course, I was in disgrace with the chaperones. As I might as well be hanged for a sheep as for a lamb—though there's not much lamb about Lady Susan—I became reckless, and started "fives" on the billiard table until a sheet of plate glass had been broken, and the ivory balls chipped in several places. Then I instigated the Major to refuse Faith's invitation to learn a new Patience, and ensconced him peacefully with *Ruff's Guide to the Turf*, while Dolly Thurston and I played cat's-cradle to the huge disgust of Massey, who was too unsophisticated to conceal his feelings, whereas you might put me on the rack, and I would wear the same expression that I do at a performance of Wagner. But my crowning indiscretion came after a dinner at which the Major and I broke all records of joviality, owing to our being temporarily freed from our respective encumbrances, and reveling instead in the smiles, he of Sybil with her sporting tastes, I of Dolly, who was punishing Massey for a display of jealousy by appreciation of my vein of humor. When the male element was left to itself and Mr. Bellew's cigars, the Major mixed what he called a " stirrup cup " out of numerous liqueurs, and fortified by this I marched into the hall at 10.15 P. M. and proposed "dark room," a game I have never found to fail as a source of innocent amusement. It takes the form of clearing the largest available room of superfluous furniture, extinguishing every ray of light in it, and then setting the players in their stockinged feet to escape noiselessly without being caught by one of their number, who delays his entrance in the first instance into the room until the others shall have concealed themselves in any recess that strikes the individual fancy. The last person caught takes on the duty of catcher in the next round.

In spite of the remonstrances of the chaperones against so terrifying a form of entertainment, the Major was appointed catcher by general acclamation. His heavy breathing, as he crept round and round the big central table of the dining-room, cleared of its appointments for the purpose, in pursuit of a faintly rustling petticoat, materially assisted the intended victims. Then he could be heard swearing softly to himself as he ran from the sideboard into a screen, and thence cannoned off into the fire-irons, and his progress was so audible that every one eluded his clutch save myself, who was preoccupied with my efforts to

solve the problem whose hand it was I had found myself holding for a brief period behind the window curtains. My turn as catcher ended in disaster and disgrace, for I adopted the original plan of taking up my
position full length under the table, from which point
of vantage I seized the first available ankle. There
was a scream and a plunging noise, followed by a confused uproar, during which, with the rushing as of a
mighty wind, the whole human contents of the room
fled from all points of the compass into the hall, to be
met by the hostile public opinion of the outraged
mothers, since the spoil of my ingenuous tactics proved
to be Clive Massey, who, taking advantage of the opportunities offered by the game to make his peace with
Dolly Thurston, was interrupted by my assault at an
inopportune moment, and found himself unable to
avoid dragging her to the ground.

We failed to clear ourselves of the suspicions resting on us, individually and collectively. Dolly was
packed off to bed like a naughty child, the Bellew girls
came under their mother's displeasure for no other
reason I could see than that they had not given cause
for anxiety, and Clive and I were fixed with the cold-
est looks, he because he was ineligible, and I for having dared to originate so compromising a game.
Griffiths alone had indulgence extended to him, an
illustration of the irony of fate, since he, above everything else, was anxious to get into Mrs. Bellew's bad
books rather than endure the baleful geniality, which
even his slow intuition told him boded no good for his
continued independence. The sole satisfactory result
traceable to the night's doings was the healing of the
breach between Massey and myself, an outcome of his
gratitude to me for giving him a chance of " letting

bygones be bygones." I showed my intention of taking an interest in the affairs of a sportsman like himself by inviting him to look me up in Jermyn Street on his return to town.

．　　　．　　　．　　　．　　　．

Clive Massey is one of those fresh, clean-limbed Englishmen, a sight of whom makes one feel proud to be their fellow countrymen. The product of public school and University, he and his kind dance, shoot, and hunt through life if the paternal income allows. If it doesn't, they gravitate into the Indian native cavalry, or the South African mounted police, or turn their hands to any job they can find in any country on the globe. They have few brains of the quality enabling them to pass examinations, and no ambitions, but put them in a tight place in an outpost of civilization, and they extricate themselves, and those depending on them, with a robust common sense and an innate courage and resourcefulness that only emerge from beneath their stolidity and reserve under the stress of danger. All the pedagogues in the length and breadth of England, relying on the arts and enticements of written and oral questions, are powerless to extract from Massey & Co. any knowledge of the kind that would seat them in Whitehall at home, or in official posts abroad. Commercially their virtues are valueless, imperially and socially they are beyond price. Not that Massey will ever feel the absence of money-making talent. He is a ward of Chancery, with a substantial property accumulating, under careful and thrifty management, fat revenues against the day when he will come into his own, and, in the eyes of the law, reach man's estate.

I never wish for a better companion at dinner than

the fellow. He begins the meal with enthusiasm, and continues on that note till the end, unlike some men I know who get anecdotal, morose, or sleepy, when they have disposed of the last course. But Massey so bubbles over with *la joie de vivre, et de la bonne cuisine* that he rouses the whole table to action. He possesses a healthy zest for amusement, and a frank enthusiasm for the enjoyments that life holds out to him, with a complete absence of that self-conscious cynicism that too often marks and mars the Oxford man. His company unseats black care from behind the horseman's back, and drives misogynists to seek human friendship, and rejected lovers to try their fate again.

I speak from recent experience, because he was my guest only the other night, having kept me to the invitation extended casually at Southlands as soon as he conveniently could, for I found, when he turned up, resplendent in a white waistcoat, that he had only been in town two days and was due back in Oxford on the morrow. He was so eager to keep the tryst that he arrived while I was completing my toilet, but his punctuality allowed me to take a hint from his costume, and discard the smoking jacket I had contemplated for full dress. I can read the signs of the times as well as any one, and Massey's general "get up" spelled two words, and two words only—"The Empire." I know better than to confine an undergraduate indoors after 9.30 P. M., especially when his Alma Mater will claim him within twenty-four hours.

Dinner provided the usual topics, the whereabouts of mutual friends, athletics, sport, and musical comedy. Mentally I went back ten years and saw myself again as a healthy animal, determined to have a good time while I was young, filled with a vague and restless curiosity concerning the world outside the University, which, from the magic environment of Oxford, appeared as "through a glass darkly." The gray walls and clustering pinnacles of that enchanted city once more surrounded me as I listened to Massey's cheerful chatter about the chances of the Boat Race, the beauty of the waitress in the "Cozy Corner" tearooms at Carfax, the best place to dine in town for 3s. 6d., and so on. He was prepared to test any and every thing in his search for what he called "Life," and I gradually gathered that he thought I might be instrumental in opening some doors for him. I felt so grateful for the sense of lightheartedness he inspired in me that I let him pursue his conversational thread unchecked, till, just when I had brewed the coffee in a scientific glass crucible that makes excellent stuff when it doesn't burst in the process, and fixed him up with a cigar about a foot long, he remarked abruptly, "I suppose you know a lot of people, Hanbury? I don't mean our sort, but actors, singers, and all that lot?"

"I meet them sometimes," I said carelessly.

"They're awfully interesting, aren't they?"

"Some of them are amusing enough."

Massey took the plunge. "You might introduce me, if you run across any when I'm around."

"I'll do anything I can, in my small way, of course," I replied. "When you mention actors, I conclude you mean the female of the species."

"Anything that comes along will suit me," was Massey's guarded reply, but I could see he was pleased. It was my turn to cross-examine him.

"You seemed to be having a good time at the Bellews'. Miss Thurston's attractive, don't you think?"

Miss Thurston's admirer blew a smoke ring, but vouchsafed no reply.

"She's supposed to be half engaged to her cousin," I went on, with studied calm. "That's the worst of relatives, they start at an unfair advantage with the use of the Christian name. It's to be hoped in her case the man won't foreclose on his mortgage just yet."

Massey's cigar ash dropped on his trousers. Otherwise he displayed commendable self-control.

"That yarn's not true," he said. "Miss Thurston told me herself that she had never cared for anybody, and that she would only marry some one she respected."

"You've known her a long time?" I queried, with a trace of malice.

"No, not so very long," he reluctantly confessed. "In fact, I met her at Southlands for the first time, but we're the best of pals now. I don't take much to the mother, though."

The picture of the lover in Keats' "Ode on a Grecian Urn" rose before me. "Forever wilt thou love, and she be fair!" I quoted under my breath, with this mental addition, "and like him you'll never get any forrader, my friend." Massey, under the combined influence of dinner, tobacco, and sentiment, had sunk into reverie, in which doubtless he was rehearsing the rôle of Young Lochinvar, a reverie which I forbore to shatter. Romantic dreams such as his are too fragrant and rare to be lightly dispelled by the cold common sense of the worldly-wise. I could have enlightened him as to his ladylove's inconstancy in the past, and exposed the absence of accurate perspective in her fancy picture of her future husband. But I refrained. Instead I gave my guest a quarter of an hour's grace, and then took him along to his chosen music hall, where a humorous fellow on the stage was breaking plates by the score. The sight restored Massey to his true self; he threw off a gravity unnatural to him, and dragged me up and down the promenade during half the ballet, greeting everybody by their Christian names, and generally behaving as though he were an admiral on his own quarter-deck.

On our parting he assured me I was the best fellow he had ever met, and with the glow of this unsought-for compliment warming the cockles of my heart, I ended the second stage of a friendship that promised me instruction and entertainment.

" Marriage is to me apostasy, profanation of the sanctuary of my soul, violation of my manhood, sale of my birthright, shameful surrender, ignominious capitulation, acceptance of defeat. I shall decay like a thing that has served its purpose, and is done with; I shall change from a man with a future to a man with a past. . . . The young men will scorn me as one who has sold out; to the women I, who have always been an enigma and a possibility, shall be merely somebody else's property—and damaged goods at that; a second-hand man at best."—BERNARD SHAW, "Man and Superman," Act IV.

FEBRUARY

I WAS having an argument to-day with Haines about Bohemianism. He said that a Bohemian was a "blighter who never washed, ate with his fingers, and let his hair grow as long as Samson's."

Haines is a master of forcible and picturesque speech, and as he warmed to his work he quite surpassed himself.

"I know the fellows," he continued. "They slouch about Soho with seedy squash hats, and seedier fur overcoats which they pinched from the last doss-house they slept in, looking like a mixture of Svengali and a ragpicker. When they feel hungry they drink absinthe, when they want money they write verses, or scrape a violin, with a sickly smile on their unshaven faces. I always give the chaps a wide berth."

I sometimes think it's a pity that Archie Haines is a stockbroker, and not a leader writer. In the latter capacity he could make any Minister of Government uncomfortable by the vigor of his style and the force of his epithets. I told Haines that he was merely hanging a dog that had been given a bad name, and that his picture was entirely insular and fantastic. Bohemianism, I tried to show him, was a point of view, and not a question of dress or personal habits. True Bohemianism is a spirit of romance which turns even the ugliest environment into "a rose-red city,

half as old as time "; a sense of eternal youth gilding
the present and future with the glow of radiant hope;
a kinship with those who add to the common stock of
gayety, and good fellowship; a standard of artistic
excellence which admits of no compromise in its ideals
—in short, a formula of life and conduct, complete
and satisfying. I'm afraid, however, that Haines remained unconvinced.

What started the discussion was the fact that,
lunching in "The Cock" on Monday, I met Steward.
After a Fleet Street crawl I had turned into the old
place, settled myself behind one of the oak partitions,
ordered the steak and kidney pudding that the habi-
tués called for, and then, casting a look around at my
neighbors, had seen the fellow grinning at me.
Steward and I were sub-editors on the *Evening Star*
together for six months in my newspaper days. In
appearance he is about thirty-five years old, small,
and pallid featured, with coal-black hair falling in all
directions, piercing eyes masked behind heavy-rimmed
spectacles, and a general air of activity and determination. He began life selling papers, got a reputation
as a smart lad, and was put in charge of the telephones
at a newspaper office, a job he varied by fetching copy
from the reporting staff at the Law Courts. A night
school gave him a fair grounding of knowledge, which
he supplemented by voracious reading until he knew
the classical authors nearly by heart, and had accumulated a vast store of general information. Then he
took to bringing in articles of various kinds of such
high quality that they finally attracted the attention of
the editor in chief, who promoted him first to the position of a reporter, and then to the "desk," as a
sub-editor.

Having passed all his existence with the smell of printer's ink in his nostrils, Steward had the qualities of a journalist implanted in him, and his quickness of judgment and keen sense of the practical enabled him to turn his talents to the best advantage. He did some amazing things in the way of "scoops" while I was his colleague. His headlines were masterpieces of pithy compression, and he could fill the least inspired "copy" with a sparkle and dash that made it the most attractive item on the page. He would scent in a three-line paragraph from an unknown correspondent the story of the week. I shall never forget how one of the other "subs" took a telephone message about a body being found in a box in a London suburb, and was proceeding to make it into a small paragraph, when Steward, whose attention had somehow been drawn to the matter, pounced upon the thing and from sheer instinct "splashed" the story on the last edition, gave it a bill, and sent out two reporters posthaste. Next day we had an exclusive column and a half of what proved to be the criminal *cause célèbre* of the year.

But above all, Steward never lost his head in one of the unforeseen crises that ever and again disturb editorial method and routine, and discover the weak places in the staff's ability to deal with emergencies. When a decision, in all probability involving war between England and another Power, came unexpectedly into the office, Steward's coolness communicated itself to every one, from the man on the "stone" to the boy at the tape. He stopped the printing machines on the instant, although the elaborate timetable and organization for catching the trains over the country was thereby thrown out of gear, and himself sent out, line by line, to the waiting compositors a masterly *résumé* of the previous negotiations, and a summary of what the news meant to Europe. To the wild messages that came from the publishing department as to the meaning of the sudden dislocation of the day's arrangements, Steward gave replies that admitted of no questioning. The prestige and circulation of the *Evening Star* alike profited by the judgment displayed. So brilliant a journalist as Steward is certain to occupy an important editorial chair before long.

But besides all this, Steward is a Bohemian to his finger-tips, by virtue of his intention to live his own life untrammeled by the conventional environment beloved of Englishmen, to which end he creates an atmosphere of his own in which to "see visions and dream dreams." A contemporary of mine at Oxford got the reputation of being a Bohemian because he usually sat in a dressing-gown, drank Benedictine after "Hall," read Verlaine, and possessed an engraving of the "Blessed Damozel." Steward is not cast in that crude image. There is a robust common sense about his unconventionality which keeps him out of the blind alleys of morbid introspection, and sensualism, in which so many wander who profess Bohemianism either as an intellectual pose, or to excuse the gratification of vicious tastes. At his flat in Chancery Lane, in the only club he frequents, " The Savage," or in the particular restaurant in Rupert Street, Soho, where he may be found nightly, Steward wears the nimbus of the social saint. He radiates wit and originality, and stimulates even in his silences. To him no man is common or unclean, and no one's credentials for friendship are questioned who gives as

good measure as he receives, and when he is piped to,
dances, when mourned to, weeps. The " chucker-out "
at a West End music hall, the ring steward of an
East End boxing-saloon, an Undersecretary of
State, a cocktail mixer in an American bar, and the
author of the most valuable copyright in Europe, are
all Steward's friends. He is a genuine citizen of Bohemia. If there is a power which can strike off the
fetters of hypocrisy and unctuous virtue in which
Imagination and Thought are confined, Steward
wields it. If there is an antidote to the compound of
scandal and sport with which Society poisons its
votaries, Steward can supply it. His presence is a
tonic, and he knows the haunts and companions to
banish dull care and duller ignorance.

As Steward and myself ate our steak pudding and
treacle roll he told me how he had come to write the
lyrics for the new " Alcazar " musical play, *The Bird
in the Bush,* the piece, by the way, in which Cynthia
Cochrane made her début under Mason's management. One of the journalist's gifts is the writing of
light verse, and the *Evening Star* rarely appears without a neat specimen of his talent on a topic of the day.
Mason, always on the lookout for fresh talent to keep
the sacred lamp of burlesque burning, suggested to
Steward, whose acquaintance he had made at a Savage Club Saturday night, that he should try his hand
at some of the songs for the forthcoming piece, and
so pleased was he with the offspring of Steward's
muse, that he handed over the entire job to my friend,
with the result that the latter is reaping the golden
harvest which is the guerdon of successful authorship
in that sphere. The best of Steward's fancies, and
one which has already captivated play-going London,

is the song sung by the " Star " to the limelight man. It runs as follows:

In the morning I am peevish, with my nerves all on the jar,
From the shopping and the popping in and out my motor car.
In the afternoon I've problems that preoccupy my mind—
Is my figure quite *de rigueur,* are my curls all right behind?
In the dusk a quiet rubber will my restless soul content;
What with playing and with paying there's no time for sentiment!
But at night I move enraptured in your limelight's ardent glare,
And my passion is a fashion that I beg of you to share.

In the daylight I am thinking of my beauty's swift decay,
And "affection" and "complexion" get in one another's way.
In the twilight I am pensive, but it's not to do with love;
"Shall I dine in silk or satin?" is the thought all thoughts above.
In the lamplight I am troubled by a lot of different things:
My digestion, Bertie's question—"Will you have the furs or
  rings?"
In the limelight you may sue me, for my heart's no longer stone.
If your notion is devotion, I'll be yours and yours alone.

At the conclusion a terrific crash indicates that the object of the appeal has thrown discretion and duty to the winds and jumped down from his perch in the wings. A second later a stage hand rushes frantically forward and clasps the leading lady in an embrace, showing that her infatuation is returned. On the first night the success of the play was secured from that dramatic moment.

Another original feature is the Limerick King, whose entrance is marked by a ballad beginning as follows:

My name is O'Shaughnessy Brown,
I own a large slice of the town.
    My ample resources
    Of motors and horses
Confer on me social renown.

I've a yacht—tho' I can't stand the sea;
I've a wife—tho' we never agree;
    I've a son in the Guards,
    Tho' his losses at cards
Would pauperize all men but me.

The papers are full of my name,
My portraits are never the same:
I'm taken on Friday
With a duchess beside me;
On Monday I pose with Hall Caine!

The gentleman goes on to tell how he made his vast
fortune by winning limerick competitions. The hold
that the rhyming craze has on him is shown by the
fact that he never opens his mouth in the course of
the play without couching his remarks in the familiar
meter which has brought him wealth.

Steward gave me to understand that he had had a
difficult task during rehearsals owing to the mutually
conflicting views as to the "business" held by Mason,
the composer of the music, and the leading performers, male and female. But Steward was determined
to have his own way, and neither the tears of the
ladies, nor the declamations of the men proved effective in moving him from the position he took up.

Another item that I gleaned during lunch at the
"Cock" was that Mason is giving a Shrove Tuesday
dance for the members of his company to cheer things
up before Lent, and Steward wants me to go as his
guest. I have long since cut my wisdom-teeth on the
Stage and its surroundings, but theatrical "hops" are
usually amusing, and I have a mind to take Massey
with me and try the "safety in numbers" theory on
his present infatuation for Dolly Thurston.

．　　　．　　　．　　　．　　　．

People never seem able to understand what I do with
myself in town. If a man doesn't follow a hall-marked
profession, such as soldiering, "bridge," or driving a
motor, they always imagine that he possesses a large
income and a taste for dissipation. When I told Mrs.
Kyles that I "wrote things," she said "Really, how

interesting," in a tone expressive of profound skepticism.   But one must make allowances for Mrs. K——, since she has been soured by her daughter Muriel, who, having "missed her market," as the saying is, has taken up philanthropy as an alternative occupation, and is rather trying at home.

It did surprise me, however, that Lady Fullard should also harbor suspicions as to my way of life. Lady Fullard is the only one of my people's friends whom I have adopted as mine.   Her house forms a sanctuary from social creditors, and her astringent remarks act as a tonic when my nervous system is exhausted by work and worry.   We mutually respect each other, without having any tastes in common, for what interests can be shared by two people one of whom ends her day (under doctor's orders) at an hour when the other is just beginning his?

"Don't you get very tired of doing nothing?" she inquired, after having rather treacherously asked me to tea.

"You cruelly misjudge me, Lady Fullard," I protested, "I'm a hard-working fellow.   Why, this week I've done a column on 'How to Crease Trousers' for the fashion page of the *Whirlwind;* 'Delia in the Cowshed' for the Saturday *Jujube;* and 'Luncheon as a Fine Art' in the *Parthenon;* far more exhausting brain work, mind you, than engrossing deeds in a solicitor's office, or pretending at being 'something in the City' when one is really nothing."

Lady Fullard did not seem impressed.

"Writing," she said in those cold, measured tones that always curdle my blood, "is merely another name for idleness.   What you want, Mr. Hanbury, is to find a nice, sensible girl and settle down.   It's very bad for a young man to wait too long. He gets spoiled and becomes unfit to make a good husband."

"Father——" I broke out, but checked myself, as I realized that though the voice was the voice of Jacob, the hands were the hands of Lady Fullard.

"I am trying to make myself worthy," I continued nervously, "of that ordeal—ideal, I mean,—but it is bound to be a long process. I'm sorry you don't think much of my efforts."

"I've been twice to the Savoy lately, Mr. Hanbury——" Lady Fullard began, and my hopes beat high that this imposing matron was about to make a dramatic confession of frailty.

"I understand," I interrupted, in order to soften the remorse I knew she must be feeling; "but let him who is without offense cast the first stone."

Lady Fullard took no more notice of my charitable intervention than to repeat her words.

"I've been twice to the Savoy lately, and I've seen you there both times. Is that what you call making an effort?"

It took me a minute to recover from the shock of Lady Fullard's oxymoron.

"Well, one must accept some invitations," I retorted, "and the Thurstons have asked me so often."

"But on the last occasion you were alone with Mr. Haines."

"I was giving him advice."

"Giving him fiddlesticks," Lady Fullard snorted. "There was a Covent Garden ball that night."

"Really, I didn't see you there," I said, with well-simulated surprise. "Which box were you in? Surely you were not the lady in the black domino who won a prize for the cake walk?"

Lady Fullard grew scarlet.

"Sir John told me what function you were bound for, Mr. Hanbury."

"Could you persuade him to give a display of thought reading at the Cripples' Fête?" I queried. "Sir John must have wonderful powers of second sight, for, as a matter of fact, I did look in to see an old friend of the family. The fact is, Lady Fullard, I'm giving myself every opportunity of finding out how unsatisfactory the world is for the unmarried man, and how none of its pleasures can equal those of home, sweet home. I go to the Savoy in order to persuade my stubborn bachelor instinct that the dinner there isn't half as good as what I might expect from a Kensington cook. I pay a visit to the stalls at a musical comedy so that I may see for myself how much nicer it would be to spend the evening by my own fireside in a room full of smoke from a defective grate, and my wife explaining to me how she can't possibly dress on 120 pounds a year."

"When a young man," said my hostess, breaking in on my defense, "who is obviously fond of feminine society,—you needn't pretend to be horrified!—makes mock of the solemnities of the married state, it usually means that there is a woman ineligible for presentation at Court occupying his attention."

Lady Fullard forestalled a violent outbreak on her hearer's part by raising her hand. "You don't require to protest your innocence, Mr. Hanbury. But you can't go on enjoying yourself forever."

Woman's intuition is man's worst enemy. Like a masked battery it makes his position untenable before ever he knows that there is a foe about. For a quick-witted person, I was fairly nonplused. It was only the thought of Cynthia Cochrane that enabled me to recover my self-control.

"I'm not enjoying myself," I stammered, "not here, at any rate. I imagined you had a better opinion of me, Lady Fullard, than to suspect me of such conduct as you have hinted at, and for which vicious hypocrisy is the only name."

To cover my tracks I prepared to launch out on a virtuous homily. Lady Fullard cut me short.

"I suspect you of nothing that I don't expect from other men. You're all alike!"

"You mustn't judge us all from Sir John's standard," I said, determined to get some of my own back.

"I prefer not to discuss my husband." Lady Fullard's tones enforced obedience.

Sir John, for all I knew, might have had a blameless past, but I wasn't going to let his wife make grave insinuations against myself, and then ride scathless away on the high horse of marital loyalty so soon as reprisals were attempted.

"It *is* more Christian," I admitted sympathetically, "to let bygones be bygones. Where we cannot speak well of a reputation we should hold our tongues about it, but I'm afraid the world, our world"—I drawled my remarks with luscious emphasis—"isn't so charitable as you, *dear* Lady Fullard!"

Lady Fullard's hand trembled as she handled the tea things. If I had not known she had been well brought up I should have ducked to avoid the silver kettle being flung at my head. Lest primeval instinct should break through the thin veneer of civilization, which is all that separates any one of us from our primitive ancestors, I hurriedly continued—

"May I bring Mr. George Burn to see you? It

would do him so much good to have the benefit of
what you have just been telling me—the bit about
scoffing at marriage meaning a tea-shop girl in the
background. He stands particularly in need of words
of warning."

Lady Fullard glanced at me with baffled fury.

"I have heard of Mr. Burn as an idle young man
for whom Satan finds more than the usual amount of
mischief."

"I don't know where you got your information
about Satan and his Unemployed Scheme," I said,
with a warmth of feeling I made no attempt to conceal, "but you've been totally misinformed about
George Burn. He's the busiest fellow I know. Why,
he gets through more *tête-à-têtes* than any three
bachelors in Mayfair. What's the matter?"

The clouds of displeasure had lifted from Lady Fullard's face, and she was smiling.

"One can't be angry with you," she began in an
indulgent voice. "You're inimitable. *I* heard about
you at the Bellews'."

"What did you hear about me?"

"Miss Thurston was telling me how badly you
behaved."

Dolly Thurston slandering me behind my back, and
after I'd perjured myself to Lady Susan by telling her
that her daughter was really serious-minded and that
it was her partners who were responsible for that
growing flightiness which her mother deplored—Dolly
who would make a Trappist monk break his vow of
silence by her naughtiness!

"Miss Thurston doesn't know what good behavior
is," I said, with quiet dignity, "and I haven't time to
teach her. But I would place no reliance on the

words of a young lady who turns the head of an undergraduate by giving him six dances as well as supper, corresponds with half the subalterns in the Guards, and cries until she is allowed a black evening frock."

"You seem to take a great interest in Miss Thurston's affairs," was Lady Fullard's comment.

"I am concerned with her moral character only," I replied. "I don't expect gratitude, but I did think she spoke the truth."

Lady Fullard made a gesture of annoyance.

"I've no patience with the young people of to-day. One's as bad as the other. Miss Thurston's a flirt and you are a philanderer, Mr. Hanbury. You'll suit one another admirably. Must you be going? Come in when you want any more lectures!"

I had risen at the moment that Lady Fullard delivered herself of her amazing assumption. I am tolerably placid and amiable, but when the elderly wife of a knight, whose sharp tongue has earned a well-deserved unpopularity, and whose relations with her husband are notoriously humdrum, has the audacity to couple my name with that of a flighty and untruthful minx, my patience is exhausted. I said good-by to Lady Fullard in tones suggestive of wounded pride. It will take a great deal more than an invitation to tea to make me darken her doors again.

.   .   .   .   .

The first intimation I received that my mother had come up to town for a few days' shopping, bringing my sister Dulcie with her, was a note asking me to bring a man to dine at the Craven Hotel with them. As I am nothing if not prompt, I drew the Club at tea-

time and got hold of George Burn. I thought it
would stimulate Dulcie to meet the real thing for once,
George being emphatically one of those fellows whom,
from some attraction indefinable and indeed inexplic-
able to the other members of his sex, no woman seems
able to resist. Whether it is that he accords each one
of them a deferential and admiring homage which
makes his acquaintanceship a precious possession, to
be guarded, if possible, from the rest of the world,
whether he has been granted an insight into the mystery of the female mind and moods which places them
at his mercy, or whether it is merely his good looks
and the assured confidence with which he treats them,
at any rate the fair creatures capitulate to him without any storming of their defenses on his part when
to most of us they would oppose a stubborn resistance
before the siege was raised, and the terms of surrender concluded. Perhaps it is that the man strongly
attracts women who is himself attracted by them, because George is always in love, and with two or three
damsels at a time. How he manages to prevent the
strings of his various *affaires* from getting entangled
I can't think. He reminds me of a juggler who keeps
half a dozen glass balls in the air simultaneously without letting one fall. I know for a fact that, at the
present time, George has romances with Lady Lucy
Goring, although the Countess of Henley would have
a fit if she knew of it; Kitty Denver, the latest heiress
from Carlton House Terrace, and to marry nobody
under a duke; Mrs. T——, who has separated from
her husband and keeps an electric face massage establishment in Bond Street; and the leading " show girl "
at the " Firefly " Theater, the much-sought-after supper companion of all the young " bloods " who are

bent on taking the shortest cut to farming in Canada, or an appearance in the Bankruptcy Court.

Dulcie deserves all that a brother can do for her. Her natural talents have lain fallow in the country amongst the chickens and dead leaves, that is all, but I have noticed on several occasions an aptitude for Society which should carry her far, if opportunity were to offer. It is because I backed George to draw out her undeveloped powers to the utmost that I invited him to meet my sister at dinner. Sure enough, I had no sooner introduced the pair than I saw with half an eye that Dulcie was going to be as amiable as she knew how, and very sweet she can be if she has any object to attain. When she wanted me to take her to Ascot last year, and get her vouchers for my club tent, she was all sunshine and smiles weeks before. Another point in Dulcie's favor is that she always does one credit, since she has the wisdom to stick to the style that suits her, and not to adopt an unbecoming mode of dress for no other reason than that the Maison This and That has decreed it shall be "the Fashion." In a white muslin and a sash Dulcie's artless simplicity is far more effective than if she were to adopt the expensive toilettes of London girls. The type that goes about in brilliant taffetas and satins, and spread-eagle hats, and puts great bunches of osprey feathers in its elaborate coiffures at night may be amusing for a bit, but in the course of nine seasons I have never met a man of judgment who contemplated spending his life in its company. He will flirt and dance with it, talk with it in the Park on a fine evening, and act as its escort at a race-meeting or a play, but when it comes to marriage, he prefers the maiden whose ideals have not been withered by the

breath of a London June, whose notion of domesticity
is other than that of an endless round of country
houses and fashionable restaurants, and whose modest
extravagance is more in keeping with his income.
The London bachelor may be self-indulgent, spoilt,
cold-blooded—frame the indictment as strongly as
you like—but he has the good sense to appreciate the
virtues he does not possess, to know that a sinner
should not mate with a sinner, but with a saint, and
that while he will never be browbeaten and hen-
pecked into affection and unselfishness, he can be
turned into a model husband by innocence and devotion.

Dulcie, in a pretty pink frock, with her dark hair
free from all abominations of ribbons and roses, was
an effective contrast to the overcurled and under-
dressed damsels with whom George spends his time.
From the moment that I saw her in the hall of the
Craven I recognized that Dulcie was quite competent
to hold her own, even against such a redoubtable foe as
George.

Besides ourselves there were the Ponting-Mallows,
he an old friend of my people, a distinguished Indian
official who had risen to be Lieutenant-Governor of
his province, and who, just before leaving India on his
pension, had married a lively little lady some thirty
years his junior.

The half-guinea dinner at the Craven is, in my
humble opinion, the best in London. Mrs. Mallow,
in black with silver round the corsage, and a bow to
match half hidden in her hair, made it seem better
than ever. I had often heard her described as " such
a dear," though why her own sex should have designated her thus, I couldn't make out, since it seemed

so much more appropriate the phrase should come from mine. Give a man or woman a good name and canonize them, and for Mrs. Ponting-Mallow the title must be a social gold mine, although I suspect she quarries a good deal besides precious metal out of it. My respected parents have always disapproved of her —not for any defensible reason, but because the lady has too much hair and too little waist—but Ponting-Mallow has been so lifelong a friend of theirs that they have been compelled to take the trimmings with the joint, and risk social indigestion.

Conversation, in the ordinary sense of the term, was really superfluous with Mrs. Mallow. She put a three-volume novel into the movements of her eye-lashes as she took her soup, and the last act of a melodrama was fully interpreted by the quiver of her lip as she conveyed to me, under cover of a babel of noise from surrounding tables, that she was misunderstood, a fact, as I assured her, the more remarkable in that she had expressive eyes.

"You men are so hard on us," murmured the little lady, in the particular undertone which is patented for the transmission of sentiments to which the reply is prepaid.

I took a gulp of champagne, heliographed for reinforcements, and replied that her sex didn't often give us the chance of being tender.

"Do you really mean that?" asked the lady, leading a black suit.

Catching her eye I nearly revoked, but managed to discard. "What do you think?"

"That you shouldn't say such things if you don't mean them." Mrs. Mallow was no novice at the game.

I had to follow suit to the heart lying on the table.
"I mean just what you want me to."

Mrs. Mallow trumped what I regarded as my trick
by a deep sigh.

Before I had time to pay my losses, Mr. Mallow
leaned across to his wife.

"Julia," he asked, "where did we get that linoleum
for the pantry?" Evidently my mother and he were
engrossed in details of household management.

Our cards were effectually scattered. Still, as I
was helping Julia Mallow into her cloak, I arranged
to call and prescribe for her parrot, whose symptoms,
disquieting to his mistress, appeared to me to point
to habitual overfeeding. I saw Mrs. Mallow and her
husband into their coupé with quite a sense of adventure, as I promised myself an intimate study at close
quarters of an unusually fine specimen of the married
minx.

As I walked George down to the Club for a rubber,
I listened for five minutes to a diatribe on the artificial-
ity of London life, and the unsatisfactory nature of
its female inhabitants, ending with a resolution on
George's part to settle down in a hunting county, and
have done with the place once and for all. I mentally
marked up one to Dulcie's credit, and said "Yes"
and "No" as my companion's pauses and intonation
seemed to demand them. About Mrs. Mallow I kept
my own counsel. George's sense of property is undeveloped, and he has a poacher's instincts.

⋅   ⋅   ⋅   ⋅   ⋅

"MY DEAR H——,

"Mason will be delighted if you will bring
your friend Massey along on Tuesday. We fore-

gather at Midnight, and our programme will
be as follows —

12 p.m.   Stirrup cups.
12.5   'The mazy."
1.   Refresh the inner man and woman.

> *Consommé en tasse.*
> *Filets de sole frits.*
> *Poulets en cocotte.*
> *Cailles.*
> *Glaces.*
> *Café noir.*
> *Veuve Clicquot.*   1900. *Magnums.*

2.15.   Cake Walk Competition, for a diamond
        bracelet and gold cigarette case, pre-
        sented by Arthur Mason, Esq., J.P.
2.45.   Speeches and thanks by the winner and
        her partner.
2.47.   Loud and prolonged applause by the
        audience.
2.50.   Ejection of the 'gentleman' who throws
        rolls under the impression that they
        are confetti.
3.   'The Lancers.'
3.30.   Sweep up the débris, which includes a
        'transformation,' four sets of 'pin-
        curls,' one lock of golden hair, one
        black 'ditto,' one dozen bunches of
        artificial flowers, one set of false teeth,
        a gentleman's wig, three sovereigns,
        a powder puff, two lace handker-
        chiefs, and a petticoat.
3.34.   Arrival of the Manager.
3.34½. Departure of the Manager.

4. Display by the comedians.

4.15. Rival entertainment by the vocalists.

4.20. 'Half-time' called.

4.30. Exit the Band, under protests.

4.35. Installation of amateur orchestra, brilliant execution of the latest waltz.

5. Grand march past and *finale*.

5.25. Eggs and bacon at the 'Junior Turf Club.'

6. Bed.

12 a.m. Soda-water and dry toast.

"*Toujours à toi*,

"FRANK STEWARD."

On the strength of this characteristic epistle, I dragged Massey away for a night from his studies at the University of Oxford, and chaperoned him to the festivity so graphically forecasted.

Like Ceylon in the hymn, a theatrical dance is a place full of "spicy breezes" where "every woman pleases, and only man is vile." But the "Alcazar" show was "top-hole." Mason had supervised the general arrangements to some purpose. Festoons of colored lights hung across the ceiling, the corridors were tropical with palms, an excellent buffet stood just off the ballroom piled with vintage wines and the best articles of diet in the catering line; the finest orchestra in the country sat on a raised dais, and, to crown the edifice of hospitality, feather fans were provided for the ladies, and buttonholes for the gentlemen. Mason and his leading lady received the guests, who were the fine flower of dramatic and critical Bohemia, with a sprinkling of the *jeunesse dorée* of Society and high finance.

In the throng was every fair face that fills its row of stalls nightly, and brings grist to the mills of the illustrated weeklies. Amongst the crowd of men were Guy Ranford, who is building up success as a playwright on his theory that love is a disease only to be cured by matrimony; Lord Matheson, a Scotch peer just of age, and an earnest student of the drama from the level of the stage-box; Julius Pryce, the noted critic who tickles his paper with a pen and it laughs with a harvest of epigrams; and Stringer, who refines sugar, but hasn't refined himself, and whose presence could only be explained on the ground that as he largely finances Mason he couldn't have been left out in the cold.

"My word, Hanbury, I'm your debtor for life," whispered Massey to me, as we made a tour of inspection, clinging to each other for moral support amidst the blaze of youth and beauty. I steered him carefully away from the heroine of the latest stage romance, who was displaying her married charms in a setting of electric blue, but I had difficulty in repeating the maneuver when he encountered a spoiled darling, wearing flame-colored chiffon under a net of lace, who could have mounted to any step in the peerage she wanted, and whom rumor said was on the point of obtaining £10,000 damages from the heir to a Marquisate. Just when Massey, in his excitement, was about to dispense with a personal introduction in order to secure himself a partner for the next dance, I ran across Drummond, whom I had scarcely seen since Oxford days. Drummond had nearly broken his mother's heart by throwing up his " cramming " for the Diplomatic Service, and joining a touring company, in the two years of his association with which

a first-hand acquaintance with life and a capacity for
sleeping upright formed the credit side of his account
with destiny.   Now he was filling a dude part in *The
Cock and the Hen* at the "Firefly," his not very ambitious rôle consisting of saying "Ha, ha!" in the
first act, and doing a Gollywog dance in the last.
Drummond lost no time in introducing my exuberant
companion to a tall girl in a harmony of green and
gold that stopped short at the ankles.   Her impudent
good looks promised to keep Massey out of mischief
elsewhere.

In the absence of Cynthia Cochrane, who was to
arrive in time for supper, I contented myself with a
"dream" in black, whose dancing had all the characteristics of a nightmare, including the falling sensation that precludes the awakening, for she caught her
foot in a passing flounce and dragged me headlong
to the destruction of several yards of expensive fabric,
and

> "With ruin upon ruin, rout on rout,
> Confusion worse confounded,"

in the case of other couples who were involved in my
calamity.   Extrication of the victims proved a task of
some difficulty, but it was expedited by the kindly
interest of the whole assemblage, which stopped its
various occupations of the moment to assist in the
work of rescue, chanting the while in uproarious
chorus the well-known refrain—

> "You'll find about the hour of four
> 'A tangled mass upon the floor,
> And the sportsman underneath is 'Archie!'"

By the time I had brushed the dust off my clothes,
put on another collar in place of the one upon which

a ton and a half of human beings had sat for what seemed to be half an hour, and generally made myself once more presentable, Cynthia had turned up, looking as fresh as paint and as pretty as a rose, although to my annoyance she insisted upon having a dance with Steward, whose determination to master every accomplishment in which he was deficient was only equaled by his inability to keep any sort of time whatever, and his tendency to sudden attacks of giddiness, during which he had to be bodily upheld by his partner, or he would have sat down there and then.

At one o'clock a general rush was made for supper, served in the big salon downstairs at three long tables. Steward had reserved places for Cynthia and myself alongside his, while opposite us was Massey, still loyal to "Green and Gold," and evidently finding no obstacle to reconciling his attachment to Dolly Thurston with a demonstration of affection toward the favorite of the moment. Cynthia and I sat for a moment spellbound by the crash of laughter and the roars of merriment which rose in a crescendo of sound to the distant roof. Few gayer sights could be imagined than that presented by the great hall lit by every color of the rainbow, the jewels on the prettiest necks in the kingdom, in spite of all their glow and luster, flashing forth less brilliant lightnings than their owners' eyes.

The supper itself lacked no feature that might make it memorable. The band in the balcony with its popular melodies sung in chorus by the revelers below; the "Widow" dry and iced to a nicety; the quails with their culinary escort of truffles and cockscombs; the crackers; and the paper hats, modeled in the fashions of all ages and nations, which were brought round with the dessert, set flowing currents of gayety and excitement that swept away the canons and conventions of the everyday world, till, at the striking up of *La Mattchiche*, a personage, in the helmet of a Roman legionary, leaped on to the table in a frenzy of Bacchic mirth, and, with one foot on an *épergne* of fruit, and the other in a finger bowl, did a *pas-seul* to the envy, and, subsequently, to the discomfort, of his neighbors. As a climax Mason was enthroned in state on the center of the festive board, while his guests marched past him with knives, forks, and spoons held at the salute.

Once back in the ballroom I found myself forming one of a large group around two young gentlemen who, each with his hands clasped under a walking stick passed across his elbows and below his knees, were engaged in the thrilling pastime known as "cockfighting." The "cake walk" competition which followed was the usual sort of thing, half graceful, half grotesque. Massey introduced a new figure by walking on his hands, his lady holding him by the legs, but the prize went to Drummond and his partner, the pair accomplishing a remarkable combination of skill and neatness. Drummond's speech of thanks was short and to the point.

"Messieurs et mesdames, ladies and gentlemen, fellow-creatures," he said, "my companion is tonguetied, I am breathless, you are all nearly speechless. Art is long, life is short, and my powers of oratory less. We thank you."

The Lancers were all that Steward had prophesied. I thought discretion the better part of valor, and sat out with Cynthia, with whom I should probably have stayed till we were swept out with the crumbs, had not a pink shoe hurtling past my head broken the thread of our conversation. I had the presence of mind to pocket it hastily as a trophy for my mantelpiece, and assume a look of anxious innocence which turned the band of searchers to disturb other couples.

I'm afraid I can't qualify as an efficient chaperon, for I failed on my departure to find any trace of Massey, save his hat, which by inadvertence he had left on a chandelier in the ballroom.

"*We behold woman at work incessantly. One man is a fish to her hook; another a moth to her light. By the various arts at her disposal she will have us, unless early in life we tear away the creature's colored gauzes and penetrate to her absurdly simple mechanism. That done, we may, if we please, dominate her.*"—GEORGE MEREDITH, "Lord Ormont and his Aminta."

MARCH

The Offices of the "Evening Star"—Mr. and Mrs.
Ponting-Mallow at home—Massey excites Suspi-
cion—and justifies it—The Correspondence of a
Comedy Queen—Steward dines out

EVER since I introduced George to Steward
one night at "The Gourmet" in Lisle Street,
Soho, where we had gone for a French dinner as a
change from the unimaginative British menu at the
Club, he has expressed a great admiration for the
journalist, so that it was at his own request I took him
round yesterday to the offices of the *Evening Star* to
show him Steward in his element.

I never set foot in Fleet Street without regretting
I am no longer an inhabitant of that delectable land.
The very atmosphere is electric with enticing whispers
for youthful hope and spreading ambition. No Siren
could play music half so entrancing to me as the roar
of the printing presses and the bustle and stir in-
cidental to the production of a newspaper. As we
climbed the stairs to the sub-editors' room, the walls
shaking and the building reverberating to the stress
and labor of the great machines in the basement,
George merely remarked that he pitied the poor devils
who had to pass their lives in such a confounded din.
To me the uproar was eloquent with a thousand
memories of the days when I sat before piles of copy
—police court "flimsies," the latest divorce sensation,
cuttings from the provincial Press, the unsolicited con-

tributions of outside men, "penny-a-liners" anxious
to increase their meager incomes by ungrammatical
accounts of fires, street accidents, and the like.   I saw
myself once more with my coat off, my hair in the
wild tangle that is the prerogative of the pressman,—
by my side a cup of tea and a plate of what was once
hot buttered toast, while the eight tape machines
round the room clicked out eternally the news of Parliament, the Law Courts, and Sport to my indifferent
ears.   With all the strain and worry, the "bloomers"
that, in spite of one's precautions, found their way
into print, and the unforeseen descent of the editor
in a whirlwind of vehemence and invective, to hurl
over our devoted heads charges of incompetence and
threats of dismissal, the life was worth living.   One
had one's fingers on the pulse of the world.   In my
heart of hearts I knew that journalism is the only
career that attracts me.   There is no other profession
in which I would more willingly win my spurs.
True, the prizes are for the few, and the majority of
journalists plod along on modest incomes all their days.
But I ask no editor's chair in which to sit in lonely
splendor, approached by my subordinates only
through the chill medium of the telephone, blue-pen-
ciling in my Olympic wisdom their most cherished
flights of fancy, and crushing their dearest schemes
of circulating enterprise.   Give me the rough and
tumble of the fray, the tussle with the chief com-
positor on the "stone" over the "make-up" of a
page, the anxious consultation as to the story of the
day, and what to bill on the last edition!   I prefer the
sunshine and shadow of the world of men to any twilight of the gods.

'After my accounts of the whirl of the journalistic

life, George was rather astonished at the halcyon
calm of the sub-editors' room of the *Evening Star*, a
calm due to our arriving between two editions. The
" Extra Special" was going through the press, and
the "Late" had not yet been embarked upon. So
Steward had his head in a bowl of vegetarian mess
that he had a partiality for, the chief reporter was
smoking a pipe in a corner, and spotting the winners
for the next day's racing with the sporting editor,
while the others, mostly new men since my time,
with the exception of Woodward and Finch, were
sprawling in various attitudes of relaxation and repose
about the room. A knot of boys, employed to run
errands, paste up the tape messages, and carry copy
to the "comps" and proof readers, were scuffling on
a long bench down the far wall, until shouted at by
one of the staff, when they relapsed into a moment's
tranquillity before starting their commotion afresh.
The warm air was redolent of the pungent odors per-
meating the newspaper office, and quivering with the
clatter of the linotypes, which came through a thin partition like the crackle of musketry.

Steward, who gave a touch of local color to the
scene by the two-days' growth on his chin, received
us heartily enough and did whatever was necessary in
the way of introductions. The visitors to the *Evening
Star* sub-editorial room are so numerous and peculiar
in the course of the day that nothing can surprise its
inmates, and even the Sand-jak of Novi-Bazar would
be greeted with yawns. Yet George's immaculate
"get-up" excited as much interest as was possible in
the stolid nature of Finch, who, wearing a handkerchief in place of a collar, and with his shirt open at
the neck, needed all the hints he could obtain from my

spruce friend for his own sartorial guidance. I exchanged greetings with Woodward, a methodical
fellow of mediocre ability, but who never made a
mistake at the "desk," and kept his billet on the
Evening Star while more brilliant men came and
went, inquired after mutual acquaintances on the Press
Club, and asked him to show George how things
were done on the smartest evening paper in Great
Britain.

"What's on?" I asked of Steward, as Woodward
complied with my request.

"Nothing of interest, my son. Hewson's off on a
story that may 'pan' out into a good murder, but
people have grown so moral that we can't raise a yarn
worth more than three 'sticks.' Now, if you'd start a
Society scandal I'd play it up for all it was worth."

Steward broke off abruptly, as though a thought
had struck him, seized a pencil, ran his fingers through
his hair, and scribbled away for a minute. Then he
read out the following:

"BACHELOR'S PERFIDY

"*Society's Favorite Leads Popular Actress to the Altar*

"Where was Mr. Gerald Hanbury at twelve o'clock
to-day? That is what the fashionable West End is
asking, the ladies with sighs, the gentlemen with feelings of relief.

"He was being married.

"Who was he marrying—a Princess of the Blood
Royal? a Countess in her own right, a Transatlantic
heiress? He was leading to the altar Miss Cynthia

Cochrane, the charming 'soubrette' of the 'Firefly Theater.'

"The ceremony took place in the Bodega. The bride, clad in clinging 'voile,' and a merino toque, was given away by her past. There was no best man, for, as Mr. Hanbury remarked to the officiating minister, 'There can be no better man than myself.'

"The happy couple have left for their honeymoon at Clapham Junction, on credit.

"No flowers, by request."

"Hang you, Steward," I said, as everybody roared, "I didn't come to be insulted."

Steward took a spoonful of his abominable diet, and called a boy.

"Here," he exclaimed, "get this set up and bring me a proof. Mr. Hanbury wants a memento of his visit."

I made a rush at the messenger, but he disappeared. I didn't know office boys could move so quickly.

I was thinking of the effective retort which, however, escaped me, when a pile of copy thrust into the central basket drew general attention. George Burn was wandering around the room like a lost soul, Steward was frowning over the illegible handwriting of an important member of the staff, every one was absorbed. I took up a reporter's notebook from the table, put down a paragraph, and, silently gesticulating to a boy, conveyed to him that I wished it put into type. The urchin grinned and went off. I leaned back nonchalantly and hummed a popular tune through my teeth.

Ten minutes passed. George, who had finished his tour of inspection, whispered to me that he had to be

at Rumpelmayer's at 5.15. I made no response. A
pile of proofs was brought in and divided out amongst
those at the table. A minute later and a big fleshy
man opposite burst into a roar of laughter. Finch
followed suit. Steward looked up angrily.

"Can't you fellows find something else to do than
to laugh like hyenas?"

"He's got even with you, Steward," spluttered the
fat man, still shaking with mirth. "How's this?"

"The friends of Mr. Steward, the well-known
journalist, will be pleased to hear that he changed his
shirt to-day and put on another pair of cuffs. There
is no truth in the rumor that he shaved. He did not.
Appearances are often deceitful, but Mr. Steward has
no appearance."

Steward swept the litter in front of him into one
mass and hurled it at my head. I dodged for the
door.

"We don't want your monkey tricks here, Hanbury," he shouted after my retreating form.

I forbore to reply; but when, on opening the
"Last" edition of the *Evening Star,* I saw my offending paragraph in the "News of the Day" column,
evidently slipped in by some mischief-loving "sub,"
I felt that I had got the best of the encounter.

   .   .   .   .   .

Mr. Ponting-Mallow is a bore. No self-respecting
husband ought to be in his wife's boudoir after three
o'clock, and yet, when I called at Porchester Terrace
at tea time, I found him there, with an Indian cheroot
in full blast, reading aloud an article from the *Eastern
Quarterly* on "Suttee and Symbolism." Ponting-

Mallow has revived the extinct fashion of side whiskers, much to the disparagement of his personal appearance, his complexion is as parched as his favorite
delicacy—Bombay duck—and he preserves a military
precision in his dress, for his frock coat is always but-
toned as tight as a tunic, and his trousers might have
been worn at the Brighton Pavilion under the Regency
without exciting comment.

Ponting-Mallow merely raised his eyebrows by way
of greeting to me, and continued his reading:

"To the early European observers the practice of
suttee—the immolation of bereaved wives on the
funeral pyre of their departed lord and master—appeared as nothing else than the rite of an ignorant
and degraded Paganism, a superstition of which the
origin might be traced to those savage times when the
death of their natural protector left the widows an
easy and immediate prey to the enemies swarming outside.   Scientific vision, however, cleared from the
mists of prejudice, sees in the ceremony of suttee a
noble tribute to the sanctity of marriage in the East,
by its insistence on the indissoluble nature of the
union, and the inability of the wife to look upon herself in any other light than that of the natural com-
plement of her husband."

An involuntary exclamation of appreciation escaped
from me. Mr. Mallow looked up. "A finely expressed——" here he paused, with an irritating trick
he has when half-way through a sentence, as if anxious
to let the weight of his words sink into his hearer's
mind—" er—truth."

"The practice seems well worth adopting here," I

suggested, " with the addition of a pyre for widowers, so that they might also display a burning affection for the dear departed."

" In the Buddhist faith, Hanbury," said my host, " the devotion of the husband to his wife's memory is presumed. He displays it best by—er—marrying again."

" Most of us must be Buddhists then, without knowing it," I responded. "It's very comforting to be able to have the sanction of religion to gratify one's own personal inclinations. But weren't the wives supposed to be capable of constancy?"

" Easterns class women with animals in—er—possessing no soul. The contact of Western civilization is gradually dispelling that idea."

" Dispelling it? I should have thought it would have confirmed them in that belief. Give me charge of an Indian Johnny for a season, and I'd convince him of the unwisdom of modifying his original estimate of the sex."

" Haven't women treated you kindly?" asked Mrs. Mallow, with a pout that was meant expressly for my benefit.

" They've led me a dog's life," I retorted.

" Ha, ha, ha!" croaked old Mallow in a fit of merriment, misplaced because a wise husband, conscious that the marriage of May and December can only be a success if the former may sometimes join hands with June, would have refrained from laughing at a young man who had come to reconcile a high-spirited and pretty woman to the incongruity of her position.

I sympathized acutely with Mrs. Mallow's predicament in being wedded to a man in whose life she had so little share that she ought never to have come into it. Mrs. Mallow and I exchanged a glance of disgust, a glance which Ponting-Mallow must have intercepted, for his mood underwent a swift transformation.

"Perhaps, Hanbury," he said, as he picked up the magazine from his knee, "when you have—er—finished your witticisms you will—er—allow me to continue!"

"On the contrary," exclaimed Mrs. Mallow, with a courage I admired, "I think you've read quite enough, and it is very kind of Mr. Hanbury to come in and amuse us."

"My dear Julia," retorted Mr. Mallow, in his best courthouse manner, "I must ask you not to—er—contradict me in my own establishment."

If the rift in the Ponting-Mallow lute widened any more, all other conversation would be engulfed in it, and my errand to Porchester Terrace remain unfulfilled. But any frontal attack, with Ponting-Mallow as firmly entrenched in his chair as the Duke of Wellington in the lines of Torres Vedras, was doomed to failure. My eye fell on the parrot I had ostensibly come to prescribe for, and inspiration seized me.

"Now, Polly, what do you think of it all?"

As I asked the question the bird uttered a bubbling noise which might have been interpreted in any sense. I moved my left eyelid in an almost imperceptible wink at Mrs. Mallow, and continued:

"There, he says he's awfully bored with us, and is simply longing to have you to himself!"

The faintest suspicion of a smile dimpled my hostess's cheek, but her husband gave no sign that my words bore other than their surface meaning. I fidgeted, and upset a teacup, but that dense old Indian

official, whose retirement from duty was obviously
due to softening of the brain, made no movement of
departure. He was only waiting for the door to close
on me to inflict a further installment of " Suttee and
Symbolism" upon his martyr of a wife. How I hated
his chutney skin and his idiotic magazine!

In despair I once again apostrophized the parrot,
who obligingly squawked in a piercing key.

" Yes, he's saying that, if he were a human being
instead of a green bird, he would take you to a
matinée at Daly's."

Mrs. Mallow bent her head as I made the audacious
proposal on the bird's behalf, and I rose triumphantly.

" I really must be going," I exclaimed, in anything
but lugubrious tones, as I stood before the little lady,
" but I hope to see you again—at Daly's," I added
under my breath.   Then I flung a last word at Ponting-Mallow:

" Good-by, sir.   I think if I were a Mahatma or
Brahmin, or whatever the fellows are called, I should
be more occupied in keeping my wife's affections
during my life than in procuring a theatrical and
revolting exhibition of them after my death."

" You'll teach us—er—many things, no doubt, when
you are married," replied Ponting-Mallow, lighting
another of his confounded cheroots.   " And learn a
few, too," he added as an afterthought.

The sarcasm was wasted on me, for I had just
caught Mrs. Mallow's eye, and when I catch an eye
like hers I don't let it go easily.

My considered judgment on Ponting-Mallow is this:
He has all the characteristics of the louse without its
pluck!

.   .   .   .   .

Clive Massey is beginning to be a source of anxiety

in many quarters. He is just the thoughtless, impulsive soul whose welfare is a concern to everybody except himself. Anyhow, I see trouble ahead, and not upon unsubstantial evidence. The first hint came to me while I was leaning over the barrier at Princes' Skating Club the other Sunday, intent on watching an elderly lady doing outside-edge backward, and picking herself up after each turn. For patience and pertinacity she was beating the record set up by Bruce and the spider. She had fallen into double figures when a well-known voice sounded just behind me. I turned around sharply to be confronted by Miss Dolly Thurston and her aunt, whose house in Cadogan Square is a favorite *pied-à-terre* of the former's when on the warpath in town. After the exchange of formal greetings, Miss Thurston dropped into confidential tones, meant for my ear alone.

"Have you heard anything of Clive Massey lately?" she inquired, with a nonchalance that showed me how much importance she attached to my answer. "Mother asked him to come to a dance, and got no reply."

"I've no more information than you have," I truthfully said. After all, there was no reason to connect the incident of the "Alcazar" ball with Massey's shortcomings as a correspondent.

"He's probably working hard," I went on reassuringly. "Hasn't he got an exam on this term?"

"Mr. Hanbury," and the emphasis in Dolly Thurston's voice rebuked my suggestion, "you don't look after your friends very well. Clive has scarcely been in Oxford at all. He finds London a pleasanter place."

"Isn't it?" I asked, with engaging innocence. I wasn't going to let the girl see I suspected anything.

"Mr. Hanbury, Clive's getting into mischief. Sybil Bellew passed him in Piccadilly when he was walking with a stage person, and he wouldn't look at Sybil."

A girl of Dolly's age doesn't concern herself with the moral welfare of an undergraduate except for the best of reasons—or the worst—it all depends on one's point of view toward the institution of marriage. Massey must have made an impression at Southlands. I paid Miss Thurston the compliment of taking her seriously.

"I'll find out everything there is to know. But young men will be young men."

"Can they only be young men with the help of young women?" asked Dolly Thurston, with an unexpected flash of wit, turning her head away a moment later, as she realized the boldness of her comment. Red-hot on the scent of an opportunity for the display of my diplomatic gifts, I forbore to reply, and rushed away with an abruptness that must have astonished my companion. I like to be in the front line of battle on all occasions.

In the next few days, from various sources, I gleaned the following facts bearing on "L'Affaire Massey":

1. Massey had been seen lunching with a vision in brick-red, and a hat festooned with cherries— "a ballet girl with a bally orchard on her head," as my informant phrased it.
2. The 'Varsity Notes in a certain flippant weekly contained the following cryptic sentence: "A popular member of the cast of the forthcoming O. U. D. S. performance of *The Merry*

Wives of Windsor is doing most of his rehearsing in town, though opinion is divided
as to whether he is rehearsing for a breach of
promise case or a Registrar's Office."

3. A mutual friend of George Burn and Massey
had accompanied the latter to buy a necklace
of uncut turquoises, which rumor said might
be seen nightly on the stage of the " Firefly "
Theater during one of the most popular numbers in *The Cock and the Hen.*

4. The hall porter at the Club had been heard to
declare to one of his satellites that Mr. Massey's young woman must be very fond of him,
to write so many letters, and send them all
round by special messenger with instructions
to await reply.

In this emergency I decided to look up Drummond,
a thing easier said than done, however. If I called
round at his rooms he was invariably out, if I sent up
for him at the " Firefly " he was either " on in front "
or absent with a cold, and his club in Leicester Square
seemed to serve no other purpose for him than to act
as a place where he might call for his letters. But I
finally ran him to earth there one afternoon about four,
to find he had just finished what he called " a light
lunch after a wet night." Judging from the array of
empty oyster shells, the skeleton of what looked like a
shark, but turned out to be a sole, the two grilled
bones that might have belonged to the mammoth they
dug up in Siberia the other day, and the bottle of
" pop " turned upside down to prove its emptiness,
any lightness Drummond had derived from the meal
could only have gone to his head.

From the glimpse I had caught of Drummond at the "Alcazar" ball, I was under the impression he had scarcely changed at all from his Oxford days, but in the cold light of the day that filtered through the diamond-paned windows I saw that Drummond's complexion was pasty, from the nightly "make-up" of paint and powder, that his hair was thinner on the top than would have been the case had he led a more normal existence, and that he wore a scarlet knitted waistcoat picked out with green spots, a watchchain of plaited hair ending in a bunch of seals, and a pair of patent leather boots with white kid "uppers."

The conversation, from my point of view, took a little time to get under weigh, because Drummond overflowed with embarrassing cordiality, and I was introduced forthwith to the other occupants of the half dining, half smoking room, that formed the chief part of the club premises, and plied with questions as to my opinion of this piece and that in which the present company were individually appearing, for the feeding of whose vanity I scattered fulsome eulogies of plays I hadn't seen and didn't want to. When I got Drummond to myself I asked him for particulars of the girl he had introduced Massey to at the ball.

"Alice Howard, you mean," said Drummond, "she's in our show. She's got a nineteen-inch waist, and takes 'threes' in shoes."

"I don't want her measurements. What's she like to talk to?"

"Saucy, very saucy." Drummond's voice had a reminiscent note. "Long eyelashes, and a short memory, narrow face and broad humor. She talks about 'her dear mother in the country,' and you think of your dear father in the city. She 'simply loves animals,' and only rides in motors. She says she's devoted to her art, yet she's quite artless. She 'knows all the ropes,' and has one of pearls. Oh, Lordie, she's a handful!"

"After that, I should know her anywhere," I exclaimed approvingly. ",Whom has she got in tow at present?"

"Don't ask me," was Drummond's weary rejoinder. "I can't keep pace with all the highfliers in our show. There's always some new boy being trotted out for my benefit when I stand 'right center' before the old rag falls on the tableau of the market place. If it isn't a photo of 'darling Bobbie' at the wheel of a Panhard, grinning like an ape at the ten-guinea hat in the foreground he hasn't paid for yet, it's sure to be 'a duck of a bracelet' from some other silly juggins, upon the costliness of which I'm expected to make appropriate comment. I rather fancy Alice has a fresh 'flame.' At least I dimly recollect being shown a bangle, or necklace, or something. But I'm fed up with all their goings-on. When it comes to the Maiden Selling Plate I'm one of the 'also-rans.'"

At the conclusion of this brilliant impromptu Drummond flicked a speck of dust off one polished boot, drew the knees of his trousers carefully up to avoid bagging, undid the last two buttons of his waistcoat, and shut his eyes. As I reached the door he began to snore. He had earned his nap.

The sequel was that Haines and myself got stalls at the "Firefly," and went to judge the case upon its merits—or rather, hers. We both spotted the young woman as soon as she came on for the song and dance, "The Boy was Black, and so the Girl looked Blue," which has helped to give *The Cock and the*

Hen a thirteen months' run. Alice Howard, wearing a short costume of black and white lozenges, her unbraided hair tied with pink ribbon, looked the very picture of designing innocence. The necklace was there, reinforced by other jewelry in the shape of a locket on a long gold chain, four bracelets, and a mass of rings. She moved as though it was an awful bore having to come on at all, and went through the inane gyrations expected of the chorus with complete indifference. We both agreed that she was a highly dangerous combination of attractions. Massey, in my rooms, had talked about life. The term "life" in the mouth of inexperienced people like himself is invariably a euphemism for "Woman," and to a superficial observer Miss Howard offered plenty of undeveloped territory for the explorer. It was this sense of the unknown in her acquaintance that would appeal to the venturesome in Massey's character.

Of course Drummond caught sight of me a few minutes later, but our attention was diverted from his pantomimic gestures of welcome by the interest Miss Howard displayed in the occupant of the stage box on the right, but whose identity was concealed from Haines and myself by our position in the stalls, until in the "foyer" during the interval we discovered Massey. The latter seemed somewhat abashed at the encounter.

"Hello, here alone?" I exclaimed cheerily.

"The other man fell through at the last moment," said Massey, with a hypocritical smirk.

"Where are you sitting?" I continued. "I haven't seen any signs of you."

"I'm in a box."

Haines intervened. "I didn't know you were a

millionaire, but if you're the fellow that Flossie of
the Ringlets has been staring at all the time, you've
made a conquest!"

Massey modestly disclaimed any responsibility, and
began a movement of retreat.

"You'll come on to supper with us?" The question was mine.

"Awfully sorry, old fellow, but I'm engaged."

"We shall probably see you at 'the Roman's'
then," I said, drawing my bow at a venture. Massey
gave a start of surprise and annoyance. Evidently
his rendezvous with Alice Howard had been anticipated. He would have to make other arrangements.
The plot thickened.

"I've got to write a note," he broke out. "See you
fellows another time," and he rushed off.

Haines and I looked at one another. "Why on
earth are we bothering about the fellow?" I asked.
"It's no business of ours."

"I rather like his young woman," Haines retorted
candidly, "and you enjoy playing the heavy father,
Hanbury. That's why we're going to see this thing
through."

So we returned to our seats when the bell rang, to
resume our Vigilance Committee work in the interests
of—Massey, I suppose. Haines fixed his opera glass
on Miss Howard so persistently that Drummond, in a
convenient interlude in the café scene, pointed out to
her the interest she was arousing, only to be rewarded
for his pains by the haughty toss of a fair head, an
indifference on the lady's part which did not last, for
she took a careful survey of Haines a moment later,
and cast a glance in his direction whenever she made
an entrance. Haines' dress clothes are a model of

tailoring, and he believes in a carnation as a buttonhole, so he deserved scrutiny. I could fancy Alice
Howard spoiling the jealous Massey's supper with
talk of a rival admirer. I certainly gave her no credit
for caring a rap about our young friend, or, indeed,
about anybody, for a heart would merely have got in
the way of her professional career.

Haines wanted to draw the various supper haunts
for the pair, but I put a stop to his malicious project.
Massey deserved a run for his money, and I was
grateful to him for giving our set conversational open-
ings that would last at least a month.

   •   •   •   •   •

Confined to my Jermyn Street rooms by a heavy
cold, and as bad a spell of raw weather as March can
show, a fit of tidying up seized me yesterday, but I
never got beyond the drawer into which Cynthia
Cochrane's correspondence had been thrust, for opening one envelope to see whether or not it was worth
keeping, I became so interested that I went on from
sheet to sheet, and letter to letter, until the afternoon
had gone, and the zeal for destruction evaporated.

Extending over the nine years during which Cynthia
and I have maintained friendship, the letters chronicle
a record of sunshine and storm, and, if fate should
ever intervene to sever my relations with the actress,
they will serve to keep for me a golden memory. I
little thought when, as a happy undergraduate, I
chased a flying hat down an esplanade it would lead
to a sentimental *impasse* with a woman destined for
high honors in a profession in which success is always hardly won. For if Cynthia's letters show me
one thing it is that the stage is conquered by something more than the possession of two rows of white

teeth and an Odol smile. When a drawing-room darling, sitting on a Louis Seize chair, in a lace frock trimmed with baby ribbon, talks about "going on the stage," she pictures herself walking on in the limelight to the soft strains of the orchestra, clad in the latest creation of Reville and Rossiter, with all her friends in the stalls applauding till their gloves split, and the rest of the company spellbound at her loveliness and grace. Then the actor-manager will lead her three times before the curtain for a further salvo from the audience, when she will be free to drive away in an electric brougham, upholstered in white satin, to sup with the Duke of Magenta Stretlitz, who will offer her the strawberry leaves directly the *poulet au diable* has been served on gold plate. As every girl I know cherishes this modest ambition, I often have occasion to recall the realities of theatrical life as depicted by Cynthia's pen.

The earliest epistles dealt with Cynthia's experiences on tour, the following being sent one September from a holiday resort just big enough to boast a pier pavilion, and to hold a troupe of White Coons as well as the *Golden Belle* company:

"I've risen to 30/- a week on the salary list, and I'm going strong. Thanks to the billstickers, and the enterprise of the advance agent, the house has been full every night, and the manager as cheerful as a cherub, such a contrast from our last stopping place, where he swore the whole time, and sacked a girl because she kissed the stage carpenter during the setting of the baronial hall.

"My chance seems a long time in coming, but as fortune, they say, knocks at every one's door once in a lifetime, he is bound to rattle on my bit of oak sooner or later, and I shan't keep him waiting longer than it takes to jump into the hall and raise the latch. I know I could do better than Grace Western, who is only playing the lead because her boy is rich, and backing her. She'll exhaust even the boss's patience, though, if she continues to carry on with a fresh fellow in every town and to fill the local papers with paragraphs about 'What the Little Bird Saw.' If the little bird saw half of Grace's goings-on he'd molt all his feathers, and take to blinkers.

"We are having the best of times, picnics, tea parties, and gayeties without end. Indeed, without such intervals of calm as we get at places like this, no one could stand the racket and rush of touring. Why, I haven't slept so well for months!"

Then there is another in a different key, when Cynthia was in a northern manufacturing town during a bleak February.

"I've never been in a more horrible place. It rains all day, and I sit wondering what sins I've committed to deserve such punishment. The 'digs' are no better—a frowzy landlady, who is rarely sober, the mirror patched with brown paper, candle grease everywhere, and the food brought up on dishes that look as though they hadn't been washed since the last tenant went. When I complained, the woman said that actresses couldn't pick and choose their lodgings, but must be thankful to find the people who would take them in at all. That's the sort of thing that makes me want to chuck the stage for good and all.

"Things aren't going smoothly in the show either.

The box office grumbles at the takings, everybody feels 'down in the mouth,' and the manager thinks I'm 'stuck up' because I won't let him make love to me. Still, it will be all the same a hundred years hence!

"We are due in the suburbs in five weeks, hurrah! Then, my dear, you shall give me supper, and we'll do a 'Covent Garden' together and I'll forget that men can be cads, and women wanton."

Ambition to succeed kept Cynthia loyal to the profession, she had pluck and faith in herself, and she pulled through where a girl with less talent or determination would have retired into private life, and a hat shop. From my privileged position behind the scenes I saw how hard was the fight.

"I've rehearsed from 9 till 3" (so ran one letter), "put in an evening performance from 7.30-10.30, saved a pal from making a fool of herself with a man who ought to have known better, and now I'm writing to you in order to let myself talk to somebody who does believe in me. When I become a 'star' won't I be good to my understudy, my word!—and to all the girls who are trying to live on less than £2 a week, and sending home a postal order to their mothers as well! I respect success more than ever now I realize how hardly it is won, and how for one victor there are ten vanquished."

Cynthia got her foot on the ladder, which was to reach to the stage of the "Alcazar," by an incident described as follows by my lively correspondent:

"Grace Western has done for herself at last. Three

nights ago she came on 'full of corn,' according to
the expressive vocabulary of the scene shifters, and
cheeked the management right and left. So, at the
end of a performance in which the gallery pelted our
leading lady with pronouns and paper pellets, Grace
was officially informed that, as her home circle must
be pining for the return of its brightest ornament,
she had better catch the night express. And now
rumor runs that her Crœsus isn't taking any more of
Grace because she smacked his face on the arrival
platform of St. Pancras for not having already horse-
whipped the London impresario of the *Golden Belle*
on her behalf.

"I am playing second lead on the strength of the
vacancy; and what follows?"

From that moment Cynthia Cochrane never looked
back. She went from second to lead, from the prov-
inces to London pantomime, and thence to the
" Alcazar," and the glory of capital letters on the play-
bills.

It was with the pantomime engagement at the Paddington "Grand," now nearly two years ago, that
Jimmy Berners appeared on the scene. Cynthia, of
course, has had hosts of admirers besides "yours
truly," but to their advances and attentions she has
presented an innocence and resoluteness baffling the
most persistent and infatuated. In many ways Cynthia, from the point of view of the stage, is peculiar.
She has always refused to acknowledge that the sign-
ing of a contract gives her agent any right to sup
with her, and, if her attention has been drawn to the
fact that the same stall has been occupied night after
night by the same individual gazing at her with

vacuous admiration, Cynthia has attributed the phenomenon to the drawing powers of the piece itself. But Jimmy Berners stood in a category by himself.

Jimmy Berners was a city solicitor, with a very large practice built up on his shrewdness, and a capital which he continually increased by his capacity for successful speculation. Excluded from the social circles, he would fain have moved in through his strongly marked Hebraic features, and the racial habits he failed to divest himself of, Berners betook himself to a free-and-easy sphere where a gentleman is permitted to wear a red silk handkerchief tucked into his evening dress waistcoat and present any lady with an article of jewelry at short notice. Proceeding behind the scenes at the Paddington " Grand " on one occasion, he had met Miss Cochrane, and, struck by her superiority to her surroundings, at once resolved to better the acquaintance. Cynthia had drawn me a portrait of him at the time.

" Such a quaint creature came to see Cissie the other night ('my latest mash,' she introduced him as), a regular Aaron, with a buttonhole as big as a cauliflower and a nose to match, his coat pinched in at the waist as though his five feet of height had been six, an amber-topped cane in his hand to make him look a ' Percy,' and a bouquet for Cissie that must have cost pounds and pounds. He stared so much at me that she got quite angry and called me a 'poaching cat.' Fancy me taking anything away from Cissie—even her reputation!"

It wasn't a case of Cynthia taking Jimmy Berners away from any one, but of Jimmy Berners throwing himself at Cynthia's head. He put a car at her disposal, and when she removed to the "Alcazar" in the spring he followed, and leased a box, which was the nearest point he could get to her. The competition at the "Alcazar" proved rather severe for Jimmy. Weighed in the managerial balance, he had been found wanting, and the stage door closed to him, until he had followed a private tip and invested a couple of thousand pounds in the shares of the theater.

Cynthia's attitude toward her persistent admirer was one of pity.

"He's so unfitted" (she wrote to me once), "for the rôle he's taken up of breaking the hearts of actresses. Those of us who do possess that unfashionable commodity will not barter it away to a Frog Prince. Still, Jimmy is a good sort, however ridiculous he may be."

In his own eyes, Jimmy Berners was not in the least bit ridiculous. He was in deadly earnest, and at last forced Cynthia to acknowledge as much, by offering her his hand—("Such a hand," as Cynthia said, "all rings and fat!"). A refusal couched in such terms as might least hurt his feelings had been to no purpose, for the unabashed Berners still remained in attendance and his car nightly stopped the way at 11.30 outside the "Alcazar" stage door.

Although I should be driven off with contumely amidst a shower of scent bottles, powder puffs, slippers and lingerie, were I to say so in the dressing-rooms of the "Alcazar," I would advise a lady of the chorus to marry Jimmy Berners before Lord Fitz-noodle. In spite of his sallow skin, Jimmy is a

" white man," and if his blood isn't blue there's plenty of it. But I should feel some hesitation in urging my point of view upon Cynthia herself. It would look remarkably as though I were using Jimmy as a cat's-paw to draw my chestnuts out of the fire. I would willingly pay the price of a massive silver candelabra, or a set of hand-painted doilies, to see Cynthia happily settled in life with a husband she could respect, even if she couldn't love him. Besides, the number of wives I know whose hearts had been given elsewhere when they married another, and now are so fond of their second best choices that they won't even let them out of their sight to attend the funeral of an old friend on New Year's Eve, or escort the governess to church, shows that there should be every hope for Cynthia. Marriage is like dipping into a lucky-bag —the smaller the hand the woman has, the less chance is there of her drawing out the stuffed monkey, or the doll which squeaks.

·   ·   ·   ·   ·

All my friends say that I spend my days in the hopeless task of trying to combine the two opposite worlds of Society and Bohemia; and they warn me against incurring social pains and penalties for attempting to reconcile such extremes of existence. They would, in effect, imprison me within the narrow confines of a particular rank in life, on the assumption, I suppose, that any one adventurous enough to stray beyond the pale of the environment into which he was born, to encounter other humanities and creeds, will return from his pilgrimage across that borderland in revolt against the code ruling his former state, and import alien ideas shocking to the tastes and habits current there. But eccentricity is not originality, just as to be unconventional does not necessarily involve an appearance in the divorce court. I have no patience with the man or woman who willfully offend the susceptibilities of friends in order to proclaim their freedom from prejudice, and assert independence. It may seem a strange thing to say, but if I were a married man anxious to prove my belief that the wedding service was the fetich of a decadent civilization, I wouldn't take " Number Two" to supper at the Savoy. In the same way were I more in sympathy with the politics of the New Cut than of Mayfair, I would prefer not to wave the Red Flag at a Park Lane dinner table. When I'm in Rome I do as the Romans do, even though the toga doesn't suit my figure, and makes walking difficult. *"Il faut souffrir pour être belle,"* and to have a good time. All the same there is no triumph so great as the attainment of the apparently impossible, the founding of a salon, say, on the ruins of the old régime. Any hostess can get dukes to meet dukes; the problem is to introduce dukes to dustmen.

All of which is a mere literary prelude to the announcement that Steward dined with me the other night to meet the Bellews. I had seen the Southlands' motor standing in Bond Street, and remembering the social obligations under which she had laid me, I waited till Mrs. B—— came out of her jeweler's, and invited her and a daughter for the following evening. Mrs. Bellew has always prided herself on keeping an open mind, which, in practice, takes the form of combining the position of Dame President of the local Primrose League Habitation with the Chairmanship of a Browning Society in Pont Street, and of letting her girls read anything they like.

Philosophers and wise men through the ages have endeavored to locate the seat of the soul in the human body, but without success. I know exactly where it lies, so I ordered the following ménu. I flatter myself that the author of *The Gourmet's Guide to Europe* couldn't beat it.

Bisque d'Écrevisses.
Sole aux Crevettes.
Perdreau Casserole.
Salade.
Glaces Orange.
Friandises.

Mrs. Bellew was obviously disconcerted by Steward's turn-down collars, and "made-up" white tie, but his tactful manner, and appropriate choice of an introductory topic dispelled her doubts, till the aroma of the crayfish soup put her quite at her ease. The fact that he was the librettist of the "Alcazar," musical play gave my old Fleet Street colleague a glamour in the eyes of Sybil Bellew, and made her ply him with erudite questions on the ways of the stage, in the framing of which she showed an alarming knowledge of the contemporary French drama, and the latest *cause célèbre.* As a type of precocious maidenhood she was new to Steward, and I could see that he was making a study of her, while he displayed an unwonted deferential manner, addressing her as " my dear young lady." Her mother was a couple of courses in getting her bearings right. Mrs. Bellew only enters on conversational duels as a principal, never a second, however unequal her powers be to sustain the position. She feels she owes it as a duty to her sex and class never to acknowledge intellectual inferiority, either in monologue or repartee. Personally, I gibber at her. She mistakes nonsense for

cleverness, just as with some people a catch phrase like
"I don't think" passes for humor.

Steward early won Mrs. Bellew's respect by defin-
ing a Conservative as "a Liberal with a public-school
education," and held her attentive to his speculation
as to the most appetizing culinary description in literature, which he decided in favor of the hermit's venison
pasty in *Ivanhoe*. We progressed through a variety
of topics, comprising the rival merits of Nikisch and
Mottl as conductors, the best wine to drink with fish,
when "rose du Barry" would come in again as the
fashionable color, the place of the nude in art (during
which discussion I tactfully engaged Sybil Bellew in a
verbal sparring match), and the Negro Problem in the
States.

By the time the last-named subject was under discussion Mrs. Bellew had thoroughly aroused Steward's
sense of mischief. He had talked his best to uncom-
prehending ears, and to find the conversation continually turned from the point at issue by fatuous
feminine interjections. No one likes to have his sallies
spoiled by another's density, least of all Steward.
Needless to say, Mrs. Bellew was enjoying herself
hugely. She was meeting on equal terms, so she
imagined, a stimulating wit and raconteur, and giving
a Roland for his Oliver. She introduced the Negro
Problem to our notice apropos of the bunches of mus-
catel and black grapes that the waiter had placed before
us, the kind of association of ideas to which she was
liable. Steward had suggested that the solution would
only come from the negro race itself, when Mrs. Bellew remarked, with an air of engaging originality,
"White is white, and black is black, you know."

"But the whiteness of the white is not equal to the

blackness of the black," Steward replied, with admirable gravity.

"How do you make that out?" queried the lady in a puzzled voice.

"When I was a child," he said, "I had a negro 'mammy' for a nurse."

"That does make a difference, of course." Mrs. Bellew was trying to regain her hold over the conversation.

"The black pigment in the skin of the negro," continued the unabashed journalist, "is responsible not only for his racial characteristics, but also for the essential qualities differentiating him from the European-bred American. The Greeks attributed definite action to the bile present in the human body, speaking of 'black care' and 'black jealousy,' physical and mental conditions which they thought arose directly from that secretion. Now, if scientists could only extract the coloring matter from the skin of the negro, there would be no such problem as we have been speaking of."

Mrs. Bellew's face lighted up intelligently. Her expression had been very downcast a moment before.

"In other words, if the negroes could be made white, there would be no longer any blacks to have a problem?"

"You take my meaning exactly." Steward didn't turn a hair as he said it.

I burst out into explosive laughter. Mrs. Bellew looked at me in astonishment. Like a drowning man I clutched at a straw—a cheese straw, and simulated a paroxysm of choking.

Mrs. Bellew must have suspected the violence of my gurglings, for she rose with a heightened color.

"Shall we go into the lounge?" she asked. "It's getting rather hot in here."

We moved accordingly. Even then Steward was not to be restrained from explaining to Mrs. Bellew, who was prepared to believe anything that fell from his lips, that the first violin was a leader of the Camorra who had murdered a Neapolitan bishop, but had had his appeal against extradition allowed. He also pointed out an elderly gentleman across the hall as the most vitriolic and celebrated dramatic critic of the day. Then he described how the reporters of his paper sat transcribing their copy with pannikins of absinthe before them, and how the staff of the postal district in which the "Alcazar" was situated had had to be strengthened to deal with the extra work entailed by the proposals of marriage that poured in for the chorus of the *Bird in the Bush*. Steward, in short, tore the veil from Mrs. Bellew's eyes, and showed her a London more wonderful than the Bagdad of the Caliph.

"It's been the most enjoyable of evenings," she exclaimed, on parting. "I didn't know you had such entertaining friends as Mr. Steward."

"I didn't know it myself," I replied, "until to-night."

Steward was thoroughly pleased with the whole thing. "East of Trafalgar Square," he told me, "one's sense of perspective is apt to get distorted."

"You mean," I interrupted, "your sense of humor is apt to get out of control west of it. It's not your fault that I'm still on Mrs. Bellew's visiting list."

But Steward wouldn't see it in that light, and began to talk of missionary work amongst the aristocracy. I know one thing. I should precious soon organize a massacre of the converts.

"For one woman who inspires us with worthy ideas there are a hundred who cause us to make fools of ourselves."— NAPOLEON BONAPARTE.

'APRIL'

Mrs. Mallow checkmates—Cynthia Cochrane makes another Conquest—"A Young Man's Fancy"

I HAVE no intention of calling at Porchester Terrace again, but I will say this for my short acquaintance with Mrs. Ponting-Mallow—it has taught me that a pretty woman is a law unto herself. If she likes to darken her eyebrows, powder her face thickly against the rigors of an English spring, and go about with individuals other than her husband announcing that she is determined at all costs "to be in things," who is to say her nay? No *man*, certainly; and for the opinion, good, bad or indifferent, of her own sex Julia Mallow doesn't care one straw. "Women are such cats," the lady once remarked to me, but she used the phrase in forgetfulness of the fact that she herself concealed the sharpest of sharp claws, and was not slow to bare them against the reputation of a rival. Where I was to blame was not in making a fool of myself—a person who isn't guilty of that in his youth is laying up the dullest of dull old ages for himself—but in thinking that nobody would see me doing it.

I had been under the impression that the invitation conveyed through the medium of the parrot when I had found myself in the boudoir at Porchester Terrace between Mr. Mallow and the deep sea had been an invitation to a matinée at Daly's, and a matinée only. Mrs. Ponting-Mallow, however, took it to include lunch before, tea afterward, and then a long hansom drive back across the Park, in spite of my obvious reluctance to go so far out of my way.

"And when are you coming again to let a quiet little mouse thank you for taking it out to see life?" asked the lady, as I was bidding her good-by on the doorstep, with an arch and fantastic playfulness that I was quite unable to parry.

I had had a full five hours of Mrs. Mallow's artificial curls and conversation, been enlightened on the ramifications of her various male friendships, entrusted with confidences on her social ambitions, her husband's shortcomings, her season's gowns, her old grievances, and her new cook, and I was in as urgent need of an armchair, a cigar, and a string of oaths, as a man with a bullet through the head is of surgical treatment. So, clutching the area rail, I murmured incoherently something about its being "no kindness at all, only a pleasure."

That little woman displayed the ruthless cruelty of Nana Sahib, and asked me to call the following afternoon. I replied that I was engaged. Would the day after that suit me? It wouldn't. Then Sunday? I should be out of town.

"Are you tired of me already?" pouted Mrs. Mallow, speaking the true word in jest.

"How can you think of such a thing?" I hastened to protest, with the hypocrisy demanded by politeness. "I'll come to tea to-morrow, if I may."

The tea wasn't such an ordeal as I had anticipated. Mrs. Ponting-Mallow at home took on a quieter tone than when abroad and bent on impressing her neighbors in theater and restaurant. Being less intent on pleasing, she pleased the more. Also, she had the tact to efface herself, and allow me to talk, with the added flattery of seeming to seek my advice on the subject of Ponting-Mallow.

I told my hostess that all husbands were trying, since only the weaker specimens of my sex surrendered the right of the bachelor to express admiration of beauty wherever found.

I hadn't meant that remark as a compliment to Mrs. Mallow, but she took it as one.

"If you were married you wouldn't be having tea in my boudoir. Aren't you pleased that you are still single?" she said, and smiled at me.

Certainly it was a new sensation to meet a woman who gave one a lead over conversational fences as Mrs. Mallow did. But I wasn't out to take risks that afternoon—or any afternoon where she was concerned. I began to be a little frightened of the lady. She put on the *ingénue* air as crudely as she did the powder on her nose.

" I don't see what being married has to do with it," I replied, with gross inconsistency, in my anxiety to disarm the compliment. " Mayn't a man and a woman have tea together?"

"Of course; there's no harm in it!" Mrs. Mallow gave me a look that belied her words. " That is, if people are sensible."

I held my peace,—not that my feelings were very peaceful. Quite the reverse.

"Are you sensible, Mr. Hanbury?" The lady cleared the obstacle with one question.

" I wasn't when I promised to come to tea, but I'm going to begin to be sensible now." With this I got up.

" Surely you're not going yet?" Mrs. Mallow struck a note of annoyance that was out of place in a frivolous conversation. " Ponting won't be back from the club for hours."

"I deeply regret having to leave you alone for so long," I said, with mock gravity, "but duty calls me away."

It did,—duty to Ponting, although that wouldn't have worried me if duty to an absentee husband hadn't also coincided with my duty to myself.

Mrs. Ponting-Mallow actually stamped her foot.

"It's too silly of you behaving like this. I thought we were going to be such friends."

"So we are," I replied, " in this way." And I shook her hand in token of departure.

"Oh, you know what I mean." Mrs. Mallow tossed her fair head with the petulance of a spoiled child.

I looked past the artificially darkened line of her brows straight into her eyes.

"Frankly, I do," I said, "but we'll play the game by my rules, or not at all."

Every man gets the luck he deserves. At the end of the street I met Ponting-Mallow.

That was to have been the end of Madame Mallow, so far as I was concerned, since enough is as good as a feast, and I had no mind to take up the rôle of " lap-dog " assigned to me. It was sheer ill-fortune, therefore, that not ten days later I should have found the lady at a subscription dance in Kensington, and that she should have nodded instant and cordial recognition from the arm of her partner of the moment. By all the canons of convention, and on the strength of such knowledge of the sex as is contained in the line, " Hell knows no fury like a woman scorned," I ought to have received the cut direct, and a contemptuous curl of the lip from Julia Mallow.

"Confound it all!" I muttered.

Haines, whose new-born enthusiasm for the "light fantastic" had been responsible for my presence there that night, caught the exclamation.

"What's up?" he asked, interested.

"That!" and I pointed out Mrs. Mallow as she swung past us.

"The very pretty little woman in the *crême de menthe* costume, who gave you the glad eye?"

Was I after all in danger of throwing away the pearl of great price?

"Is she very pretty?" I asked.

"Not so dusty!" replied Haines, who is wont to sacrifice lucidity of expression in order to indulge his fondness for verbal eccentricities.

"The other day," I explained, "I gave Mrs. Ponting-Mallow 'No' for an answer when she wanted 'Yes,' and if I retract there'll be the devil to pay. She's married."

"The devil is a lenient creditor," retorted Haines, with a pungent wit. "We all have our little accounts with him."

"I can't afford a hundred per cent for the loan. Besides, I've got no security to offer."

Haines turned an amused look on me.

"Security, Hanbury? Surely you of all people don't want security? 'Nothing venture, nothing have,' you know!"

"If that's your opinion, 'Archie," I whispered hurriedly, "I'm going to introduce you, for here she comes."

As Mrs. Mallow, *en route* for the cool corridor of the hotel, passed through the doorway against which Haines and myself stood, I waylaid her and effected my purpose.

"How strange to meet you here!" remarked the

lady, while Haines bent gallantly over her programme. The epithet jarred on me. Why not "pleasant," or even "charming"? Haines was quite right—Julia Mallow was pretty, and the vivid green of her dress suited her admirably. Was it still too late to be friends again—just friends? I compromised with my conscience, and booked a dance. Then, leaving Haines to his own resources, I went to smoke a cigarette and analyze my feelings. The process took some time.

When I retraced my steps to the scene of action I did so with the conviction that Haines had accurately gauged the situation. I had been far too precipitate in reading a woman's motives. Tied to a bear of a husband, Mrs. Mallow had only wished congenial companionship from me, and a spice of that chivalrous sympathy which a man should always be ready to extend to beauty in distress. I was prepared to offer the fullest reparation in my power. The refrain of "Kiss again with tears" kept running through my mind, as though in some way it was applicable to the situation. I couldn't see the connection. Mrs. Mallow might. I determined to ask her.

I met Mrs. Ponting-Mallow and Haines descending the stairs, as the waltz—my waltz—struck up. They looked extremely pleased with themselves—too pleased.

"You'll come and call, won't you?" Mrs. Mallow said, as I appeared.

Haines overdid the enthusiasm in his reply. Before I could stay him he was lost in the crowd pressing into the ballroom.

"Is there a convenient sofa upstairs?" I asked my partner. "I suppose we're not going to dance this?"

Mrs. Mallow gave me a curious glance. "Oh, yes, we are," she replied. "Every bar of it."

I put all the appeal I was capable of into my voice. "Won't you sit it out? I've got so much to say to you—about the other afternoon." I faltered in spite of myself.

"I insist upon dancing. It will save you making conversation to me."

Before I could probe the inward meaning of her remark Julia Mallow had dragged me into the current, and for twelve minutes by the clock I twisted and turned round that infernal room, till my collar melted and my hair stood on end. Ever and again my partner would turn up her face to smile at me, till I knew that Tantalus had had a pretty rotten time of it in Hades.

But even the agony of the dance was preferable to the tortures Mrs. Mallow inflicted on me during the interval which followed. Refusing to sit in any less conspicuous spot than the big hall of the hotel, the lady seemed possessed by a mocking spirit. I could neither make her become serious herself, nor take me seriously. So soon as ever I approached topics which promised well for an explanation on my part as to my previous attitude toward her, Mrs. Mallow steered the conversation on to the shallows, to wreck it completely on such a subject as the rival merits of Dandy Dinmonts and bobtailed sheep dogs for keeping down rats.

"I can't make you out at all," I said, disgust at Mrs. Mallow's conduct my prevailing sentiment, as I escorted her back at the summons of the band. "Once I was under the impression that we got on rather well together."

"We all form wrong judgments at times, Mr. Hanbury. Now I made a mistake about you."

"A mistake?" I repeated it feebly.

"Yes!" Mrs. Mallow gave a malicious emphasis to the simple affirmative. "Your man-o'-the-world air deceived me. I didn't really mean to frighten you, though."

In a whirl of amazement I stopped dead. "I frightened? What at?"

"At a married woman. That makes all the difference to you, doesn't it?"

Mrs. Mallow slipped from my side. When I had recovered sufficiently from the stormy emotions she had aroused to look around me, it was to see her dancing with Haines.

Scorned—and supplanted, I shook the dust of that ballroom from my feet and left.

When I next saw Haines he was eating crumpets in the club. I pounced on him in feverish curiosity and taxed him with contriving the mystery of Mrs. Mallow's callousness. Haines received the assault with the surprise of an innocent person, but his first words convicted him.

"Thank me," he said, "for saving you from your worse self. You as good as told me that you wanted rescuing from the machinations of a woman, old fellow, so I did the trick."

"It *was* a trick," I retorted, "and a dirty one."

"Come now, Hanbury, my friend, be just if you can't be generous." And Haines carefully brushed the crumbs off his coat. "You were hovering on the brink of temptation, I only pushed you back into safety."

"I don't want safety."

That was the truth; I didn't.

"I knew that, but you've got it now, in spite of yourself. I gained you a moral victory at the cost of a defeat to your pride. I pictured you to the lady as a diffident Don Juan, a ' fain-would-I-rise-but-that-I-fear-to-fall' sort of person, forever tiptoeing along the pleasant paths of dalliance, but never coming to grips with the realities of temptation."

"Anything more?" I put the question in rising indignation at the monstrous part Haines had played.

"Lots!" Haines spoke cheerfully. "I laid the paint on thick. I told Mrs. Mallow that your braggadocio air was only an affectation, a mask concealing a cherub's face. Mrs. Mallow doesn't want cherubs at any price, so you got the chuck."

"And you told all this infernal pack of lies in order that you might take my place?"

Haines raised a warning hand. "Steady there, Hanbury, I wouldn't advise my worst enemy to play number three at Porchester Terrace."

"Hello!" I exclaimed. "How did your call go off?"

"It didn't." Haines' words had the ring of sincerity about them. "That husband of hers smoked like a chimney all the time, and read an article on the sources of the Brahmaputra when he wasn't scrapping with his wife over the silliest of details. I was bored stiff. Not for all the smiles in the world would I go there again. You're welcome to the billet so far as I'm concerned."

"What about 'nothing venture, nothing have,' Archie?" After the way he had treated me I was justified in quoting Haines against himself to his own discomfiture.

"India has much to answer for when it sends men home with no livers." The remark sounded irrelevant, but I knew what Archie Haines meant.

"And when they have young wives as well," I added, "the practice becomes a positive scandal."

Then we clinked teacups to the death and burial of Ponting-Mallow, C.S.I. The problem of dealing with his widow was left till the hypothesis materialized.

. . . . .

James Berners, solicitor, has a lot to learn if he thinks that, on the strength of an old friend like myself having presented Miss Cynthia Cochrane, of the "Alcazar," with a pair of earrings, he is justified in sending a diamond "dog-collar" on his own behalf. An individual who is described to his face as "silly old Gerald" is on a very different footing from one to whom the formal title of "Mr. Berners" is accorded. Berners' offering had been returned by the next post, but Cynthia had been ill-advised enough to dispatch it with a note suggesting that there must have been some mistake on the part of the shop, and ending with the Parthian shot of congratulations to Jimmy on his, doubtless, forthcoming marriage to the lady for whom the jewelry was really intended.

"Now you've let yourself in for a dose of Berners with a vengeance," I told Cynthia, when she had finished her account of the incident, on the morning after.

Cynthia threw away her cigarette end and lit another.

"I couldn't resist giving Jimmy a dig," she said.

"That sound a dangerous game to play with a man who hasn't an ounce of humor in him, or he wouldn't be still hanging round the 'Alcazar.' If Berners could be laughed out of constancy, it would have been long ago. His persistency and obtuseness will remove far more rooted objections to his company than you entertain. Mark my words, Cynthia," and I shook a warning finger at the girl; "he'll be round here precious soon to explain that your letter was written under a complete misapprehension, and that his present was for your slender neck. What's more, if you aren't careful, he'll try to clasp it there himself."

Cynthia's adorable little face wreathed itself in smiles at the absurdity of my suggestion. Her merriment died away in a frown as the door-handle rattled, as only the door handle in flats can, and in walked Berners himself.

James Berners was wrapped in a fur coat, the impossible collar of which was formed of two seal skins, others giving each sleeve the appearance of muffs. On his head at an angle of forty-five degrees was set a Tyrolese hat, with a cloak-room ticket stuck in the band, while a shock of black, shiny curls created the impression that Nature at his birth had supplied him with lamb's wool instead of hair. He carried an ivory-topped cane in his hand, a cauliflower—or was it a tomato?—in his buttonhole, and a cigar, in an amber holder, stuck out from the middle of his pale face, with its high cheekbones, and broad-based nose, like the horn of a rhinoceros. He had but to show himself out-of-doors to become another Joshua, and make every living thing in his immediate neighborhood stand still in amazement.

In this emergency Cynthia Cochrane showed the stuff she was made of. She forestalled any remarks on the part of the apparition by rapidly conveying to Berners that he needn't have troubled to come round so early to apologize for the jeweler's stupidity, that she quite understood the annoyance he was feeling,

that she wished him every happiness in his future life,
that it was no use his taking off his coat because she
was just going out herself to do some shopping, and
that the weather was warm for the time of the year,
but that one could never be too careful.   It was
masterly, and not a Chancellery in Europe but could
have profited by the exhibition of diplomacy.

Then, however, Cynthia marred the excellence of
her performance by checking me in the act of insti-
tuting a tactful retreat in order to introduce me to
Berners.   A friend of mine had consulted Jimmy
Berners in a case of blackmail, and I had, on one occasion, inadvertently gone off with an umbrella of his
from the " Alcazar " and failed to return it because
the handle pleased me.   But as these two facts even
taken together hardly constituted acquaintanceship,
I swallowed my scruples and submitted to the formality for Cynthia's sake. I grasped a fat, flabby hand,
fringed with onyx signet rings, and remarked that I
had often heard of him from Cynthia—Miss Cochrane,
as I corrected it to, lest Berners might copy me in this,
as well as in earrings.

While Cynthia had been speaking, Berners had
never taken his gaze off her, and so manifestly was
he under the spell of her presence that he barely gave
me the courtesy of a glance lest he should lose a single
gesture or expression of his adored one.   Such
dumb devotion was touching, but it had the disadvantage of preventing the intruder from realizing that
he was as unwelcome a visitor as his diamonds had
been.

" You mustn't let me waste any more of your time,"
remarked Cynthia impatiently, after Berners had stood
in the open door for a full five minutes, as motionless

as a wooden Highlander outside a tobacconist's, and it became evident he had no intention of leaving the flat of his own initiative. "I suppose you've got your car waiting below?" she asked.

Some hidden spring in Berners' memory was touched by this question, for he advanced into the room, put his hat on the table, and spoke for the first time.

"My dear Miss Cochrane," he began, "your sending back the little gift——"

(I liked that, when at least two hundred of the "best" had gone to its purchase!)

"——has given me the pleasure of coming round in person to explain."

Jimmy spoke with an exaggerated care and precision, as though he was struggling to avoid falling into the vulgar colloquialisms more natural to him. His coarse, vigorous self, in its trappings of luxury and wealth, created the effect of a pebble set in gold. From Cynthia's own account he was none the less likable, an excellent companion, shrewd and entertaining. Only where she was concerned did his wits desert him, to give an impression of folly. And certainly he was doing a very foolish thing at that moment.

"There was no mistake, my dear Miss Cochrane," Berners continued, in what was meant to be a honied voice, but which only succeeded in being insinuating; "there was no mistake;" and diving into his pocket he produced the identical box in which the ill-omened jewelry had arrived.

Cynthia sounded a note which I had never heard from her before.

"If there was no mistake I should be very angry

indeed, Mr. Berners,—so angry that you would never speak to me again."

Berners' sallow countenance turned even paler, and took on a look of genuine alarm. His hand, clasping the box of jewelry, hovered nervously on the edge of his pocket, and then vanished into its capacious depths. His thoughtless attack on his loved one's self-respect had been repulsed with heavy loss. With its defeat, and the distress so evident in the enemy's demeanor, Cynthia's kind heart relented.

"I was sure, Mr. Berners, there must have been something wrong somewhere," she said, holding out her hand. "I don't allow anybody to insult me in that way. If you want to remain friends with me you must never give me anything—except the loan of your motor car sometimes."

Her strange visitor underwent a complete transformation. From the depths of despair he scaled the heights of joy, as, taking Cynthia's outstretched fingers, he wrung them.

"The car—that's it," Berners almost shouted. "It's waiting outside. Come along to lunch at Brighton. That's really what I came round for."

The ready hypocrisy was forgiven for the sake of the good nature prompting the request. Cynthia clapped her hands with the enthusiasm of a child.

"Oh, Mr. Berners," she cried, "how simply delightful of you. And, of course, you mean Gerald Hanbury to come too. He will behave quite nicely, and try to be amusing."

Thus prompted, Berners extended his invitation to myself—not in a very pressing manner. That could hardly be expected.

"I shan't go without you, sir," said Cynthia, turn-

ing to where I stood, reluctant to accept grudging
hospitality, and not particularly attracted by the prospect of Berners at close quarters for the best part of
a day. " You've simply got to come. You wouldn't
be so selfish as to deprive me of a treat. Yes, of
course, he'll be overjoyed to accept, Mr. Berners.
Thank you ever so much. Say ' Thank you,' Gerald."

I said, " Thank you."

Cynthia departed to the neighboring room, where
to a running commentary of delighted exclamations
she effected her toilet, and, as we judged by our sense
of hearing, threw her wardrobe into a wild tangle in
the search for necessary garments, finally reappearing
in a sable coat and toque, with a white motor veil
wrapped over her head, through which her eyes
sparkled like two stars seen through the mists of
night.

The vision of Cynthia, and her radiant spirits, ban-
ished every scruple as to the wisdom of my taking
part in an expedition headed by Jimmy Berners. I
forgot his vulgarity, and his overcoat, in the overflowing gayety of the prettiest girl in the world. To the
echo of Cynthia's laughter, and the music of her
voice, I climbed into Berners' car, and was whirled
away to Brighton with Beauty and the Beast.

Once free of London, Berners offended me less. He
couldn't help his personal appearance, although a
shrewd person, such as he was reputed to be, ought to
have toned down its effect by a quiet mode of dress,
rather than have heightened it by cramming on to his
person as much of his wealth as he conveniently could.
While Jimmy directed his conversation to his fair
neighbor I was content to turn my attention to the
scenery, looking its best on a perfect spring day, and

hold Cynthia's hand under the rug, only speaking
when she drew me into their idle chatter, or when an
assumption by Berners of undue proprietorship over
the girl led me to a vigorous assertion of my rights,
and a forcible explanation to him of the inferior position he occupied in her estimation.   But with this
one exception the sixty miles was covered amicably
enough,—Cynthia and Berners gossiping on the stage
and its concerns, and retailing an endless succession
of theatrical anecdotes that would have proved the ruin
of the editor who printed them, and made the fortune
of any counsel specializing in the law of libel.   Still,
I for one was glad when we reached the sea, and the
car came to a standstill before the glass and iron-
wrought portal of the Cosmopolitan Hotel.   Cynthia,
I have an idea, was of the same way of thinking, for
she squeezed my hand, and whispered, " So that's
over," as we disposed of our wraps before proceeding
to the sumptuous lunch which Berners had had the
forethought to order by telegraph before leaving town,
and to which, it is superfluous to add, we did the fullest justice.

It must have been half-past two before the ices had
followed the rest of the good things, and we were free
to stroll into the great lounge for coffee and cigars.
No sooner had we set foot in the wilderness of palms,
marble-topped tables, red plush settees, and Persian
rugs, crowded with a typical selection of those who
think Brighton and the Cosmopolitan the only place
in which to spend a week-end, than my heart sank to
my boots, and would have gone even lower were such
a feat possible.   For there, inside the central cluster
of tropical plants, from which she could command
every one and every thing, was seated, beyond all

manner of doubt, the rotund and majestic form of
Lady Fullard, her gaze riveted—and for this small
mercy I was devoutly thankful—on the contents of
the daily paper—the advertisement columns, probably,
in search of a new domestic, since Lady F——'s un-
controllable temper and sarcastic wit keep her fre-
quently occupied in that direction. Sir John sat by
her, and his health was responsible, no doubt, for the
amazing phenomenon of his wife's presence at the
Cosmopolitan—of all places. They must have lunched
upstairs privately, for there had been no sign of them
in the restaurant. Why couldn't the tiresome old man
have looked after his ailments better, and spared a
worthy young man acute mental torment? So I
thought, as I looked around for a secluded table out
of the Fullards' range. A sense of what sort of tale
Lady Fullard would tell of my association with a person of Berners' stamp, who looked like a son of Shy-
lock and the Queen of Sheba, dressed as a combination of stage coster and a millionaire from the Far
West, with his crimson waistcoat, check suit, and the
precious stones he scattered over his tie and fingers,
brought out all the coward in me. I made for a shel-
tered corner in an alcove, Cynthia following obedi-
ently enough. But Berners was up in arms at once.
He had come to Brighton with Cynthia to be seen,
and he wasn't going to hide his light under any bushel.
He protested, and loudly, that "it was a bit thick to
come all the way from town to see the swells, and then
creep behind a whacking great palm."

Suspecting that there was a method in my madness,
Cynthia Cochrane backed up my choice of a resting-
place, but nothing would satisfy Jimmy Berners, whose
obstinacy grew with every persuasive word addressed

him, but that we should sit out in the open, where
Lady Fullard would have seen me one moment, and
invented a string of innuendos and hypotheses about
my companions the next. But all chance of our carrying the day with Berners was lost when a group of
persons in the distance, whom I instantly recognized
as Mason, the proprietor of the " Alcazar," with some
members of his company, caught sight of Cynthia
Cochrane, and signified, by violent gestures, that she
and her friends should join forces with their party.
Cynthia could hardly refuse to sit with her own manager, even for my sake.

"Go along to Mason," I whispered to her, " and
take him my love. I'm going into the hall to wait for
you. There are some people I know sitting by, and I
daren't face the music with that," and I pointed sur-
reptitiously to Berners, who with his hands in the
armholes of his waistcoat displaying a yard of the
gold cable he used as a watchchain, was standing
jealously by till my secret colloquy was ended.

I reached the front hall by a circuitous and stealthy
route, and began a comprehensive study of the time-
tables, steamship guides, and excursion notices hanging on the walls, until I knew exactly the number of
times one changed between Dunfermline and Killaloe,
and the cost to a farthing of every circular tour in the
United Kingdom. I was beginning to go over the
west-coast watering places and their lists of attractions, for the third time, when a sudden end was put
to my researches. Lady Fullard swept out of the
lounge. I tried to hide my head in a guide-book.
Vain folly!

"Is that you, Mr. Hanbury?" she asked, raising
her glasses to survey me the better.

I would have denied the fact if I could, but I couldn't. Lady Fullard knew I wasn't a twin.

"Are you staying here?" Lady Fullard went on.

"Only for the day."

I saw she was about to ask another question. A courage born of despair rose in me. "By myself," I added. "My tonsils are a little weak and require sea air."

I gave a feeble cough to prove the truth of my assertion. Tonsils, I believe, were to be found in one's throat. Or was it jonquils? The doubt confused me.

"My mother," I said, "wished to be remembered to you. I must go off and fetch her; good-by."

"But a moment ago you had come down here alone, Mr. Hanbury!" pursued Lady Fullard, with unfeminine logic.

"When I said I was in Brighton alone," I stammered, "I meant I was with my mother."

"What *do* you mean, Mr. Hanbury?"

The waiter, coming up to Lady Fullard, saved me from an answer, which, for the life of me, I was unable to frame. I felt grateful to him. A second later I could have slain the idiot, as he held out a silver salver upon which lay a gold net purse containing a powder puff. It was Cynthia's.

"This was found under your chair, madame," the man explained.

Lady Fullard glared menacingly at him.

The fellow paused with a puzzled expression. "Weren't you lunching with this gentleman?" and he turned inquiringly to me. What a question to ask!

"Gerald, where are you?" rang out in Cynthia's clear tones. "Hurrah, there's my purse, I thought you had it, Gerald. I beg your pardon," and catching sight of Lady Fullard the girl stopped short.

Cynthia Cochrane made a perfect picture, her cheeks flushed with health and happiness, her eyes flashing the most dangerous of glances, distinction and grace in every line and pose of her figure. Even Lady Fullard's grim features relaxed. As for me, I didn't care what happened.

"Lady Fullard," I explained, "may I introduce Miss Cynthia Cochrane of the 'Alcazar,' one of my oldest friends! Cynthia, this is Lady Fullard, who lectures me, disapproves of my goings-on, and thinks I'm an idle scapegrace! Tell her I'm not as bad as all that."

For a moment the two women faced each other in an embarrassed silence, then Lady Fullard took Cynthia's hand in hers and patted it.

"I'm glad to have met you, my dear," she said, almost tenderly. "I thought what unusual ability you showed when I saw your performance the other night. I'm sure you're as good as you're pretty. Friendship with you won't do Gerald Hanbury any harm."

Cynthia's exuberant spirits had given place to a more subdued mood as the elder woman was speaking.

"Thank you for saying such good things," she said softly. "People aren't always so sympathetic to those of us on the stage as you are. I'm very grateful to you, not only for my own sake, but for Gerald's as well, dear Lady Fullard."

A wave of appreciation for Lady Fullard's action overwhelmed me.

"I'll never forget your saying that to Cynthia," I muttered, my voice unaccountably gone; "you're a brick!"

"I must go back to Sir John," remarked Lady Fullard, with a touch of inconsequence that was the truest tact. "He'll think I've got lost," and with a parting smile at Cynthia she moved away.

When she had passed out of sight I turned to Cynthia, her gayety evaporated, her head downcast.

"My dearest Cynthia," I said in the steadiest tone I could command, "you'll never score a bigger triumph than you have just won."

And if she lives to be a hundred she never will.

* * * * *

A successful son, I take it, falls in with his parents' wishes, when they coincide with his own, and conceals any divergence of opinion that may disclose itself between the generations, by saying little though he may think the more. If so I am a failure. I went down to spend Easter at home, knowing very well that I was giving hostages by affording my father and mother the opportunity they had long awaited for personally pressing on me their views as to my future, matrimonial and professional, and which my talents as an elusive letter writer had hitherto postponed. But I stood sorely in need of a spell of quiet after my anxious time with Mrs. Ponting-Mallow, and the charm of the country in April called me with an insistence which I, hardened Cockney though I was, could not disregard. It is easy to be wise after the event, but, had I known what was in store for me by the domestic hearth, I would have shrunk to a shadow on the flagstones of London before accepting the treacherous hospitality of my parents.

My father is an easy-going country gentleman, ready to let things slide if he can thereby escape an argument—in political phraseology a "peace at any price"

man. On his own initiative he would never have sent
the ultimatum of January last, with its reflections on
my bachelor state, since his cause of complaint against
me is my taste for literature. My father's outlook
on life is that of the dweller on the soil. The growth
of social forces seeking to break the spell cast by the
land over its occupants fills his kindly soul with fear
lest he and his should be torn from their ancient seat.
The part played by the Press in hastening this divorce
between the land of England and its owners has im-
bued him with a hatred of journalism and all its works.
That his only son should have joined the forces of
the enemy has been the severest trial of his middle
age. Moreover, the profession of letters is associated
in my father's mind with disreputable surroundings.
He labels any one who dips a pen into an inkpot as an
outsider, and a slouch hat, unshaven cheeks, and ram-
shackle costume as inseparable features to his con-
ception of a journalist as to Haines' idea of a Bohemian. My father's idea of success is peculiarly his own.
If he is to acknowledge ability it must proceed along
recognized lines. Thus he sets his seal of appreciation on the position of a Steward of the Jockey Club,
and withholds it from George Meredith's. "Any
boy can write," is his point of view, "since it only
means thinking of the proper words; but it takes a
man to judge a horse." And in the same way, a
deputy-lieutenant looms larger in his eyes than the
Member of Parliament for the county. Whatever
error in birth or upbringing went to the endowing of
me with the temperament of a Bohemian, my father,
at any rate, is not responsible for it. I am, and always shall remain, a problem to him; although I doubt
whether I shall justify the suspicion he harbors that,

when, in the fullness of time, I succeeded to the Place and its acres, I shall cut down the trees in the park to make paper pulp with, and erect a printing machine in the musicians' gallery. Pride of ancestry is not weakened by being planted alongside the modern spirit in the soul of a man. I will never degrade the heritage handed down to me by the long line of Hanburys, dead and gone, whose portraits keep ceaseless vigil, from the walls of my home, over the fortunes of their latest descendant.

I have noticed that fathers never dictate to daughters in the way that mothers do to sons. A man realizes that his womankind can manage much better for themselves than on any advice he is competent to offer. But a woman is always prepared to lay down laws of conduct for a sex whose standards are as remote from hers as the customs of the Fijians from those of the natives of Lapland. My mother's amiable theory is that once get me married, and every anxiety on her and her husband's part of which I am the cause will be removed. To her marriage is an institution which strains one's nature free of impurities. A man goes into it riotous, extravagant, self-indulgent: he comes out a churchwarden, carrying the offertory bag.

Setting out with this goal in sight, my mother during the whole of my stay at Easter let no opportunity pass of airing her views. No allusion was too slight, no occasion inappropriate for her to read me a homily on the virtues acquired by " double harness," and the vices accruing from single-blessedness. The number of promising careers amongst our acquaintances shattered by the latter state of affairs filled me with surprise. People I had never suspected of possessing any brains apparently would have been in the forefront of their professions had they only married in their twenties.   Even our solicitor was quoted as a potential President of the Law Society but for his confirmed bachelor instincts, which had kept him in a small country town because the hunting was good. I knew for a fact that the man had run away with a client's wife when still articled, so he had shown good intentions which might have been allowed to discount his later bachelor behavior.   When I laid stress on this point in his favor my mother's only form of argument was to rebuke me for my bad taste.   So like a woman to shirk the issue on a question of morality!

But if my Easter troubles had ended there I shouldn't have minded. A violent acquiescence in those prejudices which he disguises to himself as " patriotism " will always turn my father's thoughts from my concerns, and I can generally silence my mother for a time by a feigned surrender. I had, however, other things on my mind, beginning with George Burn, who was with us, in compliance with my sister Dulcie's request that I would bring some man to balance an old school friend of hers, Miss Audrey Maitland by name, who was staying over the holidays. I obeyed the more willingly for George's own sake. For the last two months George has been steering an erratic course between Lady Lucy Goring and Kitty Denver, the Transatlantic heiress, and I owed it to him to give him a change of diet.   It is a great fault of George's that he can do nothing by halves. He must not only devour the oyster, but the shell as well. And he was aided in his inclination for Dulcie's very attractive company by the development of quite a new side to her character, a tendency to feminine deceit, coupled with a masculine directness of action when it served her purpose. The first we knew of a picnic in the pine woods was Dulcie's luncheon announcement that Audrey Maitland and myself had planned it the night before. Besides the awkward assumption of intimacy it raised between us two, whoever heard of a picnic in April, and in a pine wood of all places, where the "needles" spike every portion of one's anatomy, and form undesirable ingredients of the salad and the pudding? When the event came off Dulcie made no attempt at diplomatic evasion of the duties of chaperonage devolving on her, but disappeared with George "to look for nests," leaving Miss Maitland and myself to clear away the débris of lunch, and bore each other with abstract topics of the kind indulged in by the Sunday papers—"Is love at first sight possible, or desirable?" and "Do red-haired girls make the best wives?" On another occasion, when Miss Maitland was lying down with a headache, Dulcie invited me to motor over to pay a call some ten miles away with so touching an exhibition of sisterly solicitude that I threw up an expedition I had planned with the keeper, only to discover too late that I was expected to drive the car, while she sat behind with George. I gave them the worst jolting they're ever likely to have in their lives.

The onlooker, they say, sees most of the game, but I was puzzled to know what the game was, and especially the part George was playing in it. Full of spirits and bubbling over with vivacity in the company of the ladies, George in the smoking-room was to all intents and purposes dumb. After one cigarette he would wander away on some vague errand or other, muttering an explanation of which nobody caught the purport. The errand always seemed to end up near

Dulcie.   His sense of humor deserted him, too, and
he became a fierce champion of the rights of women,
interspersing his argument with a mass of irrelevant
observations about the unappreciativeness of brothers,
and the curse of inappropriate flippancy.   In short,
George's behavior was a powerful plea for the adoption by Western Europe of the Oriental custom of
keeping women in strict seclusion.

But, besides the effect which it might have on
Dulcie's impressionable and untried feelings, George's
conduct had a more serious side.   His defection left
me stranded.   Rather than become a target for my
parents' arguments, I gave Miss Audrey Maitland
the benefit of my society for more hours than I care
to confess.

I had been seriously annoyed at finding I was expected to play host to a girl friend of Dulcie's, when
I had hoped for a week's peace from the sex, and I
had resolved to do as little as I conveniently could in
the "squire of dames" line, and leave the visitor to
find her chief companionship in her workbox and the
piano.   Upon reading Dulcie's letter, I made up my
mind to dislike Miss Maitland, and it was just as well
I settled that much beforehand, or, upon being introduced in the hall, I might have been tempted into a
contrary opinion.   Audrey Maitland had the oval face
of a Botticelli, a rosebud mouth round which the
dimples lurked, a coquettish turn of the head, and
shapely figure held erect, a frankness of manner that
suggested the most agreeable companionship, and a
trick of raising the eyes when she answered a question
that made one want to ask several more.   I was so
prepossessed in the girl's favor that I only just
stopped myself in time from offering to show her the

stables. Instead, I looked over her head (it barely reached my shoulder) to inquire whether the tap in the bathroom was in working order. That Miss Maitland giggled showed she had a sense of humor— I can forgive much for a sense of humor— much, yes, but not a lowering of my own standard of self-respect. To employ a military metaphor, I retired in disorder from the encounter.

Beauty and brains don't usually go together, but Audrey Maitland was as intelligent as she was good-looking. She had more than a nodding acquaintance with the great classical authors, and took a real interest in the affairs of the world, in contrast to Dulcie, who never opens a paper from one year's end to the other. But Miss Maitland wasn't in the least bit a "bluestocking," nor an intellectual *poseur;* her tastes in art and literature being her own, and not some one's else. In fact, she won my respect by telling me that she thought Ruskin a bore, and that the place of honor on her shelves was held by *Tom Jones.*

We all, even the youngest of us, are liable to make mistakes, and the first evening at dinner I concluded that, because in a pale blue dress and with a fillet of ribbon across her forehead she looked a fit subject for a sonnet, I could unload any nonsense on to Miss Maitland. Under cover of the butler's clattering the fish knives together on the sideboard I said something about country air suiting the complexion.

"I suppose," remarked Miss Maitland, "you begin by telling every girl that she looks nice."

"If I can," I replied.

"You don't give my sex much credit for intelligence."

"Because if I draw a conversational check on in-

telligence it is invariably returned to me marked ' No
account.'   I don't put you in that category."

" You've merely varied the form of compliment to
suit the situation.   I think compliments silly."

" So do I, only it's the fashion to pay them."

" You say that," remarked Miss Maitland, " so that
I may admire your candor.   I believe you're one of
those men who make love to every woman they
meet."

The insinuation stung, and I laid myself out during the next week to prove to the girl its falsity.   I
call most of Dulcie's friends by their Christian names,
but " Audrey " never crossed my lips.   I may have
thought of Miss Maitland as " Audrey " once or twice,
once certainly when I was shaving, for I came down
with a gash across my cheek as " wide as a church
door," but I was punctilious in keeping up the outward forms of distant acquaintanceship, a task made
the more difficult through George's occupation with
Dulcie.   Even when it poured with rain the whole
of one day I never suggested " cat's-cradle " or
picquet, lest she might have suspected me of getting
up a flirtation.   It is true that we did stay up over the
billiard-room fire the last night, till my mother sent
her maid down to ask my companion when she was
coming up to bed.   As it was only 12.30 it struck me
as unnecessary surveillance, but I daren't object, and
then have my romantic tendencies flung in my face.

For two hours that evening I sat in an armchair
on the opposite side of the hearth, and left the choice
of topics to the lady, severe self-discipline on my part,
the more so as black suited Audrey Maitland to
perfection, and she had had the forethought (to call it
" coquetry " would be treating her as she treated me)

to put a red pompon in her hair. We wasted an hour and a half of precious solitude before a gorgeous wood fire, which invited the building of cloud castles— wasted it in cold-blooded common sense. I got more and more incoherent in my replies, till Miss Maitland gave up her struggle to interest me in rational subjects, and we both stared into the flames in silence.

"There was once a little man," I suddenly began, "who lived in the heart of a log all by himself, happy and free from care, until his home was put on a big hearth and burned to ashes. He found himself all of a sudden by the side of a lovely flame quivering with beautiful colors, and glowing with passion. Then his heart beat furiously, for he had never looked on anything so entrancing. 'Who are you?' asked the little man, as the flame gently caressed his cheek. 'I am the soul of the log in which you dwelt,' replied the flame. 'Come into my embrace.' Whereupon she folded him in her arms, and he passed away with her up the chimney in a puff of smoke."

"Which being interpreted means?"—queried Miss Maitland, in a drowsy voice.

"That as I can't find happiness up the chimney like my friend, I must look for it here."

To which inanity Miss Maitland's reply ought to have been interesting had not the maid aforesaid appeared on the scene and saved the situation.

Traveling back to town next morning by the early train, George had the effrontery to tell me that Dulcie and he thought I had seemed "rather gone" on the girl. In a few pointed words I explained to George how unfavorably his conduct must strike any unprejudiced observer. Not only had he flirted abominably with the sister of his best friend, but he had left that best friend to meet temptation single-handed. But George, like the crafty criminal he is, reserved his defense, and read the *Morning Post*.

Easter, from every point of view, had been a complete failure.

" Woman is a comedy, which the wise critic hisses off the stage."
—" The Commonplace Book " of Archie Haines.

MAY

*The Philosopher in Hyde Park—"East of the Sun,
West of the Moon"—Massey champions the
Stage—A Dialogue at a Dance*

THE London season has begun in earnest, and
the air is charged with the electricity gen-
erated from the crowds of fashionable folk flowing
in carriages and on foot from Hyde Park down Piccadilly and through the Squares, filling the clubs and
restaurants all day with well-dressed idlers, occupying
at night every stall and box at the theaters, and then
filing up endless staircases amidst roses and smilax to
shake hands with bediamonded hostesses, and dance
till dawn. This is the time of year when the man
about town, discarding the garb of the shires or the
links, puts on a tail-coat and sits in the Park morning
and evening; when his cab fares amount to a small
fortune per diem; when his valet takes in a constant
stream of parcels full of the latest things in suits and
hosiery; when his letter box is crammed with dance
cards from hostesses he has never heard of, but who
"request the pleasure of his company"; when he
raises his hat at intervals of half a minute from morn
to eve in greeting to his numerous acquaintances;
when he eats his weight daily in salmon mayonnaise
and gooseberry tart.

George Burn holds the theory that the whole
machinery of season entertainments works to only
one end—the introducing of the eligible bachelor to

the marriageable maid. According to him, a hostess
dispenses indiscriminate hospitality in order to obtain
a background against which she can the most effect-
ively display her daughter. She scatters four hundred
invitations for a ball to secure the presence of some
half a dozen individuals in her house. Personally I
am indifferent to the motives which have procured my
attendance at any function so long as the food is good,
for it is a poor heart that never rejoices in quails and
plovers' eggs. But I believe there is something in
George's idea. Anyhow, he ought to know, for he
has been the object of goodness knows how many
match-making mammas, although he's barely twenty-
eight.

George was enlarging on the theme to me the other
morning in the Park—the place above all others
where the preliminary skirmishing takes place, and
the outposts of the rival forces of bachelors and matrons first sight one another.

"If I were a Society mother," remarked George, "I
would guarantee to get my daughter off my hands in
a single season."

This was George Burn in a new rôle with a vengeance.

"Well?" I asked encouragingly.

George saluted a passing dowager, and proceeded:

"On three mornings in the week I should take the
dear thing in the simplest toilette up and down the
Row from 11.15 to 12.30—not oftener, mind you,
otherwise she'd get the reputation of being a Park
'hack.' The men with neither birth nor 'brass'
behind them I'd just nod to, but wouldn't I smile on
a *parti?* I'd flatter him till he was in the seventh
heaven of gratified vanity, and then I'd disappear to

greet an imaginary friend, leaving him to endow my girl with all the charms he had discovered in her mother."

Here George's attention wandered for a moment to Lady Lucy Goring—under the Countess's escort. Lady Henley is blissfully ignorant of George's existence, so the latter had to be content with a stolen glance.

"You had just left your daughter alone," I ventured to remind him.

"Only for five minutes," replied George, acting the careful chaperon to perfection. "The roses in the girl's cheeks should not waste their sweetness on the desert air of female luncheon parties and afternoon 'At Homes,' where the only men present are either prehistoric, or married, or both. Her freshness should be preserved for the functions frequented by bachelors. As for chaperoning at balls, I'd see everything without being seen."

"Quite right, your motto being 'I'm there, if I'm wanted,'" and I patted George's knee. "The modern Jason wants to win his Golden Fleece without encountering the dragon on guard. Go ahead!"

"I'd trust my charge's good sense not to give supper to a penniless subaltern, nor to encourage attentions from a man who wouldn't pass muster in the Royal Enclosure at Ascot, and I'd spend my time telling those ladies who had announced themselves in the *Morning Post* as forthcoming hostesses, how pretty their daughters were. Above all, I would never pose before the eyes of a critical world as my girl's rival for its admiration. I'd wear black velvet to set off her white frock, and let my tiara draw attention to her unadorned wealth of hair."

"What about the entertaining you would do?" I asked, chiefly to prevent George from catching sight of Miss Kitty Denver, who, with only a maid in attendance, was coming our way. That young woman had not made the journey from Carlton House Terrace for nothing.

"Oh, the usual things," remarked my unsuspecting companion. "A couple of Saturday dinner dances, to which the most exclusive woman of my acquaintance should bring on her party of young people, half a dozen Sunday lunches for a favored few, a very small and select musical 'At Home,' a table at the Eton and Harrow match to collect autumn invitations at. And I tell you," exclaimed George, "my success with my eldest daughter would so smooth the path of her sisters, that from St. George's, Hanover Square, to Holy Trinity, Sloane Street, the bells of the fashionable churches should ring out in my praise."

"Hello!" I said in astonishment at George's temerity. "Have you got more daughters coming out?"

"Lots," he replied wildly. "There's Kitty Denver; I must go and walk with her."

"And run into the arms of Lucy Goring farther down, and make her so jealous that Lady Henley will probably discover the whole affair?"

"Not much," said the irresponsible George, as he prepared to leave, in spite of my warning. "I shall keep my weather-eye open, and dodge around a tree trunk on some excuse or other when I'm in the danger zone, or else drag Kitty off to the Serpentine. I've run the pair too long together to be caught out now. So long." And with a wink worthy of the rejuvenated Faust, George was gone to his gambling with loaded dice.

But if George, with all his knowledge of the working of the female mind, is eminently capable of looking after himself, there is one of my friends who isn't —Major Griffiths.

Mrs. Bellew's arrival in town at all, with the fall in agricultural rents having halved her husband's income, goes far to substantiate George Burn's view of the Season as a matrimonial agency. Yesterday, in the Park, I was just recovering from the shock of learning that my favorite partner of last year had got engaged—without my leave—to a staff officer in Cairo, and the Major was pouring into my ear his hopes of pulling off a "double event" in the Derby and Oaks, when the good lady, with Faith and Sybil Bellew, descended on us in a whirlwind of chiffon and lace. Like the friend I am, I at once tried to head Mrs. Bellew off on to small talk and scandal, but she was not to be turned from her purpose by trivialities, that purpose being the securing of the Major for a theater party. Now Griffiths has an abhorrence of such evenings, for he objects to the substitution of a hurried meal, with little port and less cigar, for his club house dinner and the comfortable hour and a half following. In plays his taste runs to a party of four men at a musical comedy with a pretty chorus, rather than to a representation of simple English life during which he is flanked by an *ingénue* and her mother. He likes to spend the intervals between the acts in the company of liqueur-brandies, not of ladies.

Mrs. Bellew showed no mercy, however, to the Major's improvised excuses.

"I simply insist upon your coming," she said, with

an affectation of playfulness that ill-concealed the
determination beneath. "It will take you away from
your horrid club."

Some women—Mrs. Bellew is one of them—resent
the bachelor's club, for the same reason that huntsmen
do a fox's earth—because it lets the hard-pressed
quarry escape. The Major's club wasn't "horrid."
As a matter of fact, it was mine also. I told Mrs.
Bellew as much.

"We can't have you interfering," she replied.
"You're a hardened sinner."

"In what respect?" I asked, aggrieved.

"We all know that you run away from our society
to play billiards."

I do nothing of the sort, but Mrs. Bellew has never
forgiven me for spoiling her plans over Sybil.

"But the Major," the lady went on, "is so good-
natured that he won't think of disappointing us."

Mrs. Bellew could only descend to flattery of set
purpose. I began to perceive how accurately George
had dissected a mother's mind.

The Major, meanwhile, stood by, like a naughty
schoolboy, shuffling his feet. With all our boasted
superiority of sex, what children we are where women
are concerned. There was the Major, a blustering
soldier with a record of distinguished service behind
him, as helpless as a newborn infant before Mrs.
Bellew. He didn't want to accept her invitation, she
knew that he didn't want to accept it, and yet in spite
of his protests that he was dining that night with an
old friend, that he was under doctor's orders not to
stay up after ten o'clock, and that he had to be in
Ireland on business, Griffiths was forced to submit to
the dictation of a woman, five feet four inches in

height, whom he could have swung over his shoulder
with ease, had such a monstrous notion ever occurred
to him. Her task accomplished, Mrs. Bellew swept
on down the Row in insolent triumph, leaving the
Major mopping his brow, and myself chuckling at his
discomfiture.

All the same, if Mrs. Bellew succeeds in marrying
the Major to Faith, it will be a public scandal. What
the poor fellow wants, but what apparently he can't
get, is to be left alone. He is about as much domesti-
cated as a lynx, a talent for brewing punch and bluffing at poker being slight foundations on which to
build up married happiness. If Mrs. Bellew must
find a partner for her daughter, in heaven's name let
her get some one nearer the girl's age, and leave a
whisky-and-water-worn veteran in peace!

With men like George Burn and the Major causing
me so much anxious thought, I make it a rule to go
into the background during the Season, and play the
part of spectator of the "great game." One keeps
out of danger oneself, and sees all sorts of funny
things. As a result, I can forecast most of the Society engagements that take people by such surprise
in the autumn, and I'd guarantee to draw up the cause
list of the Probate, Divorce and Admiralty division
of the High Court of Justice with accuracy, merely by
keeping my eyes "skinned" from the beginning of
May to the end of July. When a married woman
night after night makes her home in ballrooms, she
can't have a particularly happy one of her own; when
a girl's face lights up with animation as a certain partner claims a dance, I'm not astonished when I fall over
her foot in the darkest corner of the conservatory
about 3 A. M.

My observation has led me to draw up a short list of rules for dancing men and débutantes respectively:

RULES FOR DANCING MEN

If you are introduced to the belle of the ball, or the most sought-after heiress of the day, don't grumble if you can't get supper with her at the first time of asking.   She probably has other partners besides yourself.   N.B.—If you are in the Household Cavalry or heir to a peerage, this advice can be neglected.

When you have exhausted the topics of " the floor," "the band," and the theaters she has seen, a good question to put is "Do you believe in love at first sight?" You are unlikely to meet a girl who has no views on this subject, and it also has the advantage of leading on to other matters of interest.

The aphorism "Women are like nettles; they need grasping firmly," is a dangerous one to act upon indiscriminately—if you want invitations.   "*Qui embrasse, s'embarrasse,*" as Haines says.

Don't despise débutantes.   They will grow into women—probably pretty ones.

Never specialize.   Other women don't like it.

Never compete.   It ruffles the hair.   Also, if you supplant all your rivals, you find yourself loaded with unpleasant responsibilities.

If you don't know your host, shake hands with all the waiters.   It will save you missing him.

Women prefer a rat-catcher who makes love to them to an Adonis who doesn't.   Join the ranks of the rat-catchers.

Should a chaperon accost you with "I want to introduce you to a charming girl," demur until the girl in question has been pointed out. Your ideas of charm probably differ.

RULES FOR DÉBUTANTES

Never let one man monopolize you. It's awkward for you when he doesn't happen to be present.

Always tear up your programme. It saves the memory—and your reputation for truthfulness.

Go back to your chaperon between the waltzes. It is a pity to make her climb the back stairs in search of you.

Cultivate dimples. They are irresistible.

Should a partner tear your dress, smile sweetly and say, "It doesn't matter, it's only an old rag." He will think what an unspoiled, simple nature you have, and probably propose.

If your powers of conversation should fail, use your eyes. Their eloquence is unmatched.

Don't dance only with soldiers. Civilians cause much less anxiety to their wives.

To be smart one needn't necessarily say things that make other people smart.

When a man pays you open compliments you may be quite certain he thinks you a fool. Cut his next dance; he will deserve it.

. . . . .

Haines is no exception to the rule that Londoners know very little about their own city, for when I last suggested taking him to the Soho haunts of my newspaper days, he asked whether he hadn't better leave his watch and chain at home and take a knuckle-duster. Haines and his kind, if by any chance they are compelled to cross a line drawn from Oxford

Street to Trafalgar Square, do so with an acute sense
of discomfort at their surroundings, and a desire to
return with all speed to the familiar landmarks of the
fountain in Piccadilly Circus, or the arch on Constitution Hill. They hurry down the Strand like fugi-
tives from justice, intent only on transacting the business which has compelled them to traverse pavements
crowded with men and women of unknown aspect,
and ignorant that the most delectable spots imaginable lie beyond the arbitrary boundary set up by Fashion. The strange domain spreading around Covent
Garden and behind Leicester Square is a No Man's
Land, a literary and artistic Alsatia, comparable in its
diversity with the Latin Quarter alone. One door in
a narrow street admits you to the meeting place of a
select coterie of authors and actors, where one may
hear the best of conversation and mimicry; by entering another, you can get the finest French cooking for
a few pence—dandelion salad, kidneys that melt in
the mouth, an *omelette aux fines herbes* worthy of
Paillard's, and eat the whole in a cosmopolitan company ranging in status from a comedian at the music
hall around the corners, to a *mannequin* at Lucille's.

Haines, perhaps, is hardly the person to appreciate
the pleasures of Bohemia, since socially he is a
materialist, a believer in the cutlet for cutlet principle
of existence, and gives dinners to be dined, calls to be
asked again, making it his rule to see the " tat " in
prospect before he offers the " tit." He has a frank
contempt, which he shares with my father, for all the
artistic fraternity. So far as he is concerned, the
world of ideas does not exist. He recognizes no
success but the worldly one; to form any value of a
reputation he must translate it into pounds, shillings

and pence. Dante to him is a grim figure crowned
with bay leaves, whose meeting with Beatrice forms
the subject of a famous picture; Shakespeare is a
dramatist whose plays are acted at His Majesty's
Theater. Archie Haines is an invaluable tonic to a
fellow like myself, for his attitude toward life knocks
all the conceit out of one. When a morning's inspiration has filled me with a hope that I may some day
achieve a measure of fame, Haines' question. "Been
scribbling lately, old man?" reduces my work to its
proper proportions.

But this Philistinism has not prevented Haines from
breaking his orthodoxy on occasions, and accompanying me to Roche's and "the Gourmet," rambling at
all hours of the day and night through the strange,
ghost-ridden purlieus of Covent Garden and the
Strand. We have lunched at the Yorick Club, and
supped at the Beefsteak, and in the space of eight
hours have seen more of mankind than could have
been compassed by eight months of our customary
routine of hunting, shooting, dancing, and love-
making.

It was a stroke of luck that led me to run into
Steward the other night outside the stage door of the
"Alcazar" when Haines happened to be with me,
because I should never "of malice aforethought" have
arranged a meeting between persons of such antago-
nistic intellectual standpoints. Haines was taken at a
disadvantage owing to the green felt hat and flannel
suit he had put on in deference to my objection to his
original choice of dress clothes and an opera hat for a
tour of the town, so instead of assuming a "Weary
Willie" expression of well-bred superciliousness, he
returned Steward's greeting with warmth, and showed

no sign of astonishment when Mason, the lessee and manager of the "Alcazar," loomed up out of the shadows masking the stage entrance in his massive dignity of rings and shirt-studs, and genially shook hands all round without any formality of introduction.

"We're just off to my place for a business chat," Steward remarked to me, "but you and your friend won't be in the way if you care to come round too."

Haines gave me a wireless telegraphic dig in the ribs to signify his assent, so we all linked arms and stormed Steward's rooms in style.

The seal of that extraordinary man's originality was stamped over his abode. A common, self-contained flat had been transformed into something unlike anything Haines had ever seen. The hall was spanned by one of those arches of Moorish fretwork in which hung a heavy curtain of Eastern stuff glittering with a shower of golden sequins. Across one wall stretched a rug of brilliant coloring, the product, so Mason assured me, of the Shah's own factory in Teheran; on the other the only ornament was an exquisite reproduction of a Holy Family by Murillo, before which burned a row of candles in an enamel setting. The pulses of Steward's visitors quickened in response to the cunning suggestion of mystery he had contrived to convey by his scheme of decoration. The first object that caught the eye as the door of the sitting-room opened was a bronze replica of the life-size head of the Cæsar from the Vatican, placed on an ebony pedestal to let the representation of immortal majesty command the senses. Across the mantelpiece ran a fine Flaxman plaque, while in front of the fireplace stood a club fender, the seat upholstered in dark red morocco to match the prevailing tint of the room.

Bookcases spread around three-quarters of the wall
space, ending in a large bow window before which
velvet curtains fell. An old oak knee-desk had been
drawn aside from its usual place of honor by the
window, to make way for a supper table laden with
sandwiches and fruit, displayed on cut glass and silver
dishes of quite unusual workmanship. A profusion of
long, low-lying armchairs showed that the presiding
deity of this combination of luxury and comfort was
a man.

Steward had given character to the chamber by
some unexpected touches. On the walls were posters
by Willette and Dudley Hardy, a framed " Contents
Bill " of the *Evening Star* announcing the relief of
Mafeking, and menus of Savage Club guest nights. A
shelf held the gloves with which Jake Peters won the
world's heavy-weight championship in Chicago, and
a mummied cat, unearthed in making the Law
Courts' excavations. On the cottage grand piano, a
pair of stuffed bantam cocks crowed dumb defiance at
each other, and raised their steel-shod spurs for battle.
Well-controlled eccentricity, bizarre common sense,
were the impressions given by this remarkable apartment, the effect of which was heightened by the con-
trasted simplicity of the bedroom opening out of it, in
which the only furniture were a camp bed and a
Service chest of drawers.

I waved my hand with a showman's gesture for
Haines' benefit.

" This is the real thing, my young friend. On the
right " (here I indicated Cæsar) " you will observe
the death-mask of our host's maternal grandfather;
on the left is a frugal meal provided on the principle
that ' better is a dinner of herbs where love is, than

a stalled ox and hatred therewith.' All the proceeds
of writing a few catchy lyrics for the light opera
stage!"

Haines' disconcern at the difference between his
idea of a literary den and the reality was comical.
His gaze wandered round and round the room.

"It certainly seems a paying job," he remarked at
length.

"Never forget, my dear fellow," came the voice of
Mason from the recesses of the armchair in which he
had sunk with a cigar, "that if the rewards of theatrical management and authorship are sometimes great,
so are the responsibilities. There is the popular taste
to gauge, the welfare of the profession to secure, the
artistic standards to be maintained. The talents to
win success——" But here Steward, who had just
donned a purple-lined smoking jacket, cut the impresario short.

"None of that, Mason. If you want to get out the
Vox humana stop, you don't do it here. I don't
much mind looking at you, but I'm hanged if I'll
listen to you elevating the masses. What about those
new songs? I've got the idea for one number, just
the thing for the chorus of 'flappers.' It begins—

> 'Oh, the "dolce far niente"
> When the maiden isn't twenty.'

It wants a slap-dash accompaniment on these lines,"
and, going to the piano, Steward thumped out a succession of tuneful chords, till the fighting cocks rocked
again. A sudden burst of sound from the hall interrupted the improvisation, the door flew open, and a
woman's voice exclaimed, "You *are* enjoying yourselves. I thought you told Kit and me, Mr. Steward,

we should be the only guests, and we find the place overflowing."

I turned in alarm. "Well, I'm damned," I said feebly, and fell into a chair. It was Cynthia—Cynthia in a crimson opera cloak, and wearing my earrings.

Her face lit up with smiles.

"Why, if it isn't dear old Gerald! Gerald, I am glad to see you."

Steward surveyed us with an amused expression. "Right again, it is dear old Gerald, and that's dear old Haines, and in that chair, trying to attract your attention with a fat forefinger, is dear old Mason."

Cynthia turned to her companion, none other than the "Alcazar" leading lady. "Is he often taken like this?" and she pointed to her host. Then she placed one hand on my head and gently stroked it. "Don't be absurd, Mr. Steward, I've known this boy for years."

"That's no reason why you should ruffle my hair!" I spoke gruffly.

"Diddums didn't like it," mimicked Steward. Haines and Mason both laughed.

I sprang to my feet. "If you've no sense of the ridiculous, Miss Cochrane, I have. Please to remember that you are in the presence of strangers."

Cynthia made a face at me—an outrageous action on her part. "Gerald, they're not strangers. I've had tea with Mr. Mason heaps of times, and your friend there has such a nice face I couldn't feel strange with him."

"That's right," broke in Haines enthusiastically. "You come and have a sandwich with me, and we'll forget that dignified dog, Hanbury!"

"When it comes to sandwiches, I've got no dignity," I shouted, and made for the table. "Here's a toast!" and I filled a glass with champagne, the rest of the company following suit. "Man and the confusion of Woman."

"I call that downright ungallant," growled Steward, munching a lobster patty.

"Gerald doesn't mean all the nasty things he says," Cynthia made reply in those caressing tones of hers. A mist swept across my sight, but with an effort I brushed it away.

"I'll give you another toast," I said. "Miss Cochrane—the confusion of all of us." Every glass was drained. Silence ensued for a space while we devoured the good things Steward had provided.

"Some one play something," Mason began at last, producing a large case of cigars from his pocket. "We've got a 'première danseuse' here, and the opportunity is not to be missed."

Now Haines, for all his Philistinism, has an incomparable knack of taking the poorest tune, supplying the rhythm and swing it lacks, and weaving a harmony of sound to set lame folks dancing, and dumb folks singing. From a merry jingle he will swing into a "can-can," thence into a "tarantella," turn that fierce, passionate music into the dreamiest waltz, from which he will glide into the sobbing refrain of a Neapolitan love song. On this occasion he seated himself at the piano, flourished his hands about in caricature of a famous maestro, ran up and down the scales lightly once or twice with a tantalizing mastery of touch, as a preliminary to the most seductive melody it had ever been the lot of any of us to hear. To the echo of the silvery notes all of us in our

several ways paid homage; Mason's eyes closed in
reverie, Steward's keen expression relaxed in a far-
away vision of the Palace Beautiful, Kit of the "Alcazar," whose soul was in her feet, beat soft time to
the magical music, while Cynthia and myself sat
before the wreckage of the supper lost in daydreams.

"Great Scott, the fellow can play!" muttered
Mason, half to us, half to himself, and dissolved .the
spell which bound the room. The time quickened,
and a wicked little note crept into the soft bars of
the treble to wake our slumbering selves responsive
to its call. A dry whisper of enticement ran round
the circle as the power of the chords gripped it, giving to each one the fruit of the Tree of Knowledge of
Good and Evil. The sins of all the cities stalked in
our midst. Haines was unlocking doors that are best
kept bolted and barred.

"Stop that infernal noise," shouted Steward in a
harsh voice I scarcely recognized as his, "before you
drive us mad. Play something that Kit can dance
to."

The rebuke was effectual. The dreadful music
changed to the glory and sunshine of a Southern Car-
nival. In our ears rang the shouts of the masquerad-
ers, in our nostrils rose the scent of the perfumed
South, for Steward had placed a lighted pastille on a
shovel, filling the air with aromatic odors. I hastily
cleared a wide space free of chairs and et ceteras as Kit
rose to her feet and began to dance, slowly, almost
mechanically, in obedience to the fascination of the
music, with no volition of her own to direct her movements. I believe she was in a species of hypnotic
trance, or she would never have done what she did,
for although I have seen gipsies in Seville, Dervishes

in Algiers, Tziganes in Budapest, and the most renowned "ballerinas" of Paris and St. Petersburg, Kit of the "Alcazar" surpassed them all at the bidding of Haines.   He, equally, was under some spell, for he left the rank of tolerable musicians he occupies ordinarily and became inspired.   In a mist of sound, Kit hovered and swayed to the call of the measure, floating in the eddying fumes of the pastille.   She alternately pirouetted and sank, her feet flickered now high, now low, till she appeared no longer a woman, but a phantom in the moonbeams.   Mason sat bolt upright staring at her as if thunderstruck at the qualities he had never seen displayed on the stage of the "Alcazar," and which, if he could conjure up in the future, would mean a fortune to the pair.   At the last, when the piano was rising to a crescendo of savage frenzy, Steward tore off his smoking jacket and flung himself into the circle, capering and leaping with a demoniac possession, lashed out of his ordered self by the wild bars throbbing with passion and abandon. With one final effort he spun his partner round at giddy speed, to hurl her into one chair and himself into another, as the music stopped with a crash.

Haines rose with a streaming forehead.   "The devil's in here to-night," he said shortly.

Mason cast an apprehensive glance around, Cynthia gave a shudder and gripped my hand.   The environment created by Steward for his own delight was, I felt convinced, the force that oppressed us.   His magnetic personality, translated into concrete form in his flat and its contents, carried us, like the Wild Ass's Skin of Balzac's romance, to a region outside ordinary human existence.   No sound from the world came through the heavy curtains; nothing in our surroundings reminded us of it. The somber coloring of the walls, the gleam of old silver on the table, the strange relics, the fantastic objects on every hand, conveyed the certainty that there convention was unknown, its code unrecognized. If the devil was in the room, as Haines suggested, he would find himself in a spot as unearthly as his own abode.

"There are no devils except those we raise for ourselves," Steward replied, with grim intensity.

A sob broke from Kit, who was in the full flood of reaction from an excitement which had overtaxed her strength.

"Don't frighten the ladies with extracts from your Bohemian philosophy," I exclaimed, with an effort at jocularity. "They're more than half persuaded that you practice the Black Art."

Mason came forward. "I'm going to take them home in my car," he said, with a gesture toward Kit and Cynthia, who was bending over her. Then he turned to Haines. "I'll give you a box for my show with pleasure, sir, whenever you care for one. You knock spots off any ivory thumper I've ever listened to, and you've given me a better opinion of my leading lady than I've ever had reason to hold before."

Haines flushed at the compliment, but remained silent. He was a little unstrung by the sensations of the night. To tell the truth, I was precious glad myself to be out in the street at the end of it all. Steward's taste for the fantastic wants tempering with fresh air. As for his mummied cat—the sooner it is cremated the better!

    .   .   .   .   .

I had forgotten all about the part I had unwittingly played in the affair of Clive Massey, undergraduate, and Alice Howard, of the "Firefly" Theater, till the following letter, bearing the Oxford postmark, recalled the whole business to my memory:

"DEAR HANBURY:

"I hope you won't think it odd of me to ask you to lend me £20. I'll take it as a very friendly act if you will, because I can't go to my people, as they will be sure to ask questions which I shan't be able to answer and respect a third person's confidences. You are a man of the world and will understand.

"Yours ever,
"CLIVE MASSEY."

I felt pleased with my reply:

"DEAR M.:

"The money is yours. Come and gnaw a bone *chez moi* and Sunday, and meet a pal of mine, Drummond, who is playing at the 'Firefly' and is full of fun.

"Yours, till hell freezes,
"G. H."

I knew that last touch would fetch Massey as no other inducement could, and sure enough he accepted, with many protestations of gratitude, by return of post, forgetting, in his haste, to stamp the envelope, and mulcting me accordingly for the luxury of obtaining a reply.

Drummond turned up first in my rooms, magnificent as usual, the details of his costume bearing the same relation of civilian dress that objects seen under the microscope do to the ordinary unmagnified world.

His coat was too pinched at the waist, the pattern of his trousers was too stripy, and his tie was a huge "four-in-hand" sticking out an inch from his neck, carrying a fox's head in brilliants as a centerpiece. I took advantage of Drummond's punctuality to run over the salient points of "L'Affaire Massey" for his benefit, hinting that if he could contrive to disillusionize Massey about the constancy of coryphées I, and many others, would be duly grateful.

The culprit arrived twenty-five minutes late, with a hair-bracelet on his left wrist, a suspicion of powder on the sleeve of his coat, and a preoccupied spirit that took no interest in Middlesex *v.* Surrey at the Oval, when that topic was broached to break an awkward. silence. I never saw symptoms I liked less in a youth of twenty-one. In desperation I unmasked my batteries, and asked Drummond whether the *Cock and the Hen* was in for a long run at the "Firefly." With the scent red-hot, Massey gave tongue, like a well-trained hound, proceeding to enlighten us on such intimate points of the piece as the new dresses for the "Bombay" number, the choice of another understudy for the soubrette part, the rumor circulating about such and such an individual in the cast.

"You might be there yourself," said Drummond, "you've got all the latest tips. Here's one for you hot from the oven—steer clear of stage ladies. The Sirens weren't in it with them; I know." And he slapped his breast dramatically.

Massey leaned across the table, and put his sleeve in the custard.

"You've met the wrong sort, then. There are girls with ideals, with ambitions to leave this world a little better than they found it."

"Yes, and themselves a great deal better off. There's one girl in our show," began Drummond, clearing his throat, "who is a born actress off the stage, whatever she may be on it. She looks a simple little thing, yet she makes others look a jolly sight simpler before she's done with them. She meets a fellow 'rolling in it' and she tells him she despises money. Of course he sets about spending as much as possible on this rare flower of unworldly virtue. Another Johnny learns that the beautiful creature with the soulful eyes can't afford a heart amidst the temptations of the theater. 'Men are so cruel,' she lisps. 'They never think of the damage they do.' He comes to the conclusion that she loves him for himself alone. But she never lets him alone."

Drummond paused for a moment to pull his cuffs straight. "Then she strikes a chivalrous man like you, *mon ami*, and she works the 'ideals' touch, talks about the struggle for success, tells you that she finds your society so precious to her in helping her to be true to her best self." Here Massey gave a jump as if he had been sitting on a "live" rail. "She yarns you all this over five-pound luncheons, and four-pound suppers, and motor car trips that cost you a 'tenner.' As the door closes on your retreating form after a long day together, she sits down and writes to another 'boy' what a mug you are, and will he take her down the river for a change. When your account is overdrawn, and you have borrowed all the money you can from friends, Miss Alice Howard says 'Goodby,' and some other fellow sits in the stall you have warmed so long."

Drummond had most certainly hit several nails very hard on the head, for Massey's face was a study. It

got more and more flushed as the graphic description
proceeded until it was nearly purple with astonishment or rage—I couldn't make out which—and its
possessor finally scattered all doubts by striking the
table such a blow that the glasses skipped in all directions.

"My God!" he shouted. "No wonder the stage
is criticised as a profession for girls, when the base
gossip of the 'wings' is repeated to damage a woman's
character by men like you."

Drummond's lips tightened, but he only shrugged
his shoulders. Massey's torrent of melodramatic
speech rushed on.

"You don't know Miss Howard. I have that
honor. She's the sweetest, dearest, honestest little
woman in the world. The things she's gone through
would knock the stuffing out of most men. A wid-
owed mother is kept from want by her sacrifices.
Alice is quite right when she says that the curse of the
profession is the malice and jealousy of rivals. I
understand her. Men like you never will. She's
above you."

"Her father is a 'bookie,' and alive and kicking,
if you want to know," Drummond replied, in as calm
a voice as he could command; "but I don't suppose
you do. And look here, if you are going to champion
the cause of every actress who lets you spend money
on her, you've got your work cut out. Also, you
needn't be rude in the process."

Massey was too enraged to accept any evidence
against the woman who had cast a spell over his young
affections. After all, I don't think at his age I should
have listened to Drummond's indictment in a becoming spirit, especially as in several particulars its truth

had caught Massey "on the raw." But I was scarcely prepared for "Sir Galahad's" attitude to myself.

"I won't take your money, Hanbury," he said. "Your invitation was nothing but a 'plant' to insult Miss Howard."

I felt justifiably annoyed.

"Don't be absurd, Massey; Miss Howard may be an angel from heaven, for all I know. Perhaps it would be a good thing if she had wings to fly away from the impressionable front row of the stalls. But you've no right to quarrel with your friends because you happen to be in love with a chorus girl."

"My only friends are Alice's," Massey replied sententiously.

Drummond whistled through his teeth. "Then you've a queer visiting list, beginning with the King of the Kaffir Market, down to the latest subaltern in the 'Blues.'"

"Shut up," I interrupted. "You've given the fellow quite a big enough dose for one day."

"Mr. Drummond's opinions are of no interest to me," said Massey, picking up his hat and umbrella, and he went with no more ceremony than a District Visitor from a cottage.

I was the first to recover the power of speech. "I'm going into action straight away. Do you happen to know Miss Howard's address?"

Drummond produced a crushed leather pocket-book, and consulted its pages. "Number 14. University Mansions," he read out, and I jotted down the particulars on my cuff.

"'Ware wire, Hanbury," Drummond went on, "and look out when you come to the water-jump, it's devilish deep and the landing's bad on the other side."

"I'll keep a good grip on the filly's mouth," I said. "Thanks, old man. I may want your help by and by."

"It's yours for the asking," and so saying Drummond took himself off. I reached for a pipe. As the smoke wreaths rose around my head, I sketched out my plans.

. . . . .

Heaven spare me from another ball like the Bratons'! I fought my way up the stairs by dint of a quarter of an hour's vigorous elbow work, only to have my toes stamped to a jelly and receive several knockout blows in the chest from couples going through the farce of waltzing. The friends I did see I couldn't reach through the crush. If I had reached them I wouldn't have heard their voices in the uproar.

Lady Braton, at the head of the stairs, was tossed hither and thither by the flood of her guests, two-thirds of whom she had never seen before, and who, on their part, didn't care if they never saw her again. Their names had been put on somebody's list to receive invitations, so they came, chattering in loud tones about their own affairs, impartially ready to criticise the hostess's diamonds, or the supper. The débutante daughter of the house stood by her mother's side, with a large bouquet in her hand to distinguish her from other girls, frightened by the whirl of strange faces surging past her, feeling as though she was at some masquerade. Lady Braton had preferred to ask strangers to her own friends, because the latter were not smart enough, and she wanted the dancing set to come and invite Miss Braton back in turn to their own entertainments. The bargain was perfectly well understood.

" To-night you are eating my cutlets," Lady Braton said in effect to every one as she shook hands, a set smile of welcome frozen on her face. " When you are grilling cutlets of your own in the next two months, think of my daughter and myself, and let us join you in picking the bones clean." And to the credit of the majority, let it be said, they would answer the appeal.

'As for myself I never touch cutlets, so I merely felt angry at being made to waste a summer's night in overheated rooms, when I might have been sleeping peacefully, or listening to George's latest romantic exploit. The crowd annoyed me. I was jammed against the wall by First and Second Secretaries to different Embassies, who regaled themselves by scandalous little stories in French about the people present. I learned that " The Captain " called twice a day at the corner house in Charles Street, and that the tall blonde, who was being chaperoned by the Dowager Marchioness of Pendinning, had begun her season as a brunette. When I escaped by main force from my compromising position, it was to fall (literally so) into the arms of a woman I can't stand, because she will always ask me to eat a plain dinner and meet a plain daughter. One can carry asceticism too far, so I make a point of refusing. Dancing was out of the question. I looked around for a supper partner. Molly Hargreaves was no good, for she looked on appetite in a man as a sign of vulgarity, and only nibbled at a quail herself; Hester Vaughan was sure to be waiting for that fellow in the 3rd Battalion. I had just fixed on a maiden whose avoirdupois promised well, when Audrey Maitland brushed past me. All thoughts of food vanished. I secured the next dance, and steered her on to the balcony.

There was an irresistible challenge to me in the poise of Miss Maitland's head with its crown of Titian red curls, in the grace with which she leaned over the balustrade watching the square below, in the soft tones of her voice which woke an answering echo in me. I struggled hard against the attraction she radiated, for I feel nothing but contempt for the man who succumbs to the fascination of a woman, and proves false to the independence which is the birthright of his sex.

"You haven't much to say to me, now I have given you a dance," said my partner, destroying the barrier of silence I had erected between us as safeguard.

"I was thinking of a topic."

"That's not a very courteous reply."

"I'm sick to death of courtesy," I said. "It's only mistaken for weakness. Give me the good old days when we seized the women we wanted, threw them across our saddlebows, and rode off in triumph."

"Mr. Hanbury!"

"I mean every word of it."

"You're a barbarian."

"We all are," I replied with emphasis. "Scratch the dancing man"—Miss Maitland drew back in disgust—"and you find the savage," I continued placidly. "We're all stained with woad, really, and we've only left our clubs in the cloakroom."

"Where do women come in this refined theory of yours?" Miss Maitland said icily. "You don't put them in a very high category if you imagine they submit to the brutality of your sex."

"Bless your heart, they much prefer to be driven

than to drive.   Look at Mrs. Fletcher there!"—a very stately woman passed across the window with the undersized individual who was her husband—"Every one knows that she runs the show, and is miserable in consequence."

"Mrs. Fletcher is Mrs. Fletcher," was the reply; "but I have a better opinion of you than you give me credit for."

"Flatterer!"

Miss Maitland looked at me with a puzzled expression.   "What do you mean?"

"I'm not going to have you turn my head with compliments, and become sentimental, against all your theories, too.   I, a weak-headed man, may succumb to the soft murmurs of the night, and the star-strewn sky, and the fascination of your presence.   You, a strong-minded woman, mayn't."

"I never heard such nonsense!" exclaimed Miss Maitland.   "I think you must be mad."

"I'm as sane as I ever am, or ever could be with you."   I spoke rapidly, for my companion showed signs of fright.   "You can't shift the blame on to me. I was doing splendidly, resisting the temptation to say how much I like you, and what a spell you cast over my senses, and then you spoil it all deliberately by telling me you have a good opinion of me.   It's too bad," and I copied Miss Maitland's example and got up.   She had turned a rosy pink.   "May I have another dance later on?"   I continued boldly.

The girl steadied her voice with difficulty.   "I'm very angry with you, and I shan't dance with you again."

Won't she, though, at the next ball I meet her at!

JUNE

" Wives are young men's mistresses, companions for middle age, and old men's nurses."—Francis Bacon, " Essays."

JUNE

*The Capture of Major Griffiths—An Actress Inter-
viewed—Family Cares—Miss Audrey Maitland
goes to Royal Ascot and returns*

W E were all sitting in the Club on Sunday, re-
cuperating, in the ecstasy of after-luncheon
coffee and cigars, from the fatigue of Church Parade,
when Haines, at his strategic position in the corner
window overlooking Hamilton Place, suddenly announced that the Major was tottering across the road
as though he had one foot in the grave and the other
in his coffin. Two minutes later Griffiths rolled into
the room much as if it had been the deck of a liner
in the Bay of Biscay, sank into the nearest chair, with
a groan, and wiped the perspiration from his face
with a bandanna as scarlet as his complexion.

"Cheer up, Major," said Haines. "Even if your
bank has 'bust' you can always borrow a 'fiver'
from your tailor!"

The Major reached out a trembling hand, sounded
a little bell on the table beside him, and ordered a
port-glassful of '48 brandy. Then he made several
ineffectual attempts to strike a match, accepted a light
from George Burn, let his cigar go out twice, and
spilled a third of the brandy over his coat as he raised
it to his lips. Altogether it was a sad sight.

"The old man's had a nasty knock," whispered
Haines. "I haven't seen him so shaky since he took
that toss with Fernie's hounds and nearly broke his
neck."

"What's wrong, Major?" I asked. "Were you 'welshed' yesterday at Kempton?"

"Have they blackballed your candidate at the Rag?" suggested George.

"Or has she refused you again?" put in Haines, capping our random remarks with one still more absurd.

The Major's reply was incredible.

"She has accepted me."

Haines bent forward. "Look here, old fellow, we were only chaffing. Don't mind that ass, George!" —George was tapping his forehead significantly.— "Let's talk about something cheerful. You'll soon feel better."

"Accepted me." The Major repeated the words with dull despair. He reminded me of a man driven mad by an appalling calamity, whose ruined brain held nothing but the last impression registered before sanity had fled. All the same, I suspected the dreadful truth. Griffiths' military training prevented him from ever doing the unexpected.

George screwed his monocle in, and looked the Major up and down.

"If you go on in that morbid strain," he said, "I shall make it my business to get a committal order signed by two magistrates, and put you in a place where you can gibber nonsense to your heart's content. But don't do it here, Griffiths, where there's a brass match-stand handy and a hot-tempered chap like 'yours truly.' You engaged!" George confronted the wretched soldier as though he were the agent of divine vengeance. "Why, you're the most confirmed bachelor I know!"

If this admonition was meant to rouse Griffiths to

a sense of his position, it failed lamentably. Instead, moistening his parched lips with another draught of liqueur brandy, he croaked out the two words " Mrs. Bellew," and then stuck fast in the effort at coherent speech.

But here I felt that I was in a position to clear up the mystery of the Major.

" Griffiths wishes to announce," I said, "that he is engaged to Miss Faith Bellew.   Isn't that it, Major? "

Thus addressed, Griffiths nodded his head in mute confirmation.

I could picture the whole scene—Mrs. Bellew standing with one hand on the Major's shoulder, stroking Faith's head with the other, and smiling in triumph on her future son-in-law. " So you are going to take my little girl from me? "—I fancied I could hear Mrs. Bellew say it—with a convenient rearrangement of the true facts typical of that modern matron, for, to speak plainly, Faith had been thrust into the Major's arms with a mother's blessing from the moment that he first made the girl's acquaintance. Mrs. Bellew has a giant's strength, and uses it like a giant.

" Who says the age of miracles is past? " asked George Burn, of nobody in particular.

" It seems funny losing you like this, Major," remarked Haines, " when you looked like staying the course."

Griffiths gave a meditative frown. The secret of his impending fate once out, he was regaining his composure.

" There's a sort of ' now-the-laborer's-task-is-done ' feeling that isn't half bad," he said. " I can look on and see you youngsters make fools of yourselves with some satisfaction."

"A queer sentiment for a newly engaged man," I remarked. "I'd be sorry for you if Mrs. Bellew heard it."

"That's a wonderful woman." The Major's voice rang with real enthusiasm. "She knows what one's going to say before one opens one's mouth. I'd barely got into the house last night when she took my hand with, 'I wonder whether you've got something to tell me?' So I had, by Gad, but not what she thought."

"What do you think she expected?" asked George, with a laugh. "A request for the loan of a sovereign to pay the hansom with? It *was* a hansom?"

Griffiths actually blushed.

"Yes. Mrs. Bellew couldn't wait till the end of the Opera."

"Of course," I said. "And you had the box to yourselves most of the time, while dear, unsophisticated Mrs. Bellew looked up her friends across the house."

"What a suspicious chap you are, Hanbury," growled the Major. "Can't you give a woman credit for wanting to see her friends?"

"Certainly," I replied. "I give a woman with marriageable daughters credit for anything."

But I didn't flatter myself that the truth of my remark penetrated very far into Griffiths' intelligence, because the mood of self-abasement in which he had entered the Club had given way to an intense satisfaction at having secured a wife. He began to enlarge on the fact, and it was thus that, bit by bit, George, Haines and myself were able to draw the whole story of his wooing from the Major without letting him realize how sorry a part he had played in the old, old game, in which Woman's duplicity is matched against Man's weakness.

Feeling that no good could result to himself from the attention which Mrs. Bellew lavished on him at every meeting, the Major had begun by spurning the invitations which, ever since the first week in May, had descended on his club and chambers from that quarter. But as the only consequence of returning no answer was that Mrs. Bellew called to make personal inquiries as to his state of health, Griffiths found it the better policy to temporize in such phrases as, " I will try to look in if I can," and " You may see me at lunch, but don't wait." Even then, at the next time of meeting, on one of those chance occasions of which the Season is so prodigal, Mrs. Bellew, instead of blaming the delinquent soldier for his non-appearance, worked on his remorse bred of encountering her with no ready excuse, and carried him off to some function at which Faith was due to appear.

" Most women would have cut me for giving 'em the chuck so often," naïvely explained the Major, " but Mrs. Bellew, like the real good sort she is, said she knew I was a busy fellow, and they were only too glad to take me when they could get me."

Mrs. Bellew added further to her prestige in her victim's estimation by giving him, whenever he did go to Green Street,—the site of her temporary abode for the season,—*carte blanche* to do as he liked, take a nap after lunch, smoke in the drawing-room, or obtain the hostess's undivided attention and sympathy for his stories, and his woes. Installed as a friend of the family, his advice sought on such intimate details of domestic economy as the choice between apple and emerald green for Sybil Bellew's new frock, and what books should be ordered from the circulating library, Griffiths turned a flattered gaze on the fair Faith, who, in obedience to the strategist at headquarters, showed a smiling face to his rubicund one. As he crunched the stuffed quail, and drank the dry champagne of the Bellew hospitality, the source of all these good things took on a more favorable guise to the Major. The lady of the house appeared no longer as an ogress in wait for his bachelorhood, but an enchantress waving soft spells of satiety and ease. Leaning back in his chair, a prime cigar from Bellew's special box between his teeth, Faith seen in profile before the window, Griffiths' thoughts turned involuntarily in the direction which Mrs. Bellew desired. That good mother, in partnership with her cook, fitted her guest with rose-colored spectacles through which marriage with the sylph in the window seat appeared highly desirable.

Accident at last accomplished what design had planned. Taken to the Opera by his would-be mother-in-law, the Major had been induced by circumstances, in which chance played no part, to accompany Faith back to Green Street in a hansom. Musing, as he explained, on a new golf grip rather than on his companion, Griffiths had clutched an imaginary brassie, only to find it was Faith's hand he had imprisoned within his. The Major felt compelled by a sense of honor to justify his involuntary action by a pretty speech, from which he progressed with fatal fluency into a tender one. A sudden jolt of the cab threw Faith against his manly chest, and there somehow she remained.

"Upon my word, I couldn't tell you how it happened," the hero of the episode assured us, " but when we reached Green Street Faith had promised to become my wife."

"And you richly deserved it," said Archie Haines, with the confidence of the man who has never been tempted.

"There, but for the grace of God, sits George Burn," remarked that individual, forgetting that, were justice meted out to him, he would be saddled with far more than a single wife.

It was an act of expiation on my part, for the mirth I indulged in, to accept the post of best man which the Major thrust upon me. I bet I make a hash of it.

. . . . .

I should probably have done nothing in the matter of Massey and his star of the stage, in spite of my emphatic statement to Drummond on the occasion of Massey's tantrums at my luncheon, had it not been for a fine day last week finding me unemployed about three o'clock, with no calls to work off my energy on. Archie Haines, who has freely prophesied a catastrophe from Massey's impetuosity throwing discretion to the winds, and his banking account into overdrafts, warned me against pulling out another fellow's chestnuts from the fire.

"You'll get no thanks from either side," he had said, "and you'll make the girl think that she's got hold of a good thing in 'mugs' if his friends start routing her up."

"But I'm only going to prospect," I protested.

"I know your sort of prospecting," Haines replied. "The next thing we'll hear of will be that you are footing a dressmaking bill, or making the fortunes of a florist."

But when my sense of adventure is once roused,

Haines could pour the wisdom of Solomon into my ears in vain. I pay the conventions an outward tribute of respect as befits a man of the world, but in reality I give them scant courtesy. In my veins flows the blood of the South. I draw nothing from the cautious and unromantic North, save my income.

On the afternoon in question, the idea of calling upon Miss Alice Howard of the "Firefly" came upon me like an inspiration. I was sick to death of fashionable gayeties, after a month's undiluted dose of them. I had danced my pumps into holes, I knew the menus of both the Ritz and the Savoy by heart, and there wasn't a resident on the roads to Ranelagh and Hurlingham who couldn't at sight have picked me out of a crowd. I had talked my tongue loose with tittletattle about the infinitely small, and the furnishing of inane replies to still more inane questions. The only sensible conversation I had taken part in in four long weeks had been with the crossing-sweeper opposite St. James' Palace, who had told me how he would solve the unemployed problem in five minutes if he was given his way. I forget his method, but it struck me at the time as salutary. Anyhow, I was ripe for mischief.

The address I had obtained from Drummond took some finding, and I wandered about for a long time in the hot June air, while London basked, and the policemen on duty seemed too sleepy to give me any information on the subject of my destination. I ran the place to earth at last near the British Museum, the garden of which looked so tempting that I was within an ace of joining the pigeons for a siesta.

University Mansions was a tall, newly erected block of flats, standing back from the main arteries of traffic. As I stood in the well of the center court, where the glare outside was tempered to a pleasing coolness by the stone-flagged floor and staircase, I looked up to the dim heights above with a sense of mystery. The faint noise of the city created peace and remoteness instead of dispelling it. For all the signs of life I heard, I might have been the only person in the building, and, although the entrance opened direct on to the street, there was no porter on duty, perhaps because it was a *cul-de-sac*. I could have burgled the place or abducted any of its inhabitants with impunity. In this spirit, I slowly mounted the stairs, listening on each landing with an eavesdropper's intentness to catch a sound I could take for company on my upward way. A thrill of utter loneliness caught at my heart, and nearly drove me to flight before I reached the top floor and Number 14. I pressed my finger on the electric bell. It tinkled faintly within, but no one came. I tried again, with a like result. More in despair than from any hope of gaining an entrance, I turned the handle of the door. I had never met a flat door before that opened without a latchkey, but, to my astonishment, that one did. On the instant I was inside, with the door shut behind me. I felt like giving Raffles points for stealth and secrecy.

For sheer untidiness, commend me to the room I found myself in. It was littered with every conceivable object, from the contents of a wardrobe to the remains of a luncheon. Dresses lay over the chairs and on the floor, a feather boa dangled from the electric standard, soiled white gloves heaped up the piano, the table was strewn with dessert and decanters, a packing-case poured its contents of straw and shav-

ings on to the hearthrug, and a fallen palm spread its
length across the sofa. The afternoon sun, filtering
through Venetian blinds, shed an unnatural light on
the scene, the greenish pallor it cast over the wreckage
of dissipation resembling the symptoms that presage
in the human body the approach of death. The first
thing I picked out was Massey's photograph on the
mantelpiece, a sprig of white heather tacked to the
frame, and " To Alice, with love from Boy " sprawling across the portrait's lower limbs, with a compromising boldness bred of a gust of affection and a new
" J " nib. I wandered off, examining the varied as-
sortment of souvenirs and knickknacks that are of
tribute to a popular actress from the butterflies and
moths that have been singed in the flame, till I came
to a standstill before a writing desk piled wrist-deep
with what I mentally summarized as " next week's
bill of fare." Sure enough on the top of the heap of
invitations to picnics, suppers, river parties, and motor
drives, my eye was caught by the familiar crest of the
seminary of sound learning in Oxford at which Massey was supposed to be acquiring a liberal education.
I say "supposed," because his education, so far, had
been much more in the hands of the young lady in
whose rooms I stood, than in those of the Fellows and
Tutors of his College. Elated by my discovery, I sat
down at the desk—and fell to the floor with a re-
sounding crash, for the chair, in keeping with its mistress's reputation for doing the unexpected, incon-
tinently gave way beneath my weight. 'At the same
moment as I struggled to my feet, by the aid of the
tablecloth, I saw Alice Howard standing in the doorway, whereupon I sank back again into obscurity, in
company with most of the dessert dishes, a half bottle

of port, a decanter of sherry, an empty magnum, and a cascade of knives and forks. The ruin was complete. Samson and the pillars of the temple were nothing to it.

"Well, of all the impudent things——!" came the lady's voice, choked with indignation, and cut short in the middle of a sentence by her emotion.

"Don't scream, for heaven's sake!" I said in sepulchral tones from underneath the tablecloth. "I can explain everything," and I struggled to my feet, this time without further damage, there being nothing else to break.

Alice Howard still maintained the same pose, but her face had gone crimson. If she had had anything in her hand she would have struck me, but, fortunately, she was in no more warlike costume than a tea-gown, being fresh roused from a beauty sleep. As she made no sign to speak, I began again.

"I could get no answer to the bell, so I was preparing to wait for you, when your inhospitable chair broke," and I held up a long splinter in confirmation.

"What business have you coming here at all?" broke out the lady, with histrionic abruptness. "If my maid were here we'd turn you out."

"I'm from the staff of the *Jujube*," I exclaimed, with an inspiration of genius, "and I want the story of your career, about a column long, anecdotes of your professional life, the proposals you have received from the peerage, any details of interest to our readers. You give me the facts, I'll put the 'snap' in."

Alice Howard looked at me with an expression in which rage and surprise fought for the mastery. I quailed inwardly, but the one and only principle in "bluffing" is to put the other person on the defensive

at the outset. I should have been a lost man if I had
let Miss Howard question my credentials, or my behavior, so, before she could get a word in, I continued:

"I'm extremely sorry if I've disturbed you, but I
thought you were expecting me after my note, so I
walked in. Really you might have replied, after I'd
given up a free afternoon to get the interview."

My antagonist threw an angry glance in my direction, but she made a distinct concession by clearing
a chair of millinery and sitting down. She wasn't
beaten yet, however.

"I shouldn't think of giving you any information,
sir, after the impudent way you've forced yourself in
here. If you wish to see me, it must be at the
theater."

"Oh, come now," I said, with some warmth, for
the port had spoiled a serviceable pair of trousers, "I'm
not a penny-a-liner after a 'stick' of news to buy myself a drink. I told you I was coming, and here I
am. I promise you a good show on the magazine
page of the Saturday *Jujube,* with an inset quarter-
column block of yourself, and a double-line heading
in great primer and pica:

"CONFESSIONS OF A COMEDIENNE

"MISS ALICE HOWARD TELLS HOW SHE WINS ALL HEARTS

"You'll get an increased salary on the strength of
it, and a year's credit from your dressmaker to boom
the firm. I came for a story, and I'm going away
with one. If you don't give me the genuine thing, I
shall write one out on my own—love letters and all—
and I'll bring the Court of Chancery down upon you,
tipstaves, process servers, and the whole gang of

thieves, by saying that one of its wards wants to elope
with you!"

Exhausted by my own eloquence, I pointed to Massey's photograph.

That was pretty rough on Alice Howard, especially
after the way I had treated her crockery, but I wasn't
going to be turned from my purpose by any one or
anything. The threat acted like magic, since the
enemy capitulated, horse, foot and artillery, and I got
the whole story of Massey's infatuation from her,
filling her so with the fear of writs of "Quo Warranto" and the jargon of Habeas Corpus, mandamus,
and the rest of it, that I felt positive she would cut
short her trifling with the infatuated idiot of an undergraduate. In her heart of hearts she was bored with
his affection, and glad to be rid of him.

But I never let her have a glimpse of my purpose,
getting the information and conveying the warning
I wished in the course of my interview. I made what
amends I could for my conduct by putting all the
favorite touches into the article—the struggling childhood, the sensational début, the past sacrifices, the
future ambitions. I gave copious extracts, some real,
more mythical, from the "charming little lady's" correspondence—the Grand Duke and his thirty-six
quarterings laid at her feet, who had to do his courtship by deputy—an A.D.C.—owing to his ignorance
of English; the humble admirer in the gallery, who
saved up his pence for violets, which he sent with a
note signed "One of the gods, to a goddess"; the
Johnny in the stalls who came in each night, halfway
through the second act, to applaud a particular song,
and who expressed his devotion in the language of
the *Family Herald*—"My heart cries out always 'I

love thee,' " and so on for four pages of clotted nonsense.   It was a handsome reparation, and I left Miss
Howard beaming.   She even went so far as to suggest that we might meet again.   But we shan't.

I drove straight round to the *Jujube,* and, having
the entrée as a regular contributor, got to the editor
at once.

"I've a good story for you, sir," I said, when we
were alone.   "An interview with the coming star of
the ' Firefly '—Miss Howard—just the thing to tickle
up the week-end subscribers.   It's full of spice."

"Miss Howard!" remarked the chief, ruminating.
" I don't recall the lady.   But I like your stuff, Hanbury, and you don't give us ' stumers.'   If Williams
has room for it, it can go in.   Tell him so from me."

Williams said he hadn't room.   But it went in all
the same, in place of the Women's Dress Column.
Women think too much of clothes, and a respectable
paper like the *Jujube* oughtn't to encourage a beset-
ting weakness of the sex.   How many married men
have been ruined, etc., etc.   That was the line of
reasoning that I took; that, and an invitation to meet
Steward at dinner, for Williams is very ambitious in
the lyric-writing line, and regards Steward as his
master.

When I met Williams at the function in question,
he told me that the inclusion of my interview had led
to letters of complaint at the consequent omission from
the *Jujube* of an article, " How to make a Directoire
Gown for half a guinea," promised in an earlier number of the paper.

Ridiculous!   As though any one can't make a
Directoire dress out of two towels and a safety pin.
Besides, the letter writers ought to have been thankful

that I had saved them from social ostracism. But
some people are never grateful.

   •   •   •   •   •

 Really, I think my family is "the limit." As
though the worries of the Season weren't sufficient to
drive one nearly wild, without having domestic
troubles added to them.

 First there's Dulcie, a dear sweet girl, and a sister
in a thousand. What must she go and do but fancy
herself in love with George Burn, one of the best, no
doubt, but a philanderer if ever there was one, a man
who can't help trying to make himself attractive
where women are concerned, and who has so squandered his affections in a score of affairs that he is
incapable of real devotion to a single object. I don't
blame George. He has the butterfly temperament,
and thoroughly enjoys being spoiled by women, who
have nothing else to spend their time in but flirting
with the first young man who knows how to behave
himself with discretion, and whose personal appearance doesn't give them away when they meet husbands
and brothers in Bond Street. When woman is fair,
man is weak, and he who won't take the "gifts the
gods provide" deserves to be exiled to the Bight of
Benin, or some equally sultry spot where feminine
society is conspicuous by its absence.

 I must confess to having misjudged Dulcie's social
possibilities. My mother's doubts about the wisdom
of bringing Dulcie up for the Season are justified.
My sister is far too ingenuous; too eager to bestow
her confidence, too unskilled in the world and its
wicked ways to give herself a fair chance. Only a
person with an independent income can afford to be
perfectly natural in London; and as Dulcie, by no

stretch of the imagination, can be called an heiress,
trouble lies before her. She takes compliments seriously, won't follow the fashion of having her hats
trimmed with the bodies of birds, and ends by making
bosom friends—because she feels sorry for her—with
that Renshaw girl, whom every one steers clear of like
the plague for her *faux pas* in Cairo. But, as I
told Dulcie, one feels sorry for lots of people without
making friends with them—the Prime Minister, for
instance, and the fellows who work lifts on the Tube.

Dulcie's first meeting with George in town wasn't a
success. I happened to be at the Steins' that night,
and saw it all. George just looked in on his way to
some more attractive show, for the Steins' set isn't his,
or mine, for that matter—but as my mother had sent
him a card, he had to put in an appearance and dance
with Dulcie. The night was very hot, and George
had a good deal on his mind, what with a "book"
for Ascot, a stack of unpaid bills, and several mothers
getting anxious as to his "intentions." Dulcie, resplendent in a new white frock—she always wears
white—was expecting him to continue their Easter
romance in the same strain in which they had left it.
I don't know what George talked about on the balcony
where the two sat right through the waltz, but he
probably let his annoyance at having to come to the
Steins' at all get the better of his manners, and was
either sulkily silent, or else perfunctorily polite. Anyhow, when the pair came back Dulcie's blue eyes
were as big as saucers, her mouth quivered at the
corners, and she pleaded a headache as excuse for an
abrupt departure home.

George and I evaded Mr. Stein's invitation to Sunday lunch which he makes a rule of pressing upon any

eligible young men who are brought to his wife's
dances whether he knows them or not, and went on
to Brancaster House. George seemed so blissfully
unaware that his conduct had been taken exception to,
or that any woman's charms were to be weighed for
a moment against those of supper, that I held my
peace like a tactful brother.

Next day I had to answer a good many questions
from Dulcie. Was Mr. Burn very popular? What
did he do with his time? (This was a poser.) Who
had he danced with afterward? Did I see much of
him? I did my best for George, since, on the altar
of my sex, I'd sacrifice truth, or anything else. "Men
liked him, women didn't; he worked hard in the city
till six, when he had a meat tea and went off to the
Y. M. C. A. or the Polytechnic; he had danced with
nobody under forty, save one débutante with a hare-
lip. I saw as much of him as was good for either of
us." I gave George such an exemplary character that
he was forthwith asked to tea by my literal little sister.

Constancy, I repeat, is not a strong point with
George Burn at any time, partly, perhaps, because
he never gives it a chance. He has "heard the chimes
at midnight" with so many girls, he has squeezed so
many soft hands in the stalls of so many theaters, and
whispered sweet nothings in so many "shell-likes,"
that he really can't remember the distinctive features
of each. Of course if I were to lay the case for George
before a woman, she would say, "Surely, Mr. Burn
can't deny that he had a flirtation with Miss Hanbury
only six weeks ago?" and dismiss my petition on his
behalf with costs. But in six weeks of the Season one
can get engaged and break it off, find the "only
woman in the world" and relegate her to the position.

of " last but one," change from blonde to brunette,
and back again, with a dash of auburn thrown in.
The world was made in six days, and the Season can
be made or marred in six weeks.

George didn't come to tea, and, worse still, when
Dulcie met him at Hurlingham on Saturday, he was
so occupied with Miss Kitty Denver that he took off
his hat as though by an afterthought.   Dulcie suddenly made the discovery that the Season without
George's company would be insupportable, and it has
been the greatest difficulty to persuade her that if
invitations have been accepted they must be complied
with.   My mother has approached me with " I can't
see what Dulcie finds in that Mr. Burn.   He seems a
very ordinary young man."   But then I never should
have expected my mother to be attracted by George.

I've done my best to deal with the situation.   Reinforcements in the shape of Haines have been brought
up, but he had the misfortune on the night he dined
with us to miss his train from Woking, where he had
been playing golf, and arrive when the fish was over.
His feelings never recovered from the shock of cold
soup, and the bone of the noble salmon which he
inadvertently swallowed in his haste to " join the
field."

If Dulcie had any sense she'd let George see she
didn't care a hang one way or the other.   For a girl
to sit moping in a corner when a particular man doesn't
dance with her, or to follow him up and down the Row
with her eyes, is to give the show away to him, and
to everybody else.   She ought to make desperate love
to the most unprepossessing person she can find, so
that George will jealously try to save her from herself.
Dulcie will soon gain experience in London.   One

can't expect the country to implant a knowledge of anything except vegetable-marrows and when to plant bulbs.

Dulcie's affairs aren't the only domestic problems troubling me. My mother insisted that my father should grace his only daughter's début with his presence—and his check-book. So, much against his will, he is up in town doing the Season, a thing he hasn't done for thirty years. Not that it involves him in much social hardship, except that he can't walk about with a spud, or smoke black twist in the "Wayfarers' Club." His arrival, by the way, in the latter place for the first time in half a dozen years created quite a sensation, for the porters imagined he was an unauthorized stranger trying to force his way into that exclusive institution. The situation was complicated by my father thinking it beneath his dignity to give his name to "the menials" on the ground that it was their business to know the members. If old Lord Dingwall hadn't happened to come out and salute the governor warmly, things might have become still more awkward.

Being on the spot, my father, naturally, has devoted a good deal of attention to me, and rarely a day has passed but I have received a visit from him, and an exposition of his views on the responsibilities attaching to the position of only son of a landed proprietor, and master of harriers. With his ingrained habit of avoiding controversy, he has talked in general terms, and with no definite personal application, until one morning at the beginning of the month, I was in my rooms putting the finishing touches to an article, commissioned by the *Whirlwind*, entitled, "If Pontius Pilate came to Peckham," when my parent walked in.

I excused myself doing more, for the moment, than greeting him, and left him to wander round the room at his leisure. While I summed up the Procurator's opinion of the salubrious suburb in a few trenchant sentences, I heard my father turn over the things on the table, finger "the picture gallery and jumble sale combined" that constituted the contents of the mantelpiece, and take his bearings from all points of the compass.

"What allowance do you get, Gerald?" he suddenly exclaimed.

I turned around in my chair, to see him holding a collection of manuscripts between his finger and thumb.

"Five hundred pounds, sir," I replied. My father always likes the old-fashioned mode of address between father and son.

"Look here, I'll make it eight hundred if you'll chuck all this," and he proceeded to drop the offending bundle to the floor. "This writing business is not much of a trade at any time. For a son of mine it's sheer nonsense."

"It's awfully good of you to make the offer, sir."— It was, for the estate hasn't been doing well for years. —"But I couldn't lounge about at home."

"There's plenty of work to be done, Gerald," replied my father, shredding some black tobacco into his pipe. "Lots to do in maintaining the traditions of our family in the country, and performing your duty as a magistrate, and landowner. Lots to do, lots to do," and he continued to mutter it for some seconds.

"When the times comes," I said, "I'll do my best; but until then, and may it be many years off yet, I can't throw up what I feel I can succeed in. What do you particularly object to, sir, in the profession of literature?"

"The loss of self-respect," replied my father fiercely. "Look at the papers. They're ruining England, and the fellows who write for them must be fools or knaves, or both."

"But I don't write for the papers, or only very occasionally," I said, to appease his wrath. "The briefs don't come, and London without a definite job of some kind is impossible."

"Ah, that's a point I want to discuss with you, Gerald," my father exclaimed, pulling at his pipe in a manner that betrayed his excitement. "Your mother and I wonder what keeps you in town so much, when there's as much sport as you could wish for at home. I hope, my boy, there's no woman in the case. I don't like to inquire too closely into your personal affairs, but," and he turned to the specimens of English beauty on the mantelpiece—"there's enough here to turn any man's head. Now, this young lady! Might I ask who she is?" And my father took up the latest photograph of Cynthia Cochrane. It was one of my days "off" in the way of luck.

"That?" I said carelessly. "That's an 'out of the past, I come to thee,' as the poem says."

My father gave a grim smile.

"The poem may say what it likes, but the date on this is only a month old. Don't let a taste for this sort of thing destroy your inclinations for orthodox matrimony. I shall never forget poor Boothby telling me, one night at the club more than twenty years ago, that the romance that runs wild is the worst preparation for the one that has to go in bit and bridle. I understood the point better when, three days later, I learned that Boothby had left his wife, and gone to Buenos Ayres with a previous attachment."

"I'll play the game, sir, never fear, when I go in to bat," I made reply; "but at present I'm in the pavilion looking on."

"Don't get out in the first over, like Boothby," said my father, with a humor evidently caught from the infectious gayety of London in June. "Remember, you've got to carry on the name of Hanbury to the next generation. Never link it to any incident which could bring discredit on it."

So saying, he knocked the ashes from his pipe and departed, leaving me with a feeling uncommonly like remorse that I wasn't cast in a mold to delight his family instincts in a more direct fashion. Why is Providence so perverse? Ten to one a son of mine will care for nothing but riding to hounds.

. . . . .

I always pity the people who fancy they are doing the smart thing at Royal Ascot when they rush down from town in a motor twice as big as the Albert Hall, make an elaborate toilet, surrounded by bandboxes and dressing cases, outside the gates of the Grand Stand, fly feverishly round the Paddock between each race, skip on and off coaches, try every club tent in turn to see which has the best strawberries, and pose below the royal box in the hopes of achieving immortality on the illustrated page of the *Daily Looking-Glass*.

No, the sensible person travels down quietly in a "special," ensconcing himself upon arrival on the roof of the Enclosure, where he gets shade, and a view of the course uninterrupted by mountains of feathers, and from which he can look down in comfort on the living whirlpool at his feet. As he begins lunch just before the last race, he takes no part in the game of grab over the lobster salad and the truffled chicken, and he sees the champagne poured over somebody else; he smokes his cigar in peace and is alert to commandeer the prettiest girl to share his aerie, while a rival admirer is lying helpless from indigestion and incipient sunstroke, with a lump of ice on his head.

It was in the latter spirit that I stage-managed a party, consisting of Dulcie, Miss Maitland, and Archie Haines to Ascot on Cup Day. Haines had been persuaded by me to give the "bulls" and "bears" a rest, in order to reward my sister for giving me an opportunity of removing the bad impression I had left with Audrey Maitland at the Bratons' ball, and my gratitude further showed itself in my self-restraint when Dulcie nearly caused us to lose the train at Waterloo by taking an unconscionable time over her coiffure.

My course of action with Miss Maitland had been decided on beforehand. I would show the girl the true repentance I felt for my previous outburst by maintaining a dignified reserve. Then, when her feminine intuition had led her to put the right construction on my silence, and to convey to me, as woman so subtly can, that the past had been forgotten, and forgiven, I would resume my real, unfettered self, win her admiration by the brilliance of my conversation, let her see that sentiment and its pitfalls were not for me, perhaps even make her regret that, in obedience to the vague dictates of an abstract mentor called maidenly modesty, she had spurned such a precious possession as my friendship might have become. So it was planned. Events, however, fell out quite differently. The dignified reserve was mistaken for sulkiness, and Miss Maitland gave her undivided attention to Haines, who, flattered by the interest his remarks aroused, surpassed himself as a raconteur, and an amusing, if cynical, critic of the follies of the day. Of any man but Haines I should have felt confoundedly jealous, but Archie has all the instincts of a monk, though his profession of stockbrokering provides him with few opportunities for indulging his peculiar tastes. In his scheme of things women are less than nothing. I wish I thought the same.

Baffled, I tried another tack, and began to compete with Haines on his own ground, crowning my wit with the aphorism, modeled on the best masters, that "the comedies of this world are the tragedies of the next." But this epigrammatic effort was regarded as irreverent by Miss Audrey Maitland, who takes a Sunday-school class when at home, and is on terms of intimacy with a leading official of the Clergy Sustentation Fund. Fortunately we arrived at our destination before my wounded vanity could precipitate a catastrophe.

As we walked from the station along the private way reserved for the holders of Enclosure vouchers, I seized my courage in both hands to inquire of Miss Maitland whether I was forgiven.

"What for?" the girl asked.

"Why, for my folly when we last met."

"When was that? I have forgotten all about it."

So, I had created such a slight impression on Miss Audrey Maitland that I was classed with the horde of casual partners of a season, my identity obliterated by the next infernal idiot to be introduced, in order that he might chatter nonsense to a girl a thousand times too good for him. I could have torn my voucher into fragments in that bitter moment, and returned to town. Much Miss Maitland would have cared!

"At the Bratons'," I replied, as calmly as I could under the knockdown blow my companion's indifference had dealt me.

"Oh, of course," Miss Maitland had the grace to smile. "You *were* rather foolish, but then you are just like the others—always saying things you don't mean."

"To girls who don't care," I added quickly.

"How strange you are, Mr. Hanbury! Why should the girl be serious when the man isn't? Nobody would be more annoyed than your philanderer at finding himself confronted with real romance, when all he wanted was a tinsel flirtation."

Here was a foeman worthy of my steel, in all conscience. Cup Day promised to be something more than a mere fashionable outing.

"Yes," I retorted, "but one must begin somehow, and flirtations, as often as not, end in engagements."

"And how many hearts," said the girl, "are not broken, waiting for that transformation to take place? For her own sake the woman must not wear her heart on her sleeve."

"The fashion would be more becoming," I remarked, "than the hideous bows people wear at present."

We were crossing the highroad to the Grand Stand, and if we outraged conventions at Ascot by seeming too serious we were liable to be refused admittance. The stewards of the Jockey Club can be very strict on occasions.

Miss Maitland drew aside to let me pay the entrance money, a masculine privilege I could easily forgo.

" Thank you, Mr. Hanbury," she murmured, so that Dulcie should not hear. " You administered the *coup de grâce* very neatly, and almost painlessly. I am grateful."

But there was a gleam of mischief in the girl's eyes that spoke less of gratitude than revenge. Well, I should not decline a further encounter, but it couldn't take place just yet, for we were fairly in the current of smart humanity pouring through the subway that leads to the paddock.

The Royal Meeting is not the time for a man to engage in gloomy speculation as to the place he holds in the estimation of the girl who is beginning to usurp the place of honor in his affections. Haines and I, having obtained the usual " good things " in the way of tips, were anxious to back our fancy without delay, but our fair companions had no thoughts beyond which of the friends whom they had seen only yesterday they should meet again, as though the surroundings of the Enclosure had some magical property in conferring on people virtues and graces which they conspicuously lacked in London itself. Anyhow, whether it was the presence of Royalty, floating like an impalpable essence in the air, or a sense of being dressed to the best advantage, Dulcie and Audrey Maitland insisted on dragging us at their heels, while they fairly reveled in their surroundings. If Haines and I had had parasols and open-work necks to our shirts we might have, too, but, condemned to the outrageous clothes that fashion decrees for our sex, we cursed and perspired, mere driftwood on the tide of pleasure. Dulcie is both curious and observant, and this combination of qualities kept us busy. She wanted to know why Mrs. Ffolliot was never seen with her husband, what gave Arthur Hammond the scar on his cheek, why the Bolton girls wore such dreadful sashes, and who rumor said was engaged to little Lord Dawlish.

For half an hour the comedy of social intercourse was played to a crowded house. We shook hands with people whom we couldn't stand the sight of, because their income ran into five figures, or their cook was a Parisian; we showered small talk on the dull and the witty alike; and made no distinction of compliments to the old or the young, the fair or the plain. Our unanimity and lack of discrimination were wonderful. The effervescence of badinage and repartee, frothy and heady, foamed over one and all. Light glances shot from eye to eye. The "frou-frou" of frill and flounce gave even the most distant handshake the semblance of a caress, imparted to the most trivial remark the spice of an epigram. Dulcie told every girl how sweet her dress looked, while Haines—and I, so far as I could without compromising myself in the eyes of Audrey Maitland—conveyed with unmistakable directness of gaze that we thought the wearer sweeter still. The grateful looks we received in return would have turned our heads had we not been seasoned—five seasons, to be exact.

Luncheon in our club tent introduced us to the "old gang"—Faith Bellew with her fiancé the Major, whom she would persist in addressing as "Joe"; Lady Susan Thurston with Dolly, the latter, from the warmth of her manner to me, evidently enjoying the fruits of my success in pricking the bubble of Clive Massey's stage-door romance; George Burn, "on his own," his presence endured by Dulcie with an expression of indifference which gave the utmost credit to her self-control, and explained by himself as due to the fact that, with the thermometer at eighty degrees in the shade, he couldn't have touched a morsel if he had had to face the crimson lake of Mrs. Denver's complexion during the meal in the box to which, at Kitty Denver's instigation, he had been invited. At any other time I should have been glad to welcome so many of those for whom I entertain the warmest regard. I was, however, gracing Cup Day with my presence, not to hear George's views on the starting gate, or Lady Susan's recipe for mayonnaise sauce, but to see as much of Audrey Maitland as I could. Short of actual rudeness, I did my best to discourage inroads on my monopoly of the girl's company, not only in the tent, but outside in the Enclosure where the social sheep were separated from the goats, and the people who talked in shrill tones about "two to one, bar one" and "the dear Queen" were limited, by an iron paling and a detachment of the Metropolitan police, to gazing on the object of their familiar admiration. My sister and Haines, however, resisted every effort at dislodgment. It was not till past four o'clock that, as we were filing through the turnstile leading to the paddock, I had occasion to address a word to a passing acquaintance, and delay Audrey Maitland for a moment of time sufficient to let the others vanish from our view.

"Quick," said Miss Maitland, "before we miss them!"

I took in the situation in a flash.

"There they go," I exclaimed, with deceitful readiness, and we hastened toward the subway, a route I had selected as best qualified' to lift the yoke of an unnatural chaperonage from my galled shoulders.

"Why, they're going to. the station!" I said, when we emerged by the entrance gates behind the Grand Stand. "They must have concluded we should follow."

"Are you certain?" asked Miss Maitland, with a lack of the implicit confidence a woman should repose in a man.

"Abso-bally-lutely! I could tell Dulcie's hat anywhere, and there's old Haines slouching along beside her!"

Before this mythical accuracy of vision my companion's doubts vanished, and without more ado we proceeded to the station where—the gods be praised— a train was standing by the London platform.

"Let's jump in here," I said hurriedly, at the door of the first carriage, which contained empty places. "The others will have got in farther down."

"Oh, but I must find Dulcie." Audrey Maitland spoke in distress.

"You'll be as right as rain. Hurry up; the guard is waving his flag."

Miss Maitland sprang into the carriage; I followed. A pause ensued, during which nothing particular happened save that the train remained stationary.

"Hasn't the engine driver seen the guard's signal?" The question came from the girl.

"He can't have," I replied cheerfully. Had I not won all along the line?

"Are you quite sure the guard was waving his flag?"

Miss Maitland's persistence over a trivial detail annoyed me. I made a slip of the tongue.

"I expect so."

"Expect?" Audrey Maitland repeated the word in a puzzled tone, then she looked at me. "But you must have seen him do it. Or were you inventing? And if about the guard, why not about the others? Mr. Hanbury, did you really see your sister?"

"Inventing?" I could do no better than that.

The truth in all its naked hideousness burst upon my inquisitor. She got up to leave the carriage. At that moment the train started, after doing all the mischief it could by its dilatoriness. Miss Maitland resumed her seat with more speed than dignity. When she had recovered her composure, she began again.

"What colored hat was your sister wearing?"

Miss Maitland was going to make certain of my guilt before she sentenced me. I couldn't for the life of me recall the niceties of Dulcie's costume, in spite of the fact that her unpunctuality in the morning should have impressed them on my masculine memory.

"Blue," I replied. "No, I mean pink."

"I see that men"—what withering scorn Audrey Maitland put into her voice—"will stoop to anything to get their way. I know now, Mr. Hanbury, how much I can trust you in future."

"Aren't you breaking a butterfly on the wheel?" I asked. "I only practiced a harmless little deception."

But to the stern judge of two-and-twenty my conduct seemed neither harmless nor petty. So for the rest of the journey I was treated as too despicable to be spoken to. I managed to mitigate my punishment by staring at Audrey Maitland. A man in the dock is justified in behaving like a criminal.

"Thank you for a most enjoyable hour," I said, as we disembarked at Waterloo. "I didn't know any woman could hold her tongue for an hour."

"Don't show yourself rude as well as untruthful," retorted Miss Maitland.

"Don't lose your temper as well as your sense of humor," I replied, and we parted.

Browbeat a woman and she learns to love you; give in to her and she despises you. That has been my experience. Although facts seem against me so far, I don't believe Miss Audrey Maitland is going to falsify it.

Jenny kissed me when we met,
  Jumping from the chair she sat in;
Time, you thief! who love to get
  Sweets into your list, put that in.
Say I'm weary, say I'm sad,
  Say that health and wealth have missed me,
Say I'm growing old, but add,
  Jenny kissed me.

LEIGH HUNT.

JULY

A Festival in Bohemia—Lords and Ladies—The Major married—A Scene behind the Scenes

I.T seems altogether wrong that a woman should be able so to affect a man's moods as to drive him from his customary social haunts to hide his wounded feelings behind a veil of Bohemianism. Yet that is what Miss Audrey Maitland has done for Gerald Hanbury, by maintaining an attitude of frigid hauteur on the occasions when she has met him since the affair at Royal Ascot. Accordingly, to mark his sense of the girl's injustice he has avoided the Park, refused all the offers of hospitality which are the birthright of the bachelor, put his dress clothes into lavender, and once again sought the company of Frank Steward, the journalist.

Since I last saw him, some two months ago, Steward has been promoted to the assistant editor's chair of the *Evening Star*, where, from eight-thirty in the morning to six in the evening, he keeps the staff at high pressure, two messengers on the run, and a " hello " girl earning every penny of her salary in the telephone exchange. And, as if his professional duties in Fleet Street were not sufficient, my friend has been hard at work for Mason of the " Alcazar," making such alterations in the leading lady's part of the musical comedy, *The Bird in the Bush,* as will fit it for Cynthia Cochrane, the change of cast involving the writing of several new songs, including a topical ditty, " That's how Cleopatra got the Needle."

But, in spite of the load of responsibilities he bears

189

as a consequence of his growing reputation, Steward contrives to fulfill all manner of engagements, and with especial zest when I appear on the scene, for he holds the theory, very flattering to my own self-esteem, that my temperament, impulsive, yet critical, intent on sucking every drop of juice from the orange the while it subjects the fruit to the closest analysis, heightens his sense of enjoyment. As for myself, I know that Society appears dust and ashes to me when in Steward's company. I breathe the oxygen of heaven, not the carbonic acid gas of earth. I am no longer a puppet dancing to strings controlled by feminine fingers, but a man filled with the wonder of life, and the strength to seize the magic thing ere it passes—with youth—forever.

To have one's name inscribed on the roll of Steward's friendship is a privilege that opens the doors of many Enchanted Gardens from which the majority of mankind is rigidly excluded. Thus it was with him that I went to the Boojum's Club, hidden away in mean streets, of which the members' list and the visitors' book between them contained every name famous for generations in all walks of life. I looked on masters of their craft at play till my head whirled with conflicting emotions, and Steward loomed before me as miraculous a guide as Mephistopheles did to Faust when the fiend showed the astonished doctor the kingdoms of the world. A halo was cast over that night's proceedings by the punch, the mellow flavor of which proved an instant anodyne for care. One buried one's face in the bowl, and withdrew, heedless of sorrow, and little wonder, for the fragrance of the draught had soothed the researches of Gibbon, and checked the garrulous folly of Goldsmith.

When we have not been feasting with those pagan gods, who, despite the assertions of orthodoxy, still linger in our midst, Steward and I have spent hours in discovering the queer haunts that lie just off the well-trodden thoroughfares, surveying the monuments of the past, disturbing memories hidden under the dust of other days. Having the traditions of London stored in his memory, the journalist can tell the history of any building, and of the men who have played a part in it, thus enriching the wanderings during which we have explored the Savoy and the Temple, mingled with the strange coteries of Bloomsbury and Wardour Street, and generally contrived to squeeze a quart of sensation into a pint pot of incident. On such occasions his conversation, based on wide views and cosmopolitan sympathies, makes Steward an ideal companion. "*Tout comprendre, c'est tout pardonner.*" He has seen men and women of every class and nationality. Understanding them, he has found something lovable in each.

But, unlike so many, my Fleet Street friend's humanity does not weaken his courage and resource. To my mind, he gave conspicuous proof of these qualities only two nights ago, when we were both present at the fête given by the proprietor of José's Hotel and Restaurant to his patrons in celebration of the twenty-fifth anniversary of his wedding to Madame José, the comely lady who superintends the comforts of the customers, checks the bills, and receipts them at one and the same time as she scolds the waiters and shrieks shrill orders in Castilian down the kitchen lift, making the long room with the gilt mirrors as redolent of her vigorous self, as it already is of garlic and red pepper. For years Steward has taken his Saturday night dinner there, because he likes to rub shoulders with the mixed clientèle of the place, and for the sake of a certain savory dish of fowl cooked with rice, cockscombs and truffles, a liking for which he acquired during a visit to Madrid as a special correspondent.

Being in his flat when the invitation to the fête in question arrived, I was included in Steward's acceptance, for, as he said to me, " Old José can't do without the little paragraphs I slip in for him when news is slack, and the ' form ' wants filling up."

In our oldest clothes, Steward and I turned up almost as ill-favored scallywags as the rest of the company. And they were a crew! Flowing black ties as big as napkins, hair as long as lions' manes, scarf pins that looked like stair rods, and ear ornaments the size of curtain rings! One bearded fellow sat in his frilled shirt sleeves, with a colored sash at the waist to keep him together, while a personage, pointed out as the conductor of a restaurant orchestra taking a night off, might have been mistaken for a hussar in his braided uniform of scarlet and blue. The few attempts at orthodox evening dress were not very successful—a would-be epicure, with no white shirt in his wardrobe, had substituted a flannel one which needed washing; another, proud in the possession of the required article, had marred the effect by writing across its starched surface in black chalk, "Felicidades "—that is to say, " All manner of happiness." The ladies were no whit behind the gentlemen in eccentricity of appearance. Scarfs over the head, long gloves, dresses low and high, from brocade to cotton, a profusion of beads and jet, gold crucifixes and bronze necklets—such were the feminine fashions which thronged José's restaurant at 7 P. M. on Tuesday. .

The · banquet to which Signor José's guests sat down in any order they pleased, was a procession of dishes which I failed to identify by the Italian of the menu, but which consisted, to my palate, of chicken, served as risotto, pilaff, and in other outlandish disguises, but still chicken. We ate the bones in the soup, the breast was minced and hashed, the legs appeared decked with little frills, and surrounded by a bodyguard of preserved cherries, until finally the carcase, in the language of Mrs. Beeton, was "garnished with greens and served hot." I was consumed with curiosity (like the first oyster) as to what further outrage could be inflicted on the domestic fowl by the wizards below, when the courses made a sudden plunge into the sweets; the quaint assemblage, absorbed hitherto in the solids, burst out into a polyglot uproar that created the same cacophony of sound as the Small Cats' House at the Zoo, and my right-hand neighbor, a buxom lady with strongly marked Southern features, began to ply me with questions as to "Vot you call dis een Inglesa?" much as if I were a pupil of the Berlitz System. I parried her linguistic problems as best I could, till Steward, providentially seated on my other side, drew my attention to the bearded person in shirt sleeves, who, having excited, by his appetite, the voracious rivalry of another picturesque swashbuckler, was engaged in a duel over the syllabub for his country's honor.

"You'll see some funny sights before dawn," whispered Steward to me.

"It'll be difficult to see anything at all," I replied, "if they smoke much of the stuff they've begun on," for the clouds in process of issuing from the mouths and nostrils of both men and women were of so.dense and pungent a nature that a smoke helmet would have been a boon. An Englishman could have equally well dispensed with the toasts, sounding to uninstructed ears like "Grazia Sancho Panza Maceroni Dan Leno," although the strange audience clashed glasses and stamped the floor in perfect comprehension of the meaning. This ritual over, the guests combined their efforts to clear away the débris of the meal with a readiness that surprised Steward and myself, till, upon the bare boards being covered with green cloths, the paraphernalia of " faro " were produced as if by magic, and the mystery explained. The real business of the night was about to be entered on, and the respectable surroundings of a restaurant turned into an excellent imitation of a Neapolitan gambling resort. José's protest in the interest of his license was speedily overborne, and he himself soon as flushed with the fever of the play as his patrons. As I stood in the background, the scene illumined by guttering candles, which had replaced the electric light from considerations of safety and the police, watching the fierce, dark faces which mirrored the passions evoked by the hazard of the game, I felt myself anywhere on earth rather than within a hundred yards of Piccadilly Circus, and when Southern blood precipitated the inevitable crisis, I acted my part with the utmost sang-froid.

Some one's stake was in dispute; every one in the vicinity, croupiers included, interfered at first with conflicting opinions, next with abuse, a blow was struck, and a sudden lurch of the disputants, by this time locked in personal conflict, upset a portion of the table, and with it " Shirt Sleeves " and the winnings he was engaged in counting. In a second he was on his feet, scowling and ominous. Before a hand could be raised to stop him, he had plunged a short knife into the shoulder of the nearest bystander, and stampeded through the frightened crowd to the upper regions.

At that moment of stress, when the air was harsh with the weeping of hysterical women, and the cries of threatening men, one individual alone rose to the height of action—Steward.

" Hi, José," he yelled, " clear the women out, and for God's sake straighten up this mess before the police get wind of it! Some one "—he went on, clearing a circle round the victim, who was squawking on the ground—"some one bind up this chap's shoulder. It's only a flesh wound. The rest come along after me."

And seizing a poker from the grate, my friend dashed toward the stairs.

Then for the gallant band, who followed Steward's leadership, and in the ranks of which I found myself next to the conductor, the splendors of his uniform dimmed by the vicissitudes of the evening, there ensued a wild hue and cry, in the course of which we ransacked cupboards, linen chests, and boxes, explored the mysteries of Madame's wardrobe, and gleaned much knowledge of the domestic economy of the Hôtel José. Beds were belabored, corners probed with the emergency weapons we had provided ourselves with, and any and every place searched where a man might lurk. Not till the attics were reached did a locked door give promise of our quarry. To Steward's hoarse command to open, the only reply was a scraping noise suggestive of a chest of drawers being dragged into position. The barrier was ineffectual, for before our united strength the whole structure gave way, and in the wreckage, revealed by the candle of the besieging force, stood the figure of the culprit, threatening us with his open knife.

Steward never hesitated an instant, although physically no match for his opponent. Dashing in, he dodged the other's thrust, and dealt a crashing blow with his poker right across the forehead of the foreigner. " Shirt Sleeves " fell like a log.

" Drag him out," said Steward, as coolly as though nothing unusual had happened. " He'll have a headache that will make him feel sick for a week, and a scar to carry to his grave. That's better than putting him in the dock, and getting this place shut up as a gambling den."

So saying, he threw his poker away and descended the stairs.

When we got below the restaurant was orderly once more, not a sign of baize or counters to be seen, and the wounded man removed to a hospital where no questions would be asked. As for " Shirt Sleeves," he was packed off in a cab with two compatriots, still half-stunned by his blow, which would serve to remind him, far better than a term of imprisonment, of the disadvantages of acting in England in the free and easy way he was accustomed to in Naples, or whichever city had had the misfortune to produce him.

Steward's only comment on the proceedings, made as we strolled away across Leicester Square, was characteristic:

" When next I dine with a gentleman in his shirt sleeves, I shoot at sight."

The incident has left me with the impression that

perhaps the charms of Bohemia have been overstated. My unconventionality stops short of knives.

.   .   .   .   .

My father at last justified his forty years' membership of the M. C. C. by securing a carriage ticket for the Eton and Harrow match at Lord's this year, the position allotted being just opposite the Grand Stand, in the critical spot for seeing the promenade and the play.   So we hired a sort of coach and wagonette arrangement, and asked everybody who had shooting or fishing to give away to come to it.   At least that was the idea, but it resolved itself into my people retiring into the covered seats of Block A away from the glare and the crowd, Dulcie and myself being left to do the honors.   Dulcie's social sense, as I have said before, is not acute, and she preferred to watch the game from the inside seat.   I was satisfied with buying a "card of the match, c'rect card," at the fall of each wicket, and hailing my acquaintances as they struggled by, for between the hours of three and six on the Friday of the Eton and Harrow, all Society is to be met with at St. John's Wood, provided the weather conditions be propitious.   This year they were the hottest in living memory.   The pitch of the pathway bubbled, the seams of the woodwork gaped, one could have cooked eggs on the brickwork of the Pavilion, and the free seats were a bank of sunshades and panamas.   The tropical heat didn't worry me, for I had an iced drink tucked away under the seat, an awning over my head, nothing to do but return the bows of parboiled partners and their mammas, and give languid attention to George Burn, who, having made the discovery that the Hanbury carriage offered the best point of vantage to which he had access, had become a fixture by my side.   I could have endured this cool imposition better had George been in his ordinary careless mood, but on this occasion he had a tale of woe to relate.   Apparently both Lady Lucy Goring and Kitty Denver were under the impression my erratic friend had proposed to them, and he was at a loss how to remove the misapprehension from their minds. George had conveyed to each that he cared for her, while omitting to mention how many others shared those same elastic affections of his.

"What happens when you meet them at the same ball?" I asked, after every available fact had been retailed to my patient ears. "You must lead a Box and Cox life keeping them apart."

"Don't laugh at me, Hanbury, there's a good fellow!" said George, making a wry face. "I'm in an awful hole.   The worst is, I find it so fatally easy to get into the good graces of the sex, that, before I know what I'm doing, I'm calling a girl by her Christian name, and asking her to a radium party at the club."

" I can't offer you any help," I made reply, " except to lend you enough to clear out of the country till the scandal has blown over."

George's expression changed.

" By Jove, talking of scandal, Hanbury, that little Ponting-Mallow woman is going the pace, from all accounts."

"Who's the fellow?" I asked eagerly.   'After all, it's never too hot to talk scandal.

" He's a soldier-man on leave from India—mustache curling to the back of his head—hat stuck over one ear—bronzed son of Mars—knows his world like a book."

" Yes, a betting-book. I've met the type."

" Well, Mrs. P.-M. was introduced to the hero at a

reception of the Society for the Suffocation of Social-
ists. She's married to a man old enough to be her
father; Rowan—that's the gallant captain—a fine
figure of a man to a woman who is unhappy at home,
is kicking his heels in London on nine months' leave,
knowing nobody except the hall porter of his club
and the cloakroom attendants at the music halls; Mrs.
Mallow is a clinging little person; the captain doesn't
object to be clung to. But the fellow ought to know
better than to run the gauntlet of Boulter's Lock with
her on two Sundays running, and give her supper at
the Continental. There you are, *mon ami!*"

"Talk of the devil——" said I at this moment, and
we both stopped our conversation to watch the offending couple pass.

Rowan was a handsome enough man in a bounder-
ish way, but he had a recklessness of gait, and an
effeminacy of dress that augured ill for his chivalry
and devotion when his vanity was sated, or his sense
of danger aroused. His companion, fluffy and petite,
had a vivacity and radiance of expression, bred of
sheer happiness at being with her soldier, that empha-
sized, by contrast, the discontented spirit she showed
in her own home. I raised my hat to Mrs. Ponting-
Mallow in my most *impressé* manner. It was none
of my business to cast the first stone, and she would
probably need all our sympathy and charity in the near
future.

Just then Massey and Dolly Thurston hove into
sight, and came to a halt below our aerie. I had not
seen the former since the good work I had accomplished on his behalf in Alice Howard's flat, but he
bore me no malice over the closing down of his
chorus-girl romance, unless any such feeling could be
read into his remark—" Been doing any more inter-

fering lately, Hanbury?" which he made while Dolly
was occupied with George.

"You can drive tandem again as soon as you like,"
I retorted on Massey, with an indifferent air, for, to
tell the truth, the love affairs of babes and sucklings
don't interest me. One sees too much of such things
in the Season to get excited over them.

I let Dulcie take the pair away for lemonade and
chocolate éclairs, and returned to George and his
scandal-mongering tongue.

"There's that Miss Maitland who was spending
Easter with you," he said, as I again joined him aloft.

I searched the crowd with eager eyes, to see Audrey
with an Eton cousin. The blue bow that was pinned
to her lace frock just matched the color of her eyes.
The recognition I got was not very cordial, but probably the heat affected her.

"Won't you come and have some tea?"

I raised my tones to carry, and gesticulated toward
Dulcie in the background.

"I'm so sorry," the reply came back.   "I've got
three tables and a coach to visit somehow."

"May I walk round with you?" I continued in desperation, for the vision was entrancing.

"Bobby is escort, thank you!"   And Miss Maitland and her Eton boy were swallowed up in the
stream flowing toward the tents on the practice-
ground.

"Weren't you rather gone on her?" asked George,
watching the retreating figures out of sight.

"Not a bit," I said with vehemence.

"That fellow Hookham wants to marry her," he
continued lightly.

"Why, he drinks like a fish!"

"It's the first I've heard of it, and I've met him pretty often."

I felt an unreasoning anger rising.

"Her people couldn't possibly let her do such a monstrous thing. I'd break every bone in his body if he dared to think of it!"

"My dear Hanbury," George interrupted, "you said a moment ago that you didn't care a scrap about the girl, and now you lose your temper because somebody else does! She can't remain single for ever just because you won't either marry her yourself or let anybody else do so."

"She's much too good to throw herself away on a fellow like Hookham."

"Jealous old ass!"

"Isn't that Lady Lucy making her way over here?" I asked George.

His face fell, but there was no escape save into the fruit salad on the seat behind. Perched up on the carriage, he was a cynosure for every eye.

"So long, Hanbury," he said, as he descended to his fate—a quite endurable one in pink muslin. "I invented that yarn about Hookham to pull your solemn leg. Anybody can see you are badly hit."

I! hit?—That's all the thanks I got for listening to George's interminable stories about himself. Next time we have a carriage at Lord's, I swear I'll put barbed wire round the box seat and keep it to myself.

.   .   .   :.   .

The duties of a best man, I've always thought, were to pay the parson's fee and kiss the bride. Nothing of the sort. He has to buy the ring, and the brides-maids' presents, keep the peace between the bride's

mother and the bridegroom's, choose the hymns and
the place for the honeymoon, and stand drinks all
round. I know all about it since the dose of experience that Griffiths' wedding gave me. I only accepted
the post of "bottle-washer in chief" because, without
my moral support, the Major absolutely refused to
go through the ceremony. And it was just as well I
did, since the Major's idea of marriage had been thus
expressed to me:

"Hang the church business, Hanbury! I'm all in
favor of trotting in and out of a registry office, and
then putting in a fortnight's salmon-fishing before
Newmarket."

"My dear Major," I had replied, "if you try to cut
out 'The Voice that breathed o'er Eden' you'll hear
a voice breathing anything but 'Eden' to you.
You've got to do the thing on the right lines, unless
you want to be like the Knoxes, who said they hated
the fuss of a society show, and were married quietly,
he in his golfing kit and she in her traveling dress,
before the Registrar of the Strand. The only present
they got was a silver-gilt porringer from an old aunt,
who, hearing that some ceremony had taken place,
assumed it was a christening, and now Millie has to
wear her wedding ring outside her glove to convince
people she really is a lawful wife."

The Major wasn't as amenable to advice as I had
imagined, or wild horses wouldn't have made me
undertake the job of overseer. He was continually
being seized with what he called "brain waves," but
which I have no hesitation in characterizing as incipient madness. It was all I could do to stop him
giving the bridesmaids brooches modeled as little
drinking horns, and one of his presents to the bride

was a combination liqueur set and card table, his excuse for the solecism being that it would be "so jolly handy in between the deals." Then he wanted "Onward, Christian Soldiers," played instead of the "Wedding March," because he liked the tune, and the gray check trousers he insisted on buying for the ceremony were only suitable for the "five-shilling ring." But I could have put up with all these aberrations of conduct if the Major had not developed a heavy sententiousness that he unloosed whenever chaff or congratulation afforded him an opening. We were spared none of the good old tags about "taking up a man's responsibilities," "life incomplete without a wife," "the joy of one's own hearth," and "the selfishness of bachelors." We all groaned under the weight of Griffiths' platitudes like toads under the harrow. As Haines said one night after the Major had left the club, "I don't mind being lectured by a qualified professor on the subject, but I do object to the most ignorant fellow in the room getting on his hind legs and talking 'through his hat.'"

The unrest of the Major was in sharp contrast to the behavior of Mrs. Bellew, whose calm indifference to the approaching event was almost indecent, if that epithet could ever be used in connection with the lady, since her grand manner brings even the vocabulary into subjection. Mrs. Bellew retained the most perfect self-control, as though marriage in her family were an everyday event, instead of a rarity to stir the blood. Through all the whirl of purchasing the trousseau and the household linen, cataloguing the presents, and receiving friends, she moved with majestic serenity. "I believe in letting a girl have her head on an occasion like this," was her explanation when I called with the bridesmaids' presents, the Major having been at his regimental dinner the previous night, and, therefore, *hors de combat* for the ensuing twenty-four hours. It was very unlike Mrs. Bellew to surrender her authority so completely, but Faith showed herself worthy of her mother's confidence. The bride-elect insisted on St. George's, Hanover Square; she chose a tiara £100 in excess of the price " Joe " had meant as the limit; her bridesmaids' costumes were selected to suit her complexion rather than theirs, and she called me "ridiculous" when I suggested that it was customary for the best man to receive a slight memento of the occasion.

I, in fact, got no consideration. Dulcie and Dolly Thurston, who were both bridesmaids, sat in my room for hours at a time when I was trying to forget my troubles in hard work, because Jermyn Street was handy for the couturière "creating" their frocks, and they liked my armchairs; I became a trustee of the marriage settlement on the insufficient ground that I had been called to the Bar; I ran out of silver thrice a day with the greatest regularity settling small bills for the Major. But the climax was reached when the florist's men dumped down a forest of ferns and flowerpots in my chambers, and ruined the carpet with their boots, under the impression that the reception was to be held there. Then I issued an ultimatum to all the parties concerned that if I wasn't left in peace till the day itself I'd see the whole show damned before I'd be best man. Those were the exact words I uttered, the scene being the Bellews' drawing-room. Whereupon Lady Susan Thurston expressed surprise at my using such language before the girls, Dulcie said " That's nothing for Gerald," Mrs. Bellew shud-

dered just as though some one had walked over her
grave and given her "goose-flesh," Griffiths looked at
Faith to see what she thought, and thus get a tip for
his future guidance, while old Bellew saved the
situation by remarking in a cheerful voice, "Quite
right, Hanbury; don't you be sat upon!"

My duties on the great day itself weren't so bad as
I had anticipated. I made certain of getting my man
to the church in time by giving him lunch at one
o'clock in the Carlton grill-room, and plying him full
of Dutch courage, as a result that I had to restrain
his impatience to be off, not he mine. I saw that the
ring was safely stowed away in one of my pockets,
whence it could be handed to him at the critical
moment, and that a check for the amount of my dis-
bursements was also in my possession. I prevented
the Major taking a hat three sizes too small for him,
and an umbrella, made in the Year One, from the
cloakroom, and stopped him telling the taxicab to
drive him "Home." Finally, I steered him safely
through the varied charms of the bridesmaids waiting
in the porch of St. George's, and landed him at the
altar rails at 2 P. M. sharp. Once there he was safe,
and I turned a deaf ear to his whispered inquiry,
"When will the starting-gate lift?" and gave my
attention to the assembling congregation.

True tō the prevailing custom, the Bellews had
asked everybody they had ever met in a 'bus in order
to secure as many presents as possible, taking the
added precaution of sending a list of the invited guests
for notice in the *Morning Post,* so that the world
might read next day how the Earl and Countess of
Henley and Lady Lucy Goring were amongst their
acquaintances, without at the same time becoming

aware that the aristocrats did not grace the ceremony
with their presence, and added insult to injury ·by
giving a *bonbonnière* of cut glass and electro-plate,
price 10s. 6d. at the stores, as the incriminating label
on the back revealed.

Faith made a handsome bride. Not even Griffiths'
best man could use the same epithet of him, but he
played his part with credit, making the sole slip of
trying to force the ring on to the bride's thumb, till
the officiating clergyman intervened before the victim
fainted. In the vestry I kissed, not only the bride,
but the chief bridesmaid, and was proceeding to make
the grand tour of the whole lot, when the utmost con-
sternation was caused by the discovery that the bridegroom had signed his name in the space reserved for
Mr. Bellew, so that technically he was his wife's
father, within the prohibited degrees of the Church,
and the marriage void. However, the Courts were
spared the decision of a nice point of statute and canon
law, and the papers "a Society Sensation" in their
"late" editions, by Griffiths correcting his mistake
with a resolution worthy of a better cause, and sweep-
ing his bride toward the aisle before the organ had
started upon Lohengrin.

The reception at the Bellews' temporary abode bore
the features inseparable from such functions—a surging throng round the bride as she greeted her friends,
cut the cake, and went away in a dress of gray foulard,
her hat of French straw trimmed with humming birds
and lilac; the private detective keeping watch over the
presents, and mistaken for a distinguished diplomat
so long as he kept his boots out of sight; the presents
themselves—the baker's dozen of fish slices and forks,
the biscuit boxes and butter dishes without end, the

volumes of their own works by unread and unreadable authors; the dressing-case, "the gift of the bride's mother to the bridegroom"; the necklace and tiara combined from the bridegroom to the bride; the mass of grotesque and useless objects, from menu holders shaped like owls, to enough sets of sleeve links to stock a jeweler's shop;—the ill-disguised hostility between the circles of Montagu and Capulet, the bridesmaids acting as lodestones for the few bachelors rash enough to appear, the champagne and the ices, and the curious, throng of the neighborhood lining the red carpet on the pavement to catch a glimpse of the festivities within, and cheer the bridal pair as they drove away for the "Continong," via the Lord Warden Hotel, Dover.

At the end of it all I found myself back in my rooms with an infernal headache, and the polish trodden off a brand new pair of patent leather boots. Such is life!

Ever since Griffiths took up the white man's burden —a wife—I have been conscious of a feeling of mental depression, accompanied by the physical phenomenon of a sinking sensation under the waistcoat. When a band of friends is reduced by even a single one of its number, the survivors begin to wonder how soon their turn will come to depart. George's romantic escapades seem less entertaining, Haines' wit less pungent, my bachelor rooms less comfortable. I have even caught myself wondering what the Major and Faith were talking about at a given moment, and whether I shouldn't, in reality, be happier with fewer impulses to gratify, and more occasions for self-sacrifice—always supposing that the right person reaped

the benefit of my reformed character. But it is the
irony of fate that when I do wish to lavish my store
of affection on a particular object, that object displays
no eagerness to receive it. Miss Audrey Maitland
doesn't think me interesting, or amusing, or a good
dancer, or, in fact, any of the hundred and one things
I am reputed to excel in, and on account of which I
am so inundated with invitations that my right hand
becomes palsied replying to them. And yet I would
sooner stand well in Audrey Maitland's opinion than
in any other woman's. It is against all my principles
to confess as much, but it is the solemn truth.

Now Cynthia Cochrane does care for me. She may
not understand me, but she appreciates my stories,
and is ready with quick sympathy when her feminine
intuition tells her I have eaten too many oysters, or
had the check, given to me by a tall stranger in the
bar of the " Criterion," returned marked " No Account.
Apply to Drawer." And it was with this craving for
sympathy uppermost that I determined to spend an
evening behind the scenes of the Alcazar Theater, and
see Cynthia make her début in the leading part of
Steward's enormously successful musical comedy, *The
Bird in the Bush.*

To watch the finished product from the stalls is one
thing; to stand behind and see the same piece built up,
like a Chinese puzzle, from chaos and incoherence,
with the aid of call boys, limelight men, scene shifters,
and the respective members of the cast hopping on
from the right wing to dovetail a few minutes into the
picture on the stage, and then whisk off on the left, is
quite another. An electric bell rings in the dressing-
rooms reserved for the ladies of the chorus, and
straightway the narrow passages of the theater are

flooded with a torrent of beauty surging toward the stage entrances. There they stand gossiping in subdued tones under the keen gaze of the stage manager and his deputy, until the delivery of their cue by the performer of the moment releases them in a hurricane of fluttering skirts and waving locks to the song and dance which depends on their efforts to tickle the fancy of the public and swell the box office receipts. That brief part played, back they rush again to resume the occupations temporarily abandoned, the needlework, the glasses of stout, the paper novels, and the gossip of the day.

The "Alcazar," as I saw it on my visit, appealed to me as a place of mystery. The dim remoteness of the "flies," in which could be discerned the figures of men moving far aloft, amidst a network of wires and beams, the lights continually changing in color and intensity in obedience to the dial of the controlling electrician, the distant murmur of the stage and orchestra, seeming like an echo from another world, so little relation had it to the life behind the scenes— all these sights and sounds filled me with an amazement which even the very material presences of Mason and Drummond, out of the cast of the "Frivolity" for a brief season, could not dispel. Of Cynthia I only caught a glimpse as she went on in front for the first time to speak the opening lines of her part. "I've just met such a nice boy, I don't think. He wanted to marry me; but when he told me his income was three thousand a year, I said to him, ' It may be love; it's not business '"—wink at the gallery, and fall into a chair with a hollow laugh expressive of disillusionment. From the applause Cynthia got as she went through this business, the audience evidently wanted to see more of her, which Drummond assured me they would do as soon as she changed into her next costume.

To commence the evening's experience, Mason took me into his private room for cigars and cocktails, and when he was called away he left me in charge of Drummond to do the rounds. I saw the art of "make-up" directed to change the chief comedian, a boyish-looking person on the right side of thirty, into an irritable fossil of sixty, who wheezed out drolleries from under a thick layer of grease paint and rouge, and a bold "transformation" with side whiskers. I passed the time of day with the "first walking gentleman," somewhat exhausted from an encore, and engaged in speculating whether he could put in a hand at poker before his next call. He sat in disarray on a large wicker property basket forming the chief article of furniture in a room singularly unattractive, with its white-washed walls and gas jet flaring in a sort of iron cage. Perspiration had plowed deep channels in the brick-red complexion that the lime-light demands in order to give the effect of natural coloring across the footlights, and had imparted a woe-begone appearance to him, which so aroused misplaced sympathy on my part that, after a whispered aside to Drummond, I sent for a bottle of the theater champagne, and summoning willing colleagues from next door, we drank to the success of the *Bird* for at least another year.

"It's a thirsty life and a short one," said Drummond, as we made our way to the wings for Cynthia's song. "Old Omar's bust ought to be placed over every stage door, since we most of us practice his philosophy.

"'Drink! for you know not whence you came, nor why;
Drink! for you know not why you go, nor where.'"

"That explains what is called 'the glamour of the stage,'" I replied, wedging myself into comparative comfort against the "slips." "We are all so desperately anxious to be on nodding terms with the devil, that we are ready to be cut by our own circle in order to develop the acquaintance."

Cynthia's song—"That's how Cleopatra got the Needle"—went with a roar from start to finish. Its point lay in the play made upon the word needle, which in the first verse was the familiar monument on the Thames Embankment, in the second was the word in its ordinary meaning as an article of sewing, and in the last was the term applied by rowing-men to the acute physical discomfort known as "getting the needle." It was this last verse which set the seal of success on the number, and it ran as follows—

"Cleopatra nowadays doesn't like romances,
Calls Mark Antony 'a bore,' says 'she never dances,'
Never thinks about her hair, or talks of tulle and trimming,
Spoils her voice for love duets by shouting 'Votes for women!'

(*Chorus*)
Cleo-Cleopatra, you're a trial to us all.
To get a vote you'll threaten, and you'll wheedle.
Though we long for peace and quiet,
You insist on row and riot;
Oh, Cleopatra, you give us the 'needle.'"

Steward had been fortunate in getting the song set to a tune which exactly suited the swing of the lyrics. Cynthia's by-play and expressive emphasis had full scope in the verses, and as a consequence three encores were insisted on, and it was twenty-five minutes before she could get "off," and invite us round to her room for a chat.

We gave Cynthia sufficient grace to enable her to effect the greater part of her change of toilette, and then marched into her dressing-room, to find her free from paint and powder, and as fresh as usual—her freshness was one of her stage assets—with a coquettish toque on her head. An old woman was hanging up the varied collection of garments in her mistress's theatrical wardrobe.

"Your reputation is made, *ma chérie*," was my greeting.

"Climbed to the top of the tree at one bound," echoed Drummond, mixing his metaphors.

Cynthia dimpled.

"It went nicely, didn't it?"

I picked up a stocking and began playing with it.

"I thought the house would have shouted itself hoarse," I said.

"They were dears. I could have hugged them all."

"You can begin on me, Miss Cochrane, if you like," insinuated Drummond, always anxious to draw himself in as a subject of conversation.

"Those who ask don't deserve to get, Mr. Drummond."

"I haven't asked," I whispered.

"Those who don't ask don't want, Gerald," and Cynthia struck at me with a hare's-foot brush, transferring a patch of rouge from it on to my hand. I wiped the stain away with the stocking.

"Lawk-a-mussy-me," cried the old dresser, rescuing the article from my grasp, "you mustn't do that." And, lest we might do any further damage, she bundled everything in the nature of clothing into the baskets and cupboards, locked each in turn, and, bidding us "good-night," went out.

A knock came at the door.

"Mason, ten to one," said Drummond. But it was the commissionaire of the theater, with a large shower bouquet of roses, tied with a crimson satin ribbon.

"Isn't it beautiful!" exclaimed Cynthia, almost snatching it from the man's hands. "Was there any message with it, Sims?"

"No, miss," replied the other. "It's just this moment come by special messenger."

"Thank you, Sims," and Cynthia gave him half a crown. The man saluted, and withdrew.

"Who can it be from?" asked Cynthia, looking to see if the ribbon gave any clew to the donor's identity. "I told Jimmy Berners never to send another flower except to my funeral, so it isn't from him!"

"What about—Mason?" suggested Drummond. "He's always there, or thereabouts."

"Of course, it's Mr. Mason," cried Cynthia. "He's so thoughtful."

"Are you quite sure it is from Mason?" I said, with nonchalance.

"What do you mean? It must have been sent by Mr. Mason."

But Cynthia belied the assurance of her words, by diving into the heart of the roses, from which she proceeded to draw forth a visiting card. The girl cast me a quick glance. Then she read the card.

"Why, it's from you, Gerald!"

Drummond looked at me with envy. "That was a happy idea of yours, Hanbury."

It was—one of my happiest.

"We don't want the 'star' to forget her old friends now that she has become famous," I said, with the assumption of a lightness I didn't feel.   Sentiment was in the air, and I have the Englishman's horror of sentiment.   Cynthia had hung her head.   When she raised it again there was more than a suspicion of tears in her eyes.

I turned to Drummond, and spoke slowly and distinctly.

"Drummond, there's some one shouting for you in the passage.   If you have the slightest regard for me, you'll close the door softly behind you."

The noises of the theater were unaccountably stilled as I made the remark, so much so that the place might have been solely occupied by mice.   It was Drummond who broke the silence that prevailed.

"Hanbury, my good friend, the loud summons rings in my ears.   I will return in ten minutes," and he vanished.

"There goes a man of tact," I said, and took out my cigarette case.

"Gerald, dear,"—Cynthia's voice shook a little,— "I never forget old friends.   It's the old friends who forget me."

"Even with that bouquet there to prove the contrary," and I pointed to it in her hand.

"It's not a question of bouquets.   Don't smoke for a minute or two," as I struck a match.   "I want to talk seriously to you."

I didn't see how my cigarette would interfere, unless "talking" was a euphemism for something else, but I obeyed.   I usually do when "Cynthia of the blue eyes and fair hair" commands.

"Do you care for me, Gerald?" Cynthia began, with disconcerting abruptness.

"You know I do, Cynthia," and I took her hand. She withdrew it.

"Really care for me, I mean, Gerald. We actresses get so much false devotion, that we suspect the genuineness of any affection. If I thought you were like the rest, Gerald, I'd tear these roses to pieces," and, letting the flowers fall to the ground, Cynthia pressed her hand over her heart in the stress of her emotion.

Success, instead of intoxicating Cynthia, was endowing her with a clearer insight than ever into the facts of life. More, she was communicating her excitement to me. But I was resolved to retain control over myself.

"My dear little girl," I said, "what on earth makes you talk like this when you ought to be in the seventh heaven of delight at your triumph?"

Cynthia regained her voice with difficulty. She was apparently on the verge of a storm of weeping. The artistic temperament exacts a heavy toll from its possessors.

"Sometimes," she began, "I think I hate the stage. Oh, it's amusing enough, and one's vanity is flattered by the pretty frocks, and the nice things people say to one. But to have a heart in it all is to be miserable. The men in my own walk of life who care for me I wouldn't touch with a barge-pole; the men I care for are in a rank where marriage with an actress is social ruin. Oh, I know that well enough. Everybody thinks I've got a price, only the nice people don't say so. If it wasn't that I take a certain pride in my profession, and that I thought you looked on me in a different way from the others, I'd drown myself to-morrow."

"Look here, Cynthia dear!" And this time when I took her hand she let it remain in mine. "You are overstrung, and tired, and don't know what you are saying. Things aren't as black as all that."

But in my heart of hearts I knew that Cynthia was right, and my doubts must have crept into my voice, because Cynthia, turning her face to mine, said:

"Gerald, I'm not a child, and I know exactly what I'm saying. However much I loved a man, if I couldn't get him on my terms, he shouldn't have me on his. I could have had a flat, and a motor-car, and furs, and jewelry from one of your sex after another. But if I descended into those depths I'd never come up again alive. Do you understand?"

"Oh, my God!" I said, and stopped. After all, there *was* nothing more to be said.

Cynthia smiled at me through the tears which welled up in her clear eyes, and spoke quite simply.

"Gerald, I care for you."

I felt like a drowning man. Audrey Maitland would never say she cared for me.

"Kiss me, Gerald, dear," Cynthia went on.

If I had had any strength left I should have pro-tested, for I couldn't kiss her without putting my arm around her waist, and I couldn't put my arm around her waist without her laying her head on my shoulder. . . .

When Drummond returned he found Cynthia dab-bing her eyes with a lace pocket handkerchief, and myself so upset as to be unable to keep a cigarette alight. For the life of me I don't remember what I said to Cynthia in those few moments, or what she

said to me. When a woman is sobbing on one's
manly chest it is apt to discompose one's thoughts.
Also, I was absorbed in the discovery that Cynthia
had ten distinct shades of color in her hair, and
the most I had met before on any one head had been
six.

"You two been enjoying yourselves?" asked Drummond flippantly. Any man of fine feeling would
have forborne to mock at what was more tragedy
than comedy, but it would have been too much to
expect the self-satisfied Drummond to have any perception for situations outside his own narrow range
of emotions.

"Mason," he went on, with irritating cheerfulness,
"is as merry as a grig over your turn, Miss Cochrane;
swears it's the best stroke of business he has done for
many a long day."

"Don't spoil the good impression you created by
your tact," I remarked, as I stooped to return Cynthia
her bouquet.

"Tact?" said Drummond scornfully. "You as
good as took me by the shoulders and turned me out."

"Well, it's a free country. Why didn't you stop?"

"What! and have Miss Cynthia tell me I wasn't
wanted! Humph!" and Drummond snorted.

I turned to Cynthia. "He's a silly fellow, isn't
he? Good-by, my dear. *A demain!*"

"*A demain,*" replied Cynthia, with the ghost of a
smile.

"Curse convention," I muttered in the passage.
"If I were worth my salt, I'd see the world damned
and a good woman saved."

"Convention, my dear Hanbury," said Drummond,
with the uncanny aphoristic wisdom he sometimes dis-

plays, "is the Providence we invoke to save us from ourselves."

I looked around at him with surprise.

"I believe you're right," I said. "The salvation of a good woman doesn't depend on the effort of a bad man."

AUGUST

" Marriage is a trial and an opportunity—"
' Hear, hear!' said I. ' A trial for the husband and——' "
ANTHONY HOPE, "The Dolly Dialogues."

AUGUST

Mrs. Mallow is found out—The Parable of the Man who did—Romance and a Cricket Week

O WNERS of grouse moors and yachts may say what they please, London in August is an extremely habitable spot. There is a spaciousness about the town that is refreshing after the crowded pleasures of the Season. The absence of one's friends, the eviction from one's club by the hands and brushes of painters and decorators, the pavements full of country cousins, the streets barricaded against traffic, are all compensated for by the added sense of freedom and the relaxation of the bonds of convention, enabling one to indulge in the luxuries of the pit of a theater, and the wearing of a flannel collar and brogues in Piccadilly. People with a spirit of adventure get that spirit pampered during a period of the year when it is no longer fashionable to be seen about and when one is expected to preserve the incognito of any acquaintances, male or female, whom one may chance upon under circumstances which, in normal times, would prove the fruitful parent of scandal. In other words, one must wait till recognition given implies recognition desired, and take a cut direct as meaning nothing more than that as the cat's away in Scotland, the mouse will play. For Mrs. Grundy is absent at the seaside during August, and the proprieties are in cold storage.

Therefore, I was not surprised when, going to a certain restaurant to reclaim a walking-stick left on a previous occasion, whom should I find seated on a divan in the vestibule but Mrs. Ponting-Mallow, though, to my own knowledge, the old Indian civilian to whom she was wedded had gone to Harrogate for the waters and a fish diet. The expectant promptitude with which the lady sat up as I walked through the swing doors from the street, and the mingled disappointment and concern which she displayed on seeing my face, reflected more credit on her heart than her head. Clearly, I was not wanted and somebody else was. Barely had I begun to murmur an excuse to justify my immediate retreat than the "somebody else" appeared from the grill-room staircase in the person of —Captain Rowan. So rumor for once had not lied, like the jade she is, and I prepared to witness the rehearsal of a Palais Royal farce.

At close quarters the Captain showed up to little advantage. The bad impression that the glimpse of him at Lord's had given me was strengthened by the fellow's ill-bred familiarity in addressing Mrs. Mallow by her Christian name, when his object—before a third party—should have been to conceal the intimacy of his relations with the lady. Mrs. Mallow, however, was too hopelessly infatuated to notice any shortcomings on Captain Rowan's part, and content to fix a worshipping gaze on the latter, as though he had been the Apollo of Phidias instead of a bad cross between the Jubilee Plunger and Count D'Orsay.

"I've been hunting for you everywhere, Julia," the Captain growled at the lady, paying not the least attention to my presence, although Mrs. Mallow had attempted an introduction. "Do you think I've got nothing else to do than hang about all day for you?"

"I'm very sorry," faltered Mrs. Mallow, her com-

posure deserting her still more at this unkind reception. "My watch was wrong."

"Always some excuse," Rowan grumbled, jingling
the coins in his trousers pockets, and scowling at the
clock. "I expect our table has gone by this time." .

"Do you mind if I leave my things in the cloakroom?" the lady asked timidly.

The Captain showed his teeth. "I'm hanged if I'll
wait another moment for you," he said.

"That's not a very considerate way to treat me
before Mr. Hanbury," Mrs. Mallow retorted, with a
show of spirit.

"Considerateness be blowed!" replied the other.
"I'm going in to lunch," and away he stamped, leaving the lady to follow as best she could.

I remained in the hall staring after the pair, lost
in speculation as to the strangeness of a woman's affections, and the nature of the inducements that a savage
like the Captain offered to Mrs. Mallow that she
should risk her reputation in his company.

The world, as is its way, had put two and two
together in the case I was considering, and made five.
The affairs of a pretty woman can never be the concern of herself alone. With every curl and dimple she
loses the right to privacy. Therefore, it was common
property that Ponting-Mallow, C.I.E., had not
allowed marriage to alter his prenuptial habits, but
that he still clung to his black tobacco, his discourses
on the depreciation of the rupee, and his aversion to
dining out, as though his young wife of seven-and-
twenty had been the wrong side of forty. He imagined that he had performed his share of the marriage
partnership when he had given the girl his name, and
a fraction of his pension as dress allowance. Mallow's
whole behavior seemed bent on proving the truth of

the French aphorism, "The bonds of matrimony are so heavy that it takes two to carry them—sometimes three." Wherefore Mrs. Mallow and the Captain in the restaurant trying to readjust the weight, and myself wondering at the perversity of things.

In spite of my natural curiosity, I made no attempt to follow up the clew put into my possession by that afternoon's meeting. But chance intervened on my behalf a few days later, as though Providence desired my collaboration in the working out of the whole affair.

The Old Welcome Club, at the Earl's Court Exhibition, is a favorite haunt of mine on summer nights, in which to create those fancies that form, when turned into salable prose, the bread and butter of the literary man. As a matter of fact, I have some ideas for a light comedy à la Wyndham, and the purple vault of the sky, spangled with glittering clusters of stars, the peaceful lawn fringed by the shifting crowds of pleasure seekers without, and the occasional melody of the band, afford a favorable medium for my imagination's growth. Thus it was that I was seated in the club enclosure, my hat tilted over my face, lost in a fairyland of my own thoughts, when a voice from the terrestrial world I had left broke in upon my musings.

"We can see here, without being seen," exclaimed the speaker—a woman—close behind me, paying no attention to the quiet figure in front.

My senses, only half roused from reverie, failed to identify the familiar accent till her companion supplied the missing link of memory by remarking, "It doesn't much matter where we settle down, so long as we sit somewhere precious soon."

Why, it was Mrs. Mallow and her Captain! I prepared to play the eavesdroppper with no more compunction than I should have felt if I had been put into a position for overhearing the plans of revolutionaries.

"Have you heard from the old man again?" began the Captain, striking a match preparatory to lighting up.

I had to strain my hearing to catch Mrs. Mallow's almost whispered reply.

"Yes, Ponting is anxious to know when I shall join him, as he doesn't like his present attendant, and he thinks I shall look after him better. Why didn't he marry a hospital nurse?" A bitter laugh ended the sentence.

"What made you ever take on the job?" Rowan asked. I had a shrewd suspicion he wished to steer the conversation off the rocks of self. If so, he was disappointed.

"I suppose I was tired of being at home," the lady replied wearily, "and took the first chance of freedom that offered. Freedom, indeed!" and again there came that laugh of disillusionment. "I didn't realize," she went on, "the greatness of my mistake till I met you, Stuart."

Here, so I judged, Mrs. Mallow attempted an affectionate clasp of her companion's hand. The endearment was lost on Rowan.

"Look here, Julia," he said, with blunt directness that showed he had collected his mental forces for a crisis; "we've been playing this boy and girl nonsense long enough."

"Stuart, what *do* you mean?" gasped Mrs. Mallow under the shock of this cold douche.

"What I say. We can't go on as we have been any longer. I'm not prepared to stand the racket of the Courts, even if you are."

"The Courts?"

"Oh, you know well enough that we've practically spent the last six weeks in each other's company. It's time to ring off."

"Surely, Stuart," and the lady's voice was tremulous with suppressed emotion, "you can't expect me to go back to Ponting when you know how I feel toward him! Ask me to do anything but that! I can't act a lie to my husband."

"One lie more or less doesn't matter," said the Captain, his annoyance increasing at the resistance he was encountering. "Anyhow, you can't stop with me."

"You're very unkind, Stuart," and Mrs. Mallow began to sob. "I t-trusted you, and now you are g-going to l-leave me."

That's where women so often make the mistake that costs them everything. They trust the wrong man. But if a fellow's tie is all right he may be the biggest blackguard under the sun for all the fair sex cares, in the same way that a girl with a "strawberry and cream" complexion is always presumed by her partners to be an angel.

"My dear Julia," exclaimed Rowan angrily, "don't make an infernal noise like that! Facts are facts. You're not going to be such a fool as to leave your husband, and I'm not going to be such a fool as to help you!"

"I've d-deceived him once," whimpered little Mrs. Mallow, oblivious of her surroundings, as she was overwhelmed by the torrent of her misery. "I shall be d-deceiving him the rest of my life if I r-return to him."

In the crises of life women are remorseless logicians. They brush aside the arguments of casuistry, to pierce to the heart of the issue. I had it in my mind to admire the skill with which the lady cross-examined herself. The Captain, however, regarded the matter very differently. Called upon to pay the price of an intrigue of which he was already tired, he found himself confronted by a display of emotion which he did not share, and a situation which his sole object was to escape from with all speed. Characteristically, he took the roughest way about it.

"If you can't control yourself," growled the Captain, "I shall leave you to yourself. As for thinking you can't go back to that husband of yours, that's all tommy-rot. You'll find lots of other fellows to play about with, and you'll not be the only woman by a long chalk who has kicked over the traces at one period of her married life, and then gone straight in double harness afterward. You thought Ponting-Mallow good enough to marry; you've got to think him good enough to live with."

If it had been a man Rowan had been talking to, he would have been lying on his back after that speech with two black eyes and a damaged nose. But the frank brutality of his words seemed to act like a cautery on poor Mrs. Mallow's bleeding affections, for after a moment's silence she checked the flow of her tears, sniffled several times as she regained control of her feelings, and finally rose to her feet with the quavering remark:

"If it makes you angry, Stuart, I'll try not to be a fool, but don't leave me here alone!"

Having silenced the opposition to his satisfaction, the Captain was all honey and treacle again.

"That's right, little woman," he said. "I knew you'd be sensible."

As I screwed round my head to catch a glimpse of the departing pair, I saw Rowan pass his arm through the lady's, and escort her out of view.

I mentioned the matter to George the next day, when I met him in Bond Street wearing a straw hat with an I. Z. ribbon, and just off to the cricket week at Henley Park, for which Lady Lucy Goring's importunity had procured him an invitation. I hadn't forgotten it was he who had first put me on the scent of the intrigue.

"If that bounder Rowan," said George, "thinks he can drop Mrs. Mallow like a hot coal as soon as he has burned his fingers, he's making the mistake of his life. She seems a pliant little thing, but she's as tough as they make 'em. If he wants a letter to his colonel, he's going about the right way to get it. And between you and me and the doorpost, Hanbury, the fellow will deserve all he gets."

"What's up?" I asked. "Do you know anything?"

"I met a messmate of Rowan's the other day, and he told me they'd done all they could to clear him out of the Service. But he has the hide of a rhinoceros, and after they'd ragged his quarters for three months on end to show him he wasn't wanted, and he still turned up smiling, they gave it up as a bad job. Roman's already broken up one happy home at Simla, and he's qualifying for a 'bust up' in another establishment besides the Mallows'."

"Any good dropping a hint as to what we know, George?"

"Don't you worry, 'young-fellow-me-lad'! Trust a woman and a Jew to manage their own affairs!"

So I left it at that.

Hang Society! What has it ever done for me except exhaust my balance at the bank, and raise my tailor's bill to a height at which I can never hope to settle it, unless I were to discover a gold mine under the pavement of Jermyn Street, or inherit a block of flats in the most eligible quarter of the town from a charitable—and fictitious—aunt. Society is an assemblage of people with more money than brains, and more leisure than either, drawn together for the purposes of mutual amusement. When the pleasures Society indulges in cease to attract him, why should a man remain in the charmed circle instead of seeking happiness outside it? That's the way I feel, and its source is Cynthia Cochrane. On that night at the "Alcazar" the barrier between us was broken down, and Cynthia's letters to me since have taken on a warmth of tone that makes coolness on my part difficult, if not impossible. Forced to spend the first half of August in town through pressure of work arising out of a wish to start my holidays with no commissions unfinished, I have had ample opportunity for considering the question of Cynthia in all its aspects. I have wandered in the parks on hot windless nights, my forehead bared to the glories of the summer sky; I have sat in my window overlooking Jermyn Street, a pipe between my teeth, heedless of the flight of time, and ever have I revolved the problem of my relations to the actress.

Why is marriage with an actress looked upon by one's womenkind as an unpardonable offense, for which no penance of bell, book and candle can atone?

I once thought it was jealousy which actuated the
hostility, jealousy against a rival who employed
weapons of direct glances, unabashed coquetry, and
feminine unscrupulousness, which the more civilized
of the sex looked upon in the same light as the
Powers of Europe do upon poisoned bullets and
picric acid bombs. But I don't think so now. The
average woman, I believe, regards the profession of
acting as in some vague way outraging the sacredness
with which her sex is vested in the eyes of men, tearing away a veil which should remain inviolate. By
conniving at this sacrilege the actress is a traitress to
her sex's self-respect. This point of view is never
defined, it rarely finds expression, but the conviction
lies at the root of the attitude which is adopted toward the stage by nine out of ten women. And it is
that factor which determines the equivocal position in
which I stand toward Cynthia. That—and the experience of Hugh Mercer, which I will chronicle here
under the title of

THE PARABLE OF THE MAN WHO DID

Hugh Mercer was at a time of life when he was free
from the impulses of youth, and not yet subject to
the vacillations of age. He had a comfortable income,
a nice little place in the best part of Surrey, and he
was an object of interest to a wide circle in town and
out. He could have aspired to the hand of a baron's
daughter, a baronet's sister, or the relict of a wealthy
stockbroker, without undue ambition being gratified
by the alliance. In fact he was a "catch," and spoilt
accordingly. But as fate willed it, what should he do
one Eastertide at Brighton but get introduced to Miss

Delia Foster, who was "resting" between her theatrical engagements! She was just such another as Cynthia, with instincts of domesticity which had not been eradicated by four years in legitimate drama, self-possessed without being bold, and a general aspect of what the Society papers describe as "being in great good looks." Mercer was in a dangerous frame of mind. He had nothing to say to the average débutante of commerce, he hated Mrs. Grundy and all her tribe like poison, and he had lost all patience with the conventional and stereotyped outlook of the dowagers who asked him to lunch in the hope that he would propose to their daughters afterward.

Delia Foster gave Hugh Mercer exactly what he wanted in the way of companionship and repartee, making him feel that at last he had found unconventionality with refinement, wit with propriety, and that marriage might begin romance, instead of end it. Without running after Mercer, Delia Foster let him see that so far as she was concerned, he was "the only pebble on the beach." A surprisingly handsome girl, she wore clothes as they were meant to be worn, and didn't put on a ball dress as though it were a *peignoir*. She had a figure which really was a figure, and her waist was not like a proposition of Euclid's "two straight lines which, being infinitely produced, will never meet." The stage had given her humanity without taking away her womanhood, grace without depriving her of virtue. She was as pretty as seven, and as fascinating as ten.

Mercer's whole education had been in the direction that his instincts, as distinct from his impulses, were to be obeyed. In one short week he had made up his mind to marry Delia, confident that his wife could

go where " Miss Foster" couldn't, and that his friends
would see in her the same charms that he did. So he
got a special license, took the manager of his hotel
as witness, sent a wire to his old mother after the
ceremony,—"Am bringing home a charming bride
from the stage for your blessing,"—and went on a
honeymoon of three days to see Delia's old company
in *The Silver King* at the Theater Royal, Glasgow.
When they came back to Eaton Place, old Mrs. Mercer had barely recovered from the hysterics into which
Hugh's telegram had sent her, and she was quite unable to receive her daughter-in-law. Thereupon Mercer installed his bride at a smart hotel, and proceeded
to break the good news to his friends.

But for the bearer of glad tidings he received a
chilling reception. The benedict cannot expect the
same consideration as the bachelor, even should he
be married to one of the most popular girls in his own
set. Until the inequality of the sexes is remedied, and
men outnumber women, mothers must reserve the
hospitality of their houses for those who can help to
relieve the female congestion at home. But when a
man adds insult to injury by marrying an actress, he
is indeed outside the pale, and, as he cannot be chas-
tised direct, he is punished through his wife. And so
Hugh Mercer found. If he called alone he was
treated as a silly young man who ought to have known
better. When Delia accompanied him people became
unaccountably shortsighted. Invitations sent out in
the name of " Mr. & Mrs. Hugh Mercer" for a
dinner party were one and all refused, " with many
regrets owing to a previous engagement." Folks were
quite ready to accept Hugh "on his own," but they
showed no inclination to extend a like toleration to

his wife. His mother did express a wish to see Hugh's bride, but Delia was so nervous that she spilled her tea during the interview, and confirmed the old lady's worst suspicions about "The Profession." Delia looked all right, and talked all right, with a great deal more sense than her censors would have shown, but she had been on the Stage, and that was enough.

Exasperated by his failure to get Delia taken up, Hugh Mercer shook the dust of London from his feet and retired to his country home, where he spared no pains to create a good impression round the country-side. Always ready to be amused, people accepted as much hospitality as he cared to offer, and criticised the hostess behind his back. The fact was that Delia's reversion from the standard type was unmistakable. She couldn't have looked like an ordinary woman had she tried for a month, and the woman out of the common is never forgiven by her sisters unless she marries into the peerage, or is born there. She was clever, without having the cleverness to conceal the fact. Had she been wiser, she would have cut off three-quarters of her lovely hair, and dyed the rest black, let out her waist three inches, worn unbecoming dresses, and aspired to no wider knowledge than the best method of cleaning cretonnes. Then she would have turned every woman on her husband's visiting list from a bitter rival into a stanch friend, anxious to show the new Mrs. Mercer that they didn't think any the worse of her because of her unfortunate ante-cedents. Women may tolerate the presence in their own sphere, by right of inheritance, of one who out-shines them, but they will never endure the importa-tion of such a "creature" from the lower stratum of society. In trying to graft his wife on to his family tree, Hugh Mercer was attempting an impossible task. He was merely running his head against a brick wall, and not doing the wall any damage. After a few months he shrugged his shoulders, and went back to his club, and his men friends, who liked Mrs. Hugh because she was amusing, and didn't mind their smoking in the drawing-room.

So far Delia had acquiesced in her husband's attempt to rehabilitate her socially, since, being genuinely fond of him, she was desirous of conciliating his friends, with the object of giving him pleasure. But when she found that no amount of deference and flattery could placate the hostility aroused by her uncommon beauty and independence of mind, Delia began to get restive. Upon her marriage she had, at Hugh's request, dropped her former acquaintances, much to her own regret, because she was a companionable person. But when no substitutes were provided to fill the vacancies so created in her affections, she announced one day that she intended resuming relations with Phyllis, and Maud, and Otto, and Julian. Naturally, Hugh didn't like the idea, and, naturally, being a man, he said so, and plunged headlong into the first serious quarrel of his married life, which Delia ended by marching straight out of the house—they were installed in Eaton Place by this time, Mrs. Mercer, senior, having decamped abroad for good.

Having tasted again the savor of the old environment, Delia found her new surroundings insupportable. She couldn't think what Hugh saw in the "snuffy" women of his set to make him tolerate the rudeness they meted out to his own wife, and the breach between the couple, once opened, rapidly and inevitably widened. The time, which Delia had found hung heavy on her hands during her imprisonment in a mode of living foreign to her temperament, and only endured for the sake of the man she had loved, resumed its swift and enthralling flight amidst the associations of her stage days. Hugh refused to meet any of the actors and actresses with whom Delia consorted, and thus deprived himself of any power to supervise her acquaintances. Before long Delia was offered an engagement which she was prompt to accept,—Hugh's remonstrances having long ceased to carry any weight, —and she was irretrievably drawn back into that profession from which Hugh, in an unfortunate moment for both of them, had snatched her. Smarting under a sense of injustice, Hugh received the assurances of his women friends that it was all Delia's fault as so much gospel truth. He was persuaded to bide his time, and then set the law in motion to regain the freedom which he should have lost only to a woman who was as dowdy as she was dull.

To this day Hugh walks his clubs with the aspect of a man who has drained the cup of life to the dregs, and found the draught exceeding bitter. Over his tombstone will be set up this inscription:

> Here lies
> HUGH MERCER,
> The man who Did
> and
> Was Done

I am still wondering why the Steins asked me down for the cricket week at Lowdon Castle, and why I accepted. In the first place, I'm no Gilbert Jessop at the national game, and if I can stay in two overs, get one run past point, "snick" another through the slips and hook a half-volley to leg, I've earned the generous applause of the spectators, and a long drink with straws in it. In the second place, I know the Steins well enough to cut them. Hermann Stein is termed euphemistically "a master of high finance," but, as Archie Haines says, "A master of high finance usually plays it very low down," and if Stein got his deserts for certain business transactions he would probably be His Majesty's guest for several years. As Society realizes that if it insisted on title-deeds to its esteem from every aspirant for its favors, it would shrink to dimensions which a single drawing-room could accommodate, a wise tolerance is shown toward the past of those who, like Stein, can feed the hungry aristocrat and rent his ancestral acres. Therefore, I thought of the millions behind my would-be hosts, and their anxiety to squander them in style, and came to the conclusion that I might go further and fare worse. To refuse the proffered hand of friendship is churlish—and, if that hand be full of golden guineas, foolish as well.

Every good deed has its reward, and the first person I encountered on the platform at Southampton, where the 40-h.p. Renault met us, was Audrey Maitland. Her delightful presence was explained on the same grounds as accounted for every other guest at Lowdon. She had come with a friend of a friend of the Steins, assured that "It doesn't matter in the least not knowing your hosts. Nobody knows. But every one stays at Lowdon, and you've done very well." The incontrovertible logic of this had brought together a tolerable house party, and not on false pretenses either, for if powdered footmen behind every chair, a display of gold plate worthy of royalty, a menu as long as one's arm prepared by the ex-chef of the Paris Ritz, motors galore and a launch always under steam be "doing you well," we *were* done well. If any charge could be brought against Stein, it was that he overdid his hospitality. For all the peace and quiet his guests enjoyed, they might have been living in Hengler's Circus, instead of in the loveliest place on the south coast. During the cricket matches against the Gentlemen of Hampshire and the Greenjackets, a band blared out popular melodies for the edification of the swarm of country folk who graced the functions. At night, if it weren't dancing in a marquee on the terrace,—the Castle battlements outlined with fairy lamps, and the trees hung with lanterns,—there was a variety entertainment by performers from town, or a display of fireworks from a raft anchored off the grounds—during which, by the by, great enthusiasm was created by a set piece representing the host and hostess, in which the portion forming the mimic Mr. Stein's nose ignited before the rest, and presented a glowing design of a striking natural feature.

The chief obstacle to everybody's enjoyment was the Steins themselves. In the fine feudal palace, over-looking Southampton Water, with its ivy-clad walls twelve feet thick, its moat, its banqueting-hall black with age, its atmosphere of stately tradition, the Steins were as much at home as slugs in a gold cup. They couldn't have chosen a setting less calculated to enhance their social worth. The Misses Stein, true Roses of Sharon, with bold black eyes, and figures that it was a positive cruelty to imprison within the narrow confines of a fashionable frock, were continually changing from one garment, fearfully and wonderfully made, into another. Mrs. Stein, bewildered by the unfamiliarity of her surroundings, was far too busy getting into bodice after bodice at her daughters' bidding, to shed luster on the social position of her masterful lord and master. And if there was one person less objectionable than old Stein—with his habitual inquiry, just as though he were the butler, whether he could do anything for one, and to which no person had the courage to suggest that he might sink himself in his own launch to the general satisfaction—it was his truly Semitic son and heir. I took a dislike to that young hopeful the moment I set eyes on him, and he did not lessen it by paying odious court to Audrey Maitland, of all people.

It is surely carrying a sense of obligation too far to return the hospitality of the father by smiling on the son, and yet I couldn't find any other reason to explain why, if Miss Maitland did not exactly let Jacob, junior, monopolize her, she went very near doing so. I had a serious bone to pick with the fellow over it. At a critical period of our match with the Greenjackets I went in to try to stop the rot in the Lowdon Castle team, caused by the bowling of a lanky subaltern from the Rifle Brigade depot, who had been slinging down fast balls with such effect that six of our wickets had fallen for 75 runs, a feeble reply to the 180 knocked up by our opponents. I was leaving the pavilion, weighted with a sense of responsibility, when I happened to see the Jew boy keeping Audrey company under the trees, and actually making her laugh. I walked to the wickets "seeing red," dug a hole in the batting-crease deep enough for Stein's grave, and smote at the first ball sent down in a blind fury inspired by the thought that I was aiming a mortal blow at his curly head. The ball missed the stumps by a hand's breadth, but I overdid my stroke to such an extent that the bat continued its wild sweep until it scattered the stumps in all directions. " Seven wickets for 75, last player o," was the cheerful announcement that greeted me on my return. I was in no mood for Miss Maitland's crocodile sympathy.

"You were so interested in Stein and his funny stories," I sputtered, in my rage and shame, "that you couldn't have seen any of the play."

Before she could turn aside the just rebuke, I had passed on to the pavilion, and the stiffest drink I could mix.

There is no surer way of getting snubbed than by offering advice to a woman on her choice of friends. Such is the perversity of the sex that forbidden fruit becomes the most desirable article of diet. I can't carry the analogy of fruit into the case of Stein, since the term applied to him sounds ridiculous. He was either prickly pear or a monkey-nut. Fortunately, however, before I took the law into my own hands, and had recourse to actual violence, Stein himself released me from the horrible position of spectator to his infatuation—a spectator powerless to intervene, lest I should incur the charge of interference.

About halfway through the ball that took place on the night of our victory over the Hampshire Gentlemen, I was standing by the garden side of the marquee, smoking a cigarette, with a recklessness of manner consequent on having cut most of my partners, when Miss Maitland walked rapidly round the corner of the tent upon me, and asked me to take her where she could rest, as she felt tired. It is a habit of mine to keep a weather-eye open for secluded spots in case a need of them should arise, so I was not long in seating the lady at the end of a pergola in the French garden, which forms one of the beauties of Lowdon—a spot where the crescent moon shone through the rose-covered roof, and the summer scents hung heavy in the air.

What was it that comprised the charm radiating from Audrey Maitland? I revolved the problem while I sat back with folded arms and watched my companion tapping on the stone causeway with one dainty foot. Distinction was written plain in every feature, in the delicate line of her nose, in the peach-bloom of her soft cheeks, in her mouth curved like a Cupid's bow, in her graceful little head set on the white pillar of her neck, and wreathed in an aureole of most delicious curls. But beauty alone can never hold my devotion, though it may attract it. I must find intelligence, an interest in things which the ancients described as "the humanities." Life is too brief to be wasted on trivialities to the exclusion of those subjects which have stirred the curiosity, and stimulated the thought, of successive generations. I prefer to talk about the achievements of great men of the past, rather than the doings of small men of the present. One may be excused for not knowing about Mr. Ponsonby de Tomkyns, but to be ignorant of Francis Bacon is unpardonable. I may chatter scandal in a ballroom with my partner of the moment, but if I am to share my library it will only be with a wife who cares as little for gossip, and as much for Edmund Burke, as I do. Audrey Maitland was a woman after my own heart. She was sweet-tempered, yet shrewd;

clever without malice; feminine without folly; neither
jealous of her own sex, nor suspicious of mine; broad-
minded, tolerant, and with interests which never run
dry even in the drought of Society, to which a worldly
mother condemned her for nine months out of
twelve. This was the considered judgment mentally
delivered during the five minutes of silence which followed after we had both taken our places on the old
oak seat in the pergola that night in August.

"What a horrible young man!" said Miss Maitland
at length, shuddering in spite of the warmth of the
incense-laden atmosphere.

"Have you only just discovered that fact?" I asked,
with a joy I tried hard to conceal.

"He tried to kiss me!" the girl went on, too absorbed in her own feelings to notice mine. "Oh, I
wish mother had never made me come down here. I
told her the Steins were quite impossible."

"Shall I go and throw the fellow into the moat?"
I suggested, with the idea of consoling her.

"And have everybody talking about why you did
it? No, thank you, Mr. Hanbury."

"I shouldn't worry long over the likes of him."

"The thought which tortures me is that I must have
made him think I was the sort of girl he could kiss."
Audrey Maitland hung her head, her cheeks pink with
annoyance.

"Did he try to make love to you?" I asked, em-
boldened to do so by the fact that her anger against
young Stein was making the girl more confidential to
me than she had ever been during the Season.

"He paid me silly compliments, but I never thought
he could be such a cad as to take advantage of my
politeness to him because he was the son of the house.

We were sitting out on the terrace when he put one horrid arm round my waist, and—and——" But here Audrey Maitland's disgust got the better of her candor, and hiding her face behind her hands she broke off abruptly.

"The brute!" I muttered. "Now if you had treated him as you have always treated me, the thing could never have happened."

Miss Maitland's hands dropped, and she turned to me.

"How have I always treated you, Mr. Hanbury?" she asked in frank surprise.

"Come," I said, "you surely don't need to be enlightened on the fact that from the moment when we first met, you have done all you could to show your dislike for me. Think of the Bratons' ball, of Ascot, of Lord's—nothing but snubs, snubs, snubs."

As I uttered the indictment a wave of such sorrow for myself swept over me that I nearly copied my companion's example and buried my face in my hands.

The girl took my outburst with due seriousness.

"I'm so very sorry you've taken it like that, only I thought from something you said to me in London that you wanted to make love to me, and of course I couldn't have allowed that."

"Of course not," I replied quickly. "You couldn't allow a man whose whole body isn't worth your little finger to have the presumption to make love to you."

"I didn't mean that at all," and Miss Maitland spoke in tones of distress. "You twist what I say so that I don't know really what I do mean. Oughtn't we to be going back?" and she made as if to rise.

"What, and run into the arms of the Stein boy again? No fear. You can't snub a fellow like him, and he'll be pestering you for forgiveness and another dance."

My diplomacy was successful, for the girl sank back again.

"May I call you 'Audrey'?" I began. "It's absurd to address each other as 'Miss Maitland' and 'Mr. Hanbury' as though we were strangers."

"I don't think I ought to," my companion replied, turning her face away so that I had no clew as to her thoughts.

"It's not a question of what you 'ought' to do, but what you 'want' to do."

"Ought I to want it?"

'Audrey Maitland might have been laughing, 'for all I knew.

"I don't presume to say, but I do,—'Audrey!'" It was a bold stroke, but it proved successful.

"Well, I suppose I will then,—Gerald. Now we really must go back."

"Is there any chance of supper with you?" I ventured, as I guided her by the longest route I could to the marquee, and the crowd, every detail of which had suddenly become hateful after the peace and intimacy of the pergola, and its roses.

"You're in a very 'asking' mood to-night," smiled 'Audrey to me. "But just for a treat you may—and a table by ourselves."

I managed it all right, and we sat in our oriel till lights shone faint and faces showed haggard as the pale dawn brightened in the sky. We ranged over every topic, surprised at the similarity of our tastes, the community of our interests and an intellectual sympathy which showed itself by one uttering the unspoken thoughts of the other. If I had admired the girl at a distance, my admiration turned to a far deeper feeling when I found how little separated us, and how much united. If her beauty had ensnared my physical nature, her wit, her sympathy, her insight led my soul in chains. I went to bed in an ecstasy of sentiment, to toss sleeplessly as my imagination re-created her charms to haunt and tantalize me.

For the rest of my visit to Lowdon I was an unsatisfactory guest. When Audrey wasn't with me—she had the cleverness not to reserve her company for me alone—I was morose and *distrait,* so much so that I nearly ran the launch aground on a sand-bank through watching the girl when I was at the helm; I was barely civil to young Stein, although I ought to have been deeply grateful for his indiscretion and its consequences; I nearly had a row with the head gardener, because he found me cutting the roses in the French garden to make into a bouquet. Altogether I was gloriously indifferent to those social amenities upon which life in country houses is established, and my obliviousness to all except the presence of Audrey was heightened by the fact that we were to be fellow guests the following month at Mr. Thurston's lodge in the wilds of Rosshire. This prospect led me to effusively thank the Steins, when the time of departure came, with a genial heartiness which so wrought upon the old man that he gave me the name of his broker and some advice as to profitable investments. If the terms of friendship can be estimated with any accuracy in pounds, shillings, and pence, fifteen per cent—that was what old Stein promised me—takes some beating.

" There's nothing in the world so noble as a man of sentiment."— SHERIDAN, " The School for Scandal," Act IV.

SEPTEMBER

Steward makes a Confession of Faith—Ben Machree Lodge, Rosshire, N.B.—George Burn's Escapade at Dieppe

AFTER the pandemonium of Lowdon and the cloying richness of the Steins' ·hospitality, I was glad to put in a quiet fortnight at home with our own partridges before migrating north to catch Thurston's salmon and stalk his stags. It is rarely that I put in an appearance at all under the ancestral roof during the autumn, so my arrival was treated by my family as a windfall, the discussion of domestic problems to be relegated, accordingly, to the background for the duration of my visit.

So hypnotic were the sounds and silences of the countryside to my urban soul, and so magical the slumber into which they lulled my senses, that it was as much as the keeper could do to rouse me to tramp through the root-fields and newly cut stubbles after the little brown birds. For the most part, I was content to drowse away the sunlit hours amidst the hum of bees, and the soothing symphonies of distant reaping machines, while Dulcie, in the summeriest of summer costumes, forgot her shattered romance of the season in her efforts to perfect her service at tennis, and take the curate's volleys backhanded. Dulcie, in fact, had developed into a furious devotee of exercise, and the spiritual affairs of the parish must have been sadly neglected, from the way she tempted the curate from his duties to run up and down the base line of the court for set after set. When I remonstrated with my sister for her action, she merely exclaimed,—with that fine disregard for the higher life which her sex can show when it conflicts with feminine inclinations, —"I'm sure Mr. Sturgis is far better playing with me than visiting tiresome old women who've nothing really the matter with them."

I was glad Dulcie should find pleasure in anybody's company—even though only a curate's. A round collar and a black straw hat don't make a man a knave in my eyes, as they most unquestionably do in my father's, but then I am not the fond parent of an only daughter. And I had sufficient faith in Dulcie's affection for her brother to believe that she wouldn't take any serious step without first consulting that natural adviser. If a girl can't be trusted to play tennis with a man without building up romance around him, especially when that man is only the possessor of an income of £100 a year, and wears gray trousers with white stripes down them, she isn't fit to be allowed outside the walls of the county asylum. So I told my father when he hinted his fears of a clerical son-in-law. All the same, it seemed a wise thing to bring another Richmond into the field, and, running over the list of possibles and probables, I suddenly called to mind Steward, tied to his pen and office, shocking callers upon editorial business by the freedom of his language, and the limitations of his costume, conducting half a dozen conversations on the telephone simultaneously, and contriving to keep a cool head and clear brain in defiance of the thermometer and his manifold duties. Steward, it is true, could hardly be looked upon in any sense as a potential relative, but I knew no one who could supply so powerful a coun-

ter-irritant to the poison of the curate's fascination—
if fascination there was—by his compelling charm of
manner. Any person of sense would prefer half an
hour of Steward to half a year of the Rev. Sturgis.
I consulted the powers that be, dispatched a perspir-
ing page boy with a telegram, and brought the journalist safe and sound to our front door at 4 P. M. on
Saturday.

None of my people had ever met the man before—
or anybody like him, but there is this sovereign fact
about my Fleet Street friend, that though a person of
no perception may begin by forming a poor opinion of
him on account of his shaggy hair, insignificant figure,
and aberrations of dress, which, on the present occasion, took the form of a gray felt sombrero and white
" ducks," no one ever labors for any length of time
under that erroneous impression. Steward, moreover,
knows his own limitations to a nicety, and confines
himself to those spheres of action in which he can
shine. Therefore he declined Dulcie's invitation to
tennis, and let the Reverend Sturgis grovel in the
bushes in search of lost balls. The exertion involved
in this task may have reacted on the latter's temper,
or perhaps he may have discerned a rival, for he
adopted a patronizing manner at the tea table toward
his original-looking neighbor, and the sarcasm of the
question he addressed to Steward was apparent to
every one.

" I suppose you don't often get into the country? "
" Not as often as I could wish," replied Steward.
" Ah, that's a pity," remarked Sturgis, idly tapping
his saucer with his spoon, and with one eye on Dulcie
to note the effect on her. " One has time really to
study one's fellow-creatures here, and, with all due

deference, that is what you gentlemen of the Press never seem to do."

The intonation given to the words expressed infinite comprehension, and infinite pity on the part of the speaker.

"Really," said Steward. "Do you find humanity a profitable field for your investigation?"

"Profitable indeed," exclaimed the other, delighted at the opportunity for delivering impromptu the subject matter for a sermon he had in contemplation. "To him who reverences the truth, and has the power to perceive it, nothing is common or unclean."

"My great cause for complaint against the clergy," interrupted the journalist, addressing nobody in particular, but so emphasizing his statement that we all paused in our various acts of refreshment to listen, "is that they can't even bless mankind without putting on full vestments to pronounce the benediction. Many of us laymen"—here Steward spoke directly to the curate, who was trying to shield himself behind his teacup,—"from our knowledge of life have small reason to receive the message of a self-satisfied Church in a thankful spirit, and we decline to receive it at all unless it is spoken by a *man*."

After which the clerical gentleman subsided to his proper conversational level, to the huge delight of my father, and with the tacit approval of Dulcie, whose fairness of judgment recognized the justice of the rebuke. Never were the old women of the village so well served by their minister as during the rest of Steward's stay at the place.

No guest could be easier to entertain than the journalist, possessed as he is of the resources of a lively and many-sided intellect, for were it only a walk round

the stables, he would invest the proceedings with
interest by a fund of information on such a topic as
that great sire of our thoroughbred stock, Eclipse.
My mother was charmed by her guest's solicitude,
which never obtruded, was always present, and
Dulcie's heart was completely won by the sympathy
and insight with which he discoursed on the care and
management of the affections at a moment when advice
on that subject was peculiarly opportune. Our household being one in which ceremony is conspicuous by
its absence, Steward was at liberty to follow his own
bent during the two days he spent in it.   He was
content to lie out on the lawns, under the limes and
elms, feed the goldfish in the fountain, modeled on
the famous basin at Versailles, smoke Havana after
Havana, and steal from Time a few uncounted hours
of reverie.   The flow of witty and shrewd speech he
was ready to indulge in for our entertainment revealed
to my people the possibilities of the English language
and the human intelligence, while Steward, on his
part, professed himself eternally grateful to me for
permitting him to see the country, and existence
generally, under novel conditions.   But I was more
than repaid for any hospitality I had offered by my
friend's defense of the Artist and Bohemian against
the attacks of the Philistine—represented by my father,
who stirred up the discussion on the Sunday night
over our coffee and cigars when we were sitting under
the rising orb of a very golden harvest moon.

My father had been rash enough—rash, that is, from
his own point of view—to express a hope that Steward,
wise with the experience of a lifetime in the ways of
literary Bohemia, would dissuade his only son from
profitless excursions into that dry and thirsty land,

when he had, in the interests of his own future as a landed proprietor, far better confine his energies to acquiring the taste for country institutions which land-owning demands. Out of deference to his guest my father refrained from imparting direct his views on journalism and authors, but the guest quickly divined them.

"Why shouldn't a man," said Steward at length, "who has talent in the direction you indicate, Mr. Hanbury,—and your son has talent,—make the best use of it? Haven't we need for pens as well as plow-shares?"

"Other men," rejoined my father, "not so fortunately placed as Gerald can tempt Providence in Fleet Street. He, at any rate, has no need to do so."

"Need!" echoed the other with an inflection of scorn. "It's not a question of 'need'; it's a question of 'must,' for body and soul to obey the mysterious force impelling them. Your son and I, sir, have heard the song of the sirens, with ears unstopped by the wax of the worldly Ulysses, and we must 'see visions and dream dreams,' appraising men and things by other standards than those of accepted success, to, perhaps, find poverty and failure at the end of all. Yet we would prefer the fate of the genius Chatterton dying of starvation at the age of twenty on a pallet of straw to that of the monarch in his palace praised by all men. The stars have called to us and we must hearken."

"The stars?" asked my mother, who takes words literally.

"Literary ambition, the spirit of Romance, Bohemia," explained Steward, with a wealth of correction.

A sigh escaped from Dulcie, who was gazing at the

journalist with an expression of concentrated fascination that spoke volumes for his magnetic eloquence.

"Are you sure you are not catching cold, dear?"
said my mother, who would have similarly interrupted
the recital of a death sentence at the Old Bailey, so
little regard had she for the solemnities. Dulcie gave
a protesting shake of her shoulders, but never took her
eyes off Steward, who had resumed his brief for the
defense.

".When I was a youth carrying copy to the printer
on a salary of ten shillings a week, I wouldn't have
sold a single one of my ideals for all the luxury you
could have heaped on me. And every year I cling
still more passionately to the ambitions and hopes,
unsubstantial, no doubt, clustering within me. You
only note, Mr. Hanbury, the outward differences between myself and your friends, the unconventionalities
of my appearance"—my father's deprecating hand
was ignored—"my irreverence toward the code of
life you obey, my disregard of the accepted laws of
moneymaking. But you have no knowledge of the
sources from which I draw a *joie de vivre,* an enthusiasm which makes your comfortable existence in
comparison the shadow of a shade, bloodless and
empty. Why, sitting in this garden, surrounded by
the dim forms of trees, and under the vast canopy of
the heavens, my pulses are tingling with the summons of the eternal spirit of youth—the Andromache
of the ages—bidding me rescue it from the clutches
of the Conventions! The Romance of the world is
a prisoner in the grasp of the ideas you stand for.
Instinctively you don't want your son to join me, and
the uncouth tribe to which I belong, in the warfare we
wage against those ideas. But he will, sir, in spite of

everything you can urge. He has eaten our salt, and his name is enrolled in our fellowship."

My father's cigar glowed crimson in the darkness as he pulled at it in dawning comprehension of the faith Steward was enunciating. But it was my mother who took up the challenge.

"We don't like Gerald," she said, "spending so much time writing articles in London, when he ought to be either working at the Bar or getting known to our tenants. Besides, ideas such as you hold prevent any one settling down to the responsibilities of life, like marriage."

"My dear madam," deferentially replied Steward, "the responsibilities of life are not kept at bay by the possession of one set of ideas rather than another. The child in each of us grows old despite any creed one may possess; but while this man only knows that all things decay, that man sees the roses on the tomb, and the life springing from the dust. To your husband details are the most important thing—the rotation of crops, the head of game, the weekly investment list. To me the years are too precious to be squandered on matters which others will accomplish on my behalf for a salary. In the cave of Aladdin I refuse to concern myself with the sacks in which the treasure lies hid. I want the treasure itself—and life is the most wonderful treasure imaginable!"

Steward threw up his arms with a gesture of despair, as though language failed to describe what he found in life.

"Life!"

The word came from Dulcie in a whisper, vibrant with emotion. She crouched in her chair, her figure rigid, her whole soul responding in an ecstasy that was agony to the gospel preached to her for the first time. In that moment to her awakening intelligence Steward was neither old nor young, handsome nor plain. He was immortal youth, that incarnate spirit of nature whom the ancients called Pan, bidding her obey her own instincts and not those of other people, and to have done with the anxieties and cares with which civilization fetters the race. As if aware of the effect he was producing on at least one of his audience, and anxious to bring the conversation down to earth before it soared beyond control, Steward did not take up the thread where he had dropped it.

"My belief," he went on, "is purely personal. I would never try to inoculate another person with it; and, besides, Gerald has an inheritance to transmit, and a name to perpetuate. But he won't make the worst husband because he has looked on the glory of the world rather than its shadows, and because the goddess of Romance has touched him with the hem of her robe. Whoever has sought beauty and found it, him shall ye reckon happy!"

The voice of the speaker died away like the murmur of the night wind among pines. We sat motionless as the stone figures one may chance on in the neglected pleasance of a deserted château. My father's bowed head rested on his hands, my mother wore an expression of puzzled awe, while Dulcie, with wide-opened eyes, sought the illimitable spaces of dreamland. As for me, Steward's inspired rhapsody was a thing of joy to raise and purify me of earthly longings. I could have sat for eons in that garden, building castles in the air out of the outlines of the trees ragged against the disk of the moon. But the hour of ecstasy passes like the rest, and my mother broke up the group from that sense of disciplinary solicitude which marks the correct hostess. The pressure of my father's hand, as he gave me a more than usually cordial grip at parting outside our bedroom doors, showed me, however, that Steward's message had been interpreted aright.

Now the question with my people is, "When will that delightful Mr. Steward come to visit us again?"

"When the harvest moon sails again in the sky!" I make reply. One Bohemian is quite enough in the family.

.   .   .   .   .

Mr. Thurston's lodge in Rosshire stands in a plantation of young spruce firs at the head of a wild glen, with a river flashing three hundred feet below. In fine weather a wonderful panorama stretches before the spectator standing at the lodge door, for straight across the gorge rises Ben Machree in rugged grandeur, its broad outline broken into spurs and shoulders where the rocky flanks protrude through their thin covering of heather. The gray desolation of the great "corrie" on the face of the mountain opposite, within which lies the sanctuary for the forest, the bright streak of a waterfall on the sheer precipice forming its right-hand wall, the purple radiance of the heather-clad slopes of low ground, the gleam of distant waters, the light and shade chasing alternately across mountain and glen, the herds of red deer to be spied with no more exertion than is involved in focusing a stalking-glass, the golden eagles circling in search of blue hares—make up a prospect to be found nowhere save in the Highlands of Scotland. Even when the storms hide Ben Machree in a winding sheet of vapor, the mist pours down the valley like an army of phantoms, and the rain lashes in fury the windows of the lodge, there is an awe that is a fascination in nature veiling her face in a white mask, and the uproar accompanying the transformation. Wealth can be put to no better use than to buy a man foothold in such surroundings as those of Ben Machree Lodge.

Inside, the place is much the same as all its kind— severely simple in its appointments, the walls lined with match-boarding, the carpets and curtains of Cameron tartan, antlers and heads everywhere. The chief feature is the veranda running round two sides of the lodge, screened with glass from the uncertain climate of the "north countree"—the receptacle for rods, lines, cardboard targets, and all the varied tackle of the chase, the chosen spot for the display of the salmon, the baskets of trout, the "bags" of grouse and ptarmigan, at the close of each day's sport, the informal smoking-room of the men at all hours, the rendezvous of the ladies after dinner, where they can listen to the recital of the incidents of stalking and fishing from the principal performers. The régime is Spartan, no culinary refinements being possible, since supplies are three days' distant, and any meat, save mountain-fed mutton and venison, unprocurable. For drink there is whisky, and plenty of it. The whole domestic economy of Ben Machree Lodge, in fact, is regulated by, and subordinated to, the interests of sport. Mr. Thurston will not tolerate the intrusion of Mayfair manners, and Park Lane pirouettings, such as are the fashion on Speyside, Deeside, and other Scottish haunts of society. Lady Susan has to leave her ball dresses and tiara in the south, champagne and other "kickshaws," in the language of the host, are strictly barred, and woe betide the guest who lags

behind in the house after 9.30 A. M., or stays up when
the order for "lights out" has been given at 11 P. M.
He, or she, is never given another chance of shooting
a "royal" in Gabrach Corrie, or hooking a fresh-run
grilse by the sunken rock in the King's Pool. So
long as the light is right for spying, two rifles have
to be out day by day with Donald and Hector on one
or the other of the beats of the forest, there are rods
wanted on river and hill-loch, and if a gun can be
spared to walk up grouse on the low ground, so much
the better for the larder, and the peace of mind of
Lady Susan and her cook. Catering in the wilderness
for a house party of eight, ten servants, and a horde of
attendant ghillies and stalkers, is not a task to be
undertaken without the assistance of good men and
true to walk anywhere from ten to twenty-five miles
a day and bring in spoils varying from a stag of sixteen stone to a jacksnipe.

With the air blowing keen off the hills, the atmosphere so clear that one can make out a raven perched
on a rock at a mile, the towering majesty of Ben
Machree, its lofty head crowned with a shifting cap
of fleecy cloud, the impressive silence of the "corries"
wrapped in "the sleep that is amongst the lonely
hills," the sight of the stalking pony picking its way
carefully up the steep track to the spot where it will
wait till the faint echo of the rifle shall summon it to
bring home the monarch of the glen, the bracing of
every muscle, and the tingling of every nerve, as the
glass is turned on a shootable stag, and one enters on
the test of endurance and skill which may last half
an hour, or half a day, before one can crawl into
range of the animal—with these sensations to put on
the credit side of the account, Scotland indeed makes

one her debtor. I should have had the time of my
life at the Thurstons' even if the Lodge had been full
of "ticket-of-leave" men and suffragettes. As it was,
I found myself in a party comprised of Massey, a
captain fellow in the H.L.I. from Fort George, a
girl whom nobody takes much notice of in London
because she is plain and dances outrageously, but who
was in her element at Ben Machree, and caught more
fish than the rest of the party put together, and, above
all, Audrey Maitland, who, if she had been fascinating
in the patchouli-laden atmosphere of the Steins, was
now ravishing in a tam-o'shanter, and a broad sash
of her clan tartan across her evening frock. Bonnie
Mary of Argyll wasn't in it with Audrey for all that
makes for the conquest of my sex.

Love-making, however, took a back place in the
twelve days of my stay in Rosshire, and had I wanted
to play the Romeo, I should have found it difficult,
for a Highland lodge does not encourage *tête-à-têtes,*
unless one is indifferent as to who overhears that
speech signifying that another mortal has been
sentenced at Cupid's court-martial. Moreover, the
will was wanting. To start off less than an hour after
breakfast in any weather, trudge up hill and down
dale behind a stalker who rivals the walking powers of
Miss Kilmansegg and her golden leg, to crawl up
drains, and lie in peat hags, crouch behind a stone on
the mountain top in the teeth of a howling gale for
two hours, and then run a mile at top speed because
the deer have shifted, sprawl down an exposed face an
inch at a time in full view of the hinds below, and, if
one is in luck, get home at 7 P. M., after an eight-mile
walk with the pony only "bogging" once—such
things are conducive to thoughts of bed rather than

tender sentiments. To complete the rout of romance, Duncan Cameron skirled his pipes round and round the dinner table during dessert, this stimulating entertainment being followed by reels in the skinning-room of the deer larder, to the light of candles stuck on to the beams from which the deer were slung, and in the presence of an audience of ghillies, who followed suit themselves as soon as the "gentry" had had their fling and withdrawn to the seclusion of the veranda and bridge.

People never do themselves justice in London, where the feverish anxiety to have a good time, and be "in the swim" at all costs, produces an effect of insincerity and heartlessness. Lady Susan, pouring out coffee at breakfast or cutting sandwiches, was the British Matron *sans peur et sans reproche,* rather than the society *grande dame,* occupied in preserving social distinctions for her caste, and in saving her daughter from the attentions of ineligibles. Dolly, struggling to cast a straight line with an eighteen-foot salmon rod, was no longer the Porcelain Princess of Charles Street, Berkeley Square. And Clive Massey became a far more presentable figure in Harris tweeds, getting a right and left at grouse, or stopping a blackcock at forty yards, than when hanging around actresses. As for myself, the world was well lost for the boisterous health and spirits that filled me from the moment I jumped into an icy-cold bath, to the time when, sixteen hours later, I thrust my tired limbs into pink pyjamas.

The first days of my visit coincided with a heavy "spate," so I turned my attention to the river, wading about in the brown flood, a watchful ghillie at my back ready to gaff my belt if my feet slipped on the

uneven bed, and one of the ladies on the bank to take
a turn in whipping the most likely pools, and shout
advice, above the roaring of the waters, when a grilse
had succumbed to the lure of the "Silver Doctor,"
and was bending the "greenheart" double in wild
rushes for freedom. As soon as the river fell, the
H.L.I. fellow and myself put in one good spell after
ptarmigan and grouse on the tops of a range of hills
where, the feeding not being so much to the taste of
the deer as that on Ben Machree, we did not disturb
the stalking. The three girls accompanying us, we
walked the seven miles in line, picking up in the three
hours of the journey grouse, hares, and snipe till the
panniers of the pony were as full as an inspector of
the R.S.P.C.A. would have permitted before institut-
ing a prosecution. After a stiff scramble we lunched
on the summit, in a wilderness of gray shingle and
rocks, looking the while from Skye to Cromarty.
Then, the party dividing into two, there ensued a confused game of "I spy" over the various peaks and
gullies of the range, much banging at the flocks of
ptarmigan, which walked at one's feet like pigeons
till roused to fly by volleys of stones, an infringement
by the Captain of the Wild Birds Protection Act
(Scotland) in securing a peregrine falcon, and a hulla-
balloo after a fox, shot by myself, who, having got
separated from the rest in pursuit of a wounded hare,
surprised Reynard as he made for his den in a rocky
cairn. We arrived home in triumph with fifteen brace
of ptarmigan, twelve brace of grouse, a couple of
snipe, five hares, a fox and a peregrine, having drunk
all the streams dry on our homeward way, the ladies
footsore, the dogs limping, and a universal sensation
of having eaten nothing for twelve hours, or tasted

whisky for twenty-four. If any other place than Scotland can give an equal meed of pleasure and pain I'd like to know of it.

My first day "on the hill," as the phrase goes, was unfortunate. After Hector had given me a long crawl over broken ground, a hind, which had been lying unperceived in the shelter of a peat bog, suddenly got our wind and gave the alarm to the beast we were stalking. Later on we sighted a nice stag lying in a "pocket" on the far side of the ground, but as the wind blew over the top on both sides, the only approach was from the "corrie" below, where the ground was too bare to permit of our remaining unseen by the quarry. It was want of tact that led Hector, after our luckless day, to expatiate on the grand heads he had stalked on this selfsame beat. I did manage to shoot an animal the next time I went out on the lower ground, seventeen stone, but a "switch," so I was still without the trophy I longed for when it was my turn again to scale Ben Machree. Of course it was a misty morning on the mountain, and, as the chances of getting anything except a chill seemed remote, I suggested to Audrey Maitland that she should put on a "sou'-wester" hat and a waterproof skirt and join me. Lady Susan made some demur, but Mr. Thurston shouted out, "A good wetting hurts nobody, and makes the hair curl," and drove the girl forth.

When we set out things were not so bad, but as we rose higher and higher up Ben Machree, in a silent line of men and ponies, the mist grew denser, until all sounds became muffled in the oppressive folds of vapor. Once we heard the half cough, half grunt of a startled hind, and the clatter of the stones as she galloped away along a precipitous track, but for the most part we moved in a dead world. At rare intervals a freshening gust of air would roll away the bank of fog like a curtain to disclose, far away, glimpses of loch and moorland and mountain-side glowing a vivid green and purple in the damp atmosphere, and murmurous with the voices of the burns hurling themselves down the heather cliffs on which we stood.

The pinnacle of Ben Machree is formed of a shattered pile of granite over a hundred feet in height, its base surrounded by huge boulders, torn from the parent block in prehistoric ages, and heaped in all directions for scores of yards. A long, natural staircase of rock leads up through the center of the mass to a deep depression at the top, from which it is customary to spy the whole range of the peak, and Gabrach Corrie itself, a vast amphitheater directly below in the heart of the mountain, always full of deer for the reasons that the grass is sweet and the wind, sucked up through the corrie as in a funnel, blows from all quarters of the compass upon the deer and protects them effectually from danger. Already that season, Hector, so he said, had abandoned half a dozen stalks there after very heavy animals, owing to the treacherous nature of the air currents. While the pony was relieved of the deer saddle and hobbled, Audrey, I, and the ghillie with the rifle, climbed to the crest of the rock to await events, the stalker going off to discover if there was any clearer view to be obtained lower down the hill. For what seemed an interminable time we sat there, marooned in a sea of mist, cut off from earth as completely as though in a balloon trying to pierce the veil which hung before us for sight or sound of man or beast or good red earth.

We had given up all hope of a stalk when, with the unexpectedness of an actor appearing through a trap door on to the stage, Hector stood beside us.

"There's a gran' beast in yon corrie," he whispered. "I'm no saying he's not a royal, but, mon, he's in a verra awkward poseetion with the puffs coming every way. I spied him through a chink in the mist. It'll be clearing the noo, I think."

As he said it, the wall of vapor broke, outlines of rock appeared on every hand, and we saw the mist swirling over the sides of Gabrach Corrie, as though from a gigantic punch bowl filled with the devil's brew. Far, far below came into view the little loch at the bottom, and the jagged pinnacles ribbing the steep descent. Sounds of life penetrated once more to the ear, the hoarse croak of a raven, the pony cropping grass at the foot of our crag, and the wail of the rising wind as it commenced its sad symphony round the bleak buttresses of stone. I turned my glass on to the depths, and the deer we had been seeking leaped into being on its powerful lens, a herd of hinds feeding along the loch shore, and scattered groups of stags, their points left to conjecture, so distant were they. We lost no time in descending from our eminence, and consigning Audrey to a vigil with the pony. Hector took the rifle, and crept forward to the edge of the abyss, with myself in pursuit. When the pillar crest of Ben Machree was out of sight above, the stalker stopped behind a projecting boulder, wriggled on to his elbow and gazed long and earnestly down the slope, here set at an angle of fifty degrees. When it came my turn to look I seemed to be in the middle of all the deer in the country, for on that day Gabrach Corrie held at least fifty fine stags, and a couple of hundred hinds, some lying in pockets and holes on the steep face opposite, some feeding on the young grass for which the "corrie" was famous, others walking to "fresh fields and pastures new."

"To your right!" hissed Hector, and, as I followed his direction, there came into view a magnificent stag, its three companions all ordinarily worth a shot, but now completely eclipsed by an animal of eleven points, and at least eighteen stone. The quartet lay about five hundred yards below and to the right on a carpet of thick heather, interspersed with granite fragments. To reach them would involve crossing a dry water course and an exposed tract of rubble and grass before the shelter of a rocky spur could be attained. Even then it was doubtful, so far as we could make out from where we crouched, whether a shot could be effected without the head and shoulders of the sportsman being visible on the sky-line. But the problem could wait, the immediate question being how to get as far. For though we might hope to escape the notice of the particular beasts we were stalking, the "corrie" was so full of deer that it would be strange if we deceived them all.

But chance helped us. We lay on the lip of an enormous cup, of which the side farthest from us had been bitten out, and at the base of this gash a pass led down to a wood, the top of which was just visible. Up this pass, about a mile and a half from us, a great concourse of deer was ascending, every stag and hind in the "corrie" becoming intent on this proceeding, with heads raised from the ground, and turned to the newcomers. In the diversion so created, we threw ourselves on our faces, and never raising a limb from the ground, but progressing as an animated pancake might be expected to do, we reached the stream bed, took a moment's breathing space, and crossed the danger zone an inch at a time, until we halted behind the projecting ridge. My hopes of a rest were disappointed, for Hector started forthwith headforemost downhill, and as he had the rifle, the glass and the flask, I had perforce to follow. When we did come to a standstill, with our heels high above our heads, and the contents of my pockets emptying themselves generously over the heather, I lay with my tongue out and my brain swimming, wondering whether my insurance premiums were all paid up, and whom I should bequeath my signet ring to—Audrey, or Cynthia. I was roused to inspect the stags through a convenient crack, where they lay not 120 yards off, my beast on the extreme left, with its head laid alongside its body, dozing. To wait in a cramped position, tortured with needles and pins, a desire to sneeze, and a burning thirst, one's pipe pressing into one's side, the rifle crushing one's thigh, the blood rushing into one's head, and grim expectancy clutching at one's heart—to endure these pangs until it should please the stag to get on its legs and offer the chance of a shot to trembling fingers and blurred brain, was to display qualities deserving canonization on the spot. I would rather have gone back to Audrey and Dewar's "Fine Blend," than have taken Quebec or shot the "eleven-pointer." As a matter of fact I did none of these things, for when, after a full hour and a half's wait, the beast rose and began to feed, I was so exhausted, and my hand so unsteady that I sighted too high, or too low, or too much in front, and, instead of falling to the report, the stag stared for a moment in sheer surprise at the unwelcome entrée to its dinner,

before stampeding up the "corrie" over its far brow,
together with every animal in the place.

"Better luck next time," gasped Hector, as we
toiled back to the cairn; "but ye pulled off too soon.
It's no so late, though. We'll have something the
day."

I put the speaker's cheerfulness down to the innate
politeness of the Highlander, and accepted Audrey's
sympathy with gloom, not even lightened by her
account of instructing the ghillie in the mysteries of
"Cat's Cradle," and we proceeded along the ridge of
the mountain in the direction in which the deer had
gone, spying some of the hinds feeding peacefully on
the flats below, but of a stag, and particularly our
stag, not a trace. Hector meanwhile took all the
precautions which a stalker loves to indulge in. He
threw up tufts of cotton grass, with which his waistcoat pocket was stuffed, to test the direction of the
wind, never suffered us to turn a corner or descend
a gully till he had searched the foreground with his
glass, chose his path so as to avoid loose stones, and
called a halt for ten minutes after sending a ptarmigan
wheeling over the sky-line. As we approached the
end of the center ridge Hector redoubled his stealth,
till he disconcerted Audrey and myself by throwing
himself full length on the ground. Our nerves
thoroughly unstrung by the maneuver, we followed
suit. And it was well we did, for between the blades
of mountain grass, which formed our temporary
horizon, we saw the three companion stags to the one
I had missed walking along a plateau which broke the
declivity of Ben Machree some ninety yards below.
The sight was so unexpected that I let them vanish
in the distance before stretching for the rifle. Putting

his finger to his lips, Hector drew the Mannlicher
from its canvas case and slipped it into my hands,
just as there appeared before us the stag we sought,
carrying its head and branching antlers proudly, and
quickening its pace to overtake its comrades. My
head cleared, I raised the rifle softly, as it came level,
aimed at the line of its shaggy neck, and shot it
through the heart. At 5 P. M. exactly my foot was
on its broad flanks and I drank "Blood on the knife,"
Hector replying in the toast of "More blood." It
was nearly six before the stag was "gralloched," fixed
on the pony, and our faces turned toward the lodge,
nine miles away.

Of that walk I cherish the pleasantest recollec-
tions, for, having got the finest head so far killed that
season on the forest, I was tramping alongside
Audrey, helping her over rough places, listening to
her gay chatter, and generally reveling in her prox-
imity. What matter, then, the mischances that befell
us, the mist coming down again at nightfall, the
lantern's refusal to throw a proper light on the rough
track, the pony "bogging" twice and having to be
relieved of its load and hauled out by main force, my
disappearance into a deep heather hole with a foot of
water at the bottom, Audrey's mishap as she crossed
the river, slipping backward off a precipitous bank up
to her waist, and at the end Lady Susan's reprimand
to me for taking so little care of the girl!

"Hang the girl, he's got the stag!" said Mr.
Thurston.

"He's got 'em both," added Massey when Miss
Maitland and her hostess were out of hearing. As,
in my soaking clothes, I was in no mood for repartee,
I let that statement pass. Anyhow, wherever the lady

may find a billet, the head's going over my writing table.

.   .·   .   .   .

When, on my return south, George Burn wrote and asked me to join Archie Haines and himself for ten days at Dieppe, my first impulse was to refuse to link my fortune to any such combination of high living and plain thinking. But it is a poor comradeship which only shows itself in times of calm, so I accepted, if only to save George and Archie from their worse selves, since I could afford to view their masculine shortcomings with an aloofness due to my wandering affections having become fixed at last. My misgivings were revived with full force upon George's appearing at Victoria Station in a large check ulster, the pockets stuffed with French novels and contraband tobacco, on his head a Homburg hat ornamented with a bunch of feathers, his luggage consisting of a disreputable kit-bag and a "hold-all," and that expression of rollicking bravado on his face which the Briton assumes to convey his anticipatory enjoyment of the pleasures of "Gay Paree." We crossed from Newhaven on a sea so smooth that a sailor's life appeared the most enviable of all, George striking a note of sincerity in his confession of regret that he was not in the Navy, by saying that he liked the "wife in every port" idea. The Hôtel des Bains had been recommended to Haines as possessing all the comforts of home with none of its rigors, so we took up our residence there for the period of our stay in the French watering place.

Why is it that the mere fact of being on the Continent makes the average Englishman feel that he is the very devil of a fellow, up to no end of mischief?

The three of us sat in the Casino, and laughed at the fathers of families who were taking a week-end away from the counters and desks where they earned the salaries to pay the rents of Balham and Tooting, pretending that they liked to strain absinthe through a lump of sugar, and casting glances right and left with the intention of conveying to the ladies that they were regular Don Juans. The folk who had landed from the cross-channel steamer, typical middle-class Britons, shy and reserved, were in two hours transformed, under the influence of the Gallic climate, into gay Lotharios out on the spree, ready to fling their francs on the "boule" tables and to offer light refreshments to the butterflies of pleasure who, in silks and satins, had fluttered into the gilded saloons of the Casino. Wherever we went—to the cafés of the Grande Rue Henri IV, to the Castle on the West Cliffs, to the forest of Arques, to the restaurant at Puys, we were dogged by our fellow-countrymen reveling in the new-found sense of freedom which comes with exile from their own convention-ridden land. They lined the morning promenade on La Plage, they sat on the beach at the bathing hour, when the native beauty of Dieppe took its plunge into the "briny," clad in rainbow-colored toilettes, complete with stockings and buckled shoes, and with the wearer's monogram worked on the right hip, and they were on the spot in smoking jackets and opera hats when the band commenced the evening's gayety sharp at nine by striking up "*Non, je ne marche pas.*"

After four or five days, however, George wanted something more exciting than studying the genus "tourist."

"I didn't come over here to behave as though I was at Margate," he announced at last. "If you fellows like to spend your time twiddling your thumbs on the beach while a sweet thing in violet skips about in front trying to avoid wetting her feet, I don't, so I'm off on my own account."

"Going off on his own account" didn't improve George as a companion, but it seemed to work wonders on his spirits. We only saw him at long intervals, when he threw out dark hints about assignations, and "the time of his life," and borrowed 100-franc notes of us. We caught a glimpse of him one night on the terrace of the Casino talking to a prepossessing female in black picked out with orange sequins, but it was only a glimpse, and as George is very English, with linguistic powers to match, and his companion looked very French, Haines and I concluded that the conversation was pretty much on the surface.

"Making an ass of himself with some woman," said Haines, and I agreed; but when George began to take all his meals out, and practically never showed up for forty-eight hours, our sense of amusement changed to one of annoyance, since Haines and I were too much alike in temperament, and we needed George as a buffer.

On the sixth day of our visit we two were sitting outside our hotel after *déjeûner*, basking in the sun, when a Frenchman came up from the Plage. His heavy mustache and "imperial," his black cut-away coat and dark trousers made him appear a painful object in the heat, and the excitement which caused him to wave his cane at sight of us taking our ease was, in our opinion, solely attributable to his sufferings. To our astonishment, as he came level with our chairs he stopped to scrutinize us, rolling his eyes about meantime, and muttering "Sacré bleus," and other expletives, for his own edification rather than ours.

"You are ze Monsieur Anglais?" he asked abruptly, in an execrable accent, looking from Haines to myself, and back again to see which claimed the honor.

"Of course we're English," said Haines. "Do we look like Japs?"

The Frenchman's further examination was not to his apparent satisfaction.

"You are not ze Monsieur!" he remarked, with a shrug, and pulling at his imperial with a perplexed gesture.

"Why did you say we were, then?" demanded Haines aggressively.

"Don't worry the fellow with your lingo," I interposed. "He doesn't understand a word of it, and he's got something on his mind."

"Ze Monsieur avec le chapeau, vere ees ee?" and our strange visitor put his hand up to the side of his head and waggled his fingers in his endeavor to express the bunch of feathers which distinguished George's hat from all others.

"My goodness!" I shouted at Haines. "He means George. I don't like the looks of this."

"Jove, you're right," and Haines slapped his knee to emphasize the force of his discovery.

The Frenchman put the right interpretation on our excitement. "Le connaissez-vous?" he demanded. "I veesh parler a leettle to Monsieur."

I tried my hand at diplomacy.

"Qu'est ce que vous voulez dire à Monsieur? Peut-etre pourrons-nous lui porter une lettre?"

The man waved his arms about as though he was signaling.

"Non, non, non!" and his voice rose an octave with each word. "Il est méchant, cet homme là. Ee ees vat you call 'a devil.' He kees my vife, I kees 'eem." And the stick was flourished to the imminent danger of our heads.

"Oh, ça ne fait rien," said Haines, using about the only French phrase he knew. In the circumstances it was an unfortunate one.

"Vat you say? You tink it nossing to kees my vife?" shouted the outraged husband, growing purple in the face, and advancing toward Haines with his fist clenched.

"Ici!" and I got up to stop the fight that seemed imminent. "Mon ami ne comprend pas qu'est ce qu'il dit—— Tell him you're damned sorry," I said to Haines in an aside.

"So I am, that I haven't kissed his wife. Tell him that!"

"Monsieur me demande exprimer son regret complet," I explained. "Understand? Comprenez?"

"All right." The Frenchman's passion subsided, with Gallic characteristicness, as quickly as it had risen. "Mais votre ami?" he went on to ask.

"Il est sur la mer," and Haines gesticulated toward the blue waters of the Channel.

"Sur la mer?" gasped our visitor, gazing spellbound at the offending element for a minute before he could recover himself to say, "'Eem I 'ave seen dans le Casino hier au soir?"

"C'est vrais, old fellow," Haines continued, "il est parti ce matin au travers la Manche avec la blanchisseuse de l'hôtel—he has gone off with the washerwoman, hasn't he?" Haines had the effrontery to appeal for my support.

I began to stammer a reluctant affirmative, but I might have spared myself the falsehood. Aghast at the Don Juan proclivities of " ze Engleeshman " who could combine conquests over his wife and the "blanchisseuse" of the Hôtel des Bains, the Mossoo was defeated without my unveracious assistance, his fury extinguished in the excess of his astonishment.

"Quel jeune homme!" gasped the Frenchman, with a tragic intensity in which unwilling admiration was blended. To the heartfelt relief of Haines and myself he made haste to beat a retreat down the path, finally vanishing from our sight on the Plage.

We still had the elusive George on our souls, fearful lest a chance meeting between the rivals might lead to a mêlée, or, worse still, publicity. No sooner was the horizon clear of the husband and his ashplant than we proceeded to make systematic search for the couple who were causing all the trouble, a task easier begun than carried to a successful conclusion, since the town of Dieppe offers many secluded spots for those who think that two is company and three the very devil. In fact, the credit of ending it all belonged to Haines, who, guided by some clairvoyant instinct, insisted on tramping across three hundred yards of shingle in the burning sun to look behind a groyne which ran from the foot of the cliffs into the sea at the extreme point of the esplanade.

"Whoop, lass! tear 'em, puppy, tear 'em!"

Leaning over the breakwater, some four feet in

height, Haines gave tongue in a note of triumph that brought me up at a trot. Sure enough, there was George, not the slightest sign of embarrassment at our magical—and inconvenient—appearance to be traced in his demeanor, sitting by the side of a plump and pleasing person, not quite my ideal of a feminine companion, but still attractive enough in a piquant, foreign way to stir feelings of envy in my manly bosom at the scapegrace George's situation. Haines evidently shared the same sentiments.

"George," he said, "there's a raging husband thirsting for your blood. Let him catch you with Madame, and you'll be carried back to England on a stretcher."

"And look here," I chimed in. "Not content with throwing us over for the whole of this trip, you do your best to drag us into an unsavory scandal over which Archie and I get all the kicks, while you pocket the halfpence; and not only halfpence, by Jove!"— for a closer inspection showed me that the lady was a chemical blonde of considerable attractions—"but gold into the bargain."

I shouldn't have said myself that, after our mode of address, any introduction was necessary to complete the formalities of the occasion. But George thought otherwise.

"Messieurs mes amis—Madame Chablis."

The introduction including us both, Haines and myself bowed simultaneously, like Tweedledum and Tweedledee. Madame Chablis showed two rows of white teeth in a smile of welcome, which remained fixed as George proceeded to explain about "le mari."

"Alphonse!" exclaimed that fiery person's wife, with a silvery laugh. "Ah, c'est ridicule!"

As her ignorance seemed bliss, Haines and I thought it would be folly to enlighten her as to her spouse's knowledge and estimate of the affair. Our duty was to George, not to a flighty Frenchwoman, and, in pursuance of that duty, we literally dragged George out of sight of Madame Chablis's waving handkerchief, and out of hearing of the cries of " A bientôt, mon cheri," with which she pursued our struggling forms.

The seriousness of the situation, enforced by every art of exaggeration, having been dinned into George's ears, he was immured in his bedroom until the evening, and then smuggled by a devious route to the night boat. Jealousy sharpens the wits, and, moreover, neither the constancy nor secrecy of Madame could be trusted, once she had rejoined her husband. Only when we were seated with our back to the cabin deck, and rugs across our knees, did we feel secure.

"What really happened?" asked Haines, anticipating me by the fifth of a second.

George had the sense not to fence with the question. He started straightaway.

" I didn't give you fellows the go-by until I'd marked out my line of advance. I spotted Madame first with that husband of hers in the Casino, so I maneuvered myself to the next place at the 'petits-chevaux,' and when she had put down a stake I did likewise, and contrived to take her hand as we raised ours together. In case she wasn't one of the 'ready brigade,' I repeated the trick, but it was all right, because, while Alphonse was talking to the croupier, she gave me 'the glad eye' and glanced at the balcony, on which we both met a moment later."

George paused, with the light of battle in his eye.

"Chablis," he continued, "looked as yellow as his name suggested when I was brought up to him five minutes later as an English 'milor,' an acquaintance of Madame's in the days of l'Exposition, but I played my part to the life, talked about 'Madame la Comtesse,' and hinted at favors to come for the husband of the lady it had given me such pleasure to meet once more. As for the luncheon at Puys, which I arranged à deux, I never believed in the 'twin souls' theory till that hour when I found that Madame and I shared the same tastes in hors d'œuvres and savories, and liked them long and lingering. After that there was no question of 'Parting is such sweet sorrow.' We had the sweets without the sorrow, the only fly in the blanc mange—if I may say so—being the necessity for avoiding Chablis."

"He evidently caught you out once," interposed Haines, "for he murmured something to us about your having 'Keesed 'ees vife.' For the honor of your country, I trust you did nothing of the sort."

"True, O King," retorted George, with a levity that mocked the gravity of the occasion. "I did overstay my welcome yesterday, for Alphonse found me saying good-night on the doorstep. I had to take a flight of steps at a bound, and do the quarter-mile inside fifty seconds to save the Frenchy from committing a breach of the peace. Still, it was worth it."

George closed his eyes in the ecstasy of recollection, fit study for a picture entitled "Warrior, rest! Thy warfare o'er."

"You've behaved simply disgracefully," I remarked.

"Disgracefully," echoed Haines, producing a pencil and pulling out his shirt-cuff. "In case I'm in Dieppe

again, though, you might give me the lady's address.
I believe I've held the 'twin souls' theory all the time,
without knowing it."

But George had dropped off into a peaceful sleep.
He was exhausted, and no wonder.

"I'm very fond of George," I said to the disappointed Haines, "but I'll never go abroad with him
again, unless he is padlocked to his lawful wife."

'And I won't.

OCTOBER

OCTOBER

The Progress of Mrs. Mallow—The Return of Major Griffiths—The Green-eyed Monster in Jermyn Street—A Crash in the Grecian Restaurant

DO you know the Ponting-Mallows?" asked Lady Fullard of me, the other day, when I had called to inquire whether Homburg had had the desired effect on Sir John's health.

"I've met *him*," I replied, with the discretion that is the better part of valor in Lady Fullard's drawing-room.

"I'm so sorry for the poor man," said her ladyship, clinging obstinately to her secret.

"Now, my sympathies are entirely with her!"

Lady Fullard looked the astonishment she felt.

"Then you *have* seen Mrs. Mallow?" she exclaimed.

"Through an opera glass—at the theater," I hastened to correct. "But my opinion is based on an acquaintance with the husband. He's an impossible person."

Lady Fullard bridled,—no other word would describe the manner in which she drew herself up, as if to repel an insinuation shocking to decency and female self-respect.

"If a woman is pretty, Mr. Hanbury," she said, "there are always men who will condone any breach of the commandments she may commit."

"And members of her own sex who will convict

her upon merely hearsay evidence. 'Woman's in-humanity to woman,'" I went on, "'makes count-less husbands mourn.'"

Lady Fullard stared at me. "The evidence against Mrs. Mallow is not hearsay—as you call it. Mrs. Bompas told me that that woman has run away with a soldier."

Had I been on the Bench, Lady Fullard's idea of what constituted hearsay evidence would have given occasion for a judicial joke and "laughter in court." In the circumstances I said nothing, but took my leave as soon as I conveniently could. Lady Ful-lard's drawing-room is like a lobster-pot—easy enough to enter, but jolly difficult to find a way out of.

I happened to be dining with Steward that night, and, mentioning the matter in the course of idle con-versation, he proceeded to evince more interest than his ignorance of the parties, or their social insignifi-cance, warranted.

"The very thing," he said, when I had done. "You can earn a little honest money before anybody comes back to town."

"What do you mean?" I asked, as well as a mouth-ful of salad permitted. "I'm not going to ferret out the private life of a friend to gratify you and your public."

"Never asked you to," Steward retorted. "I'm arranging a series of unconventional Society studies, dealing with the real thing, by folk who know what they are talking about. Wendover is describing how he shared his coronet with that kid from the 'Fire-fly,' Lady Graeme is booked for 'Pin Money, and the way I make it,' and now you come along with 'Delilah in Debrett,' a subject that will write itself."

"Delilah in Debrett?" I queried in wonder.

"Rather!" and Steward's eye flashed journalistic fire. "A *cause célèbre* in the making, the stolen sweets of the Season, the shearing of a fashionable Samson. It's great; we'll wind up with it, and boom ourselves sky-high."

"It's too great for me," I retorted, "so there!" And not another word would I say on the matter, although Steward pledged the *Evening Star's* credit up to the hilt.

Steward's suggestion, however, drove Lady Fullard's gossip still further into my thoughts, and I retired to bed with a growing inclination to satisfy myself as to its correctness.

I haven't been a reporter for nothing. A man who can work up a column and a half a day, for the best part of a week, out of a hint dropped by an inebriated cabman, and a wrong address, isn't going to be balked by a maid who says "Not at home," and an Indian civilian who refuses to reply to letters. Finding my direct way blocked, I had recourse to channels of information which are open to members of the Fourth Estate, and pieced together the following facts as being a strictly reliable sequence to the scene enacted on the lawn of the Welcome Club last August.

It had been perfectly obvious on that occasion that the scales of affection between the lady and her cavalier did not hang evenly. Mrs. Mallow, having fallen from her trivial round of tepid flirtation, and insincere acquaintanceship with people whom in her snobbish soul she despised, into a state of genuine feeling, thought the world well lost in the Captain's company. Rowan, on the other hand, was inspired

by no loftier an emotion than a desire for amusement,
and his amatory plan of campaign included, at a very
definite point on the map, -a retreat for them both,
Mrs. Mallow to her husband's arms, he to India and
his regiment. But, in defiance both of convention and
strategy, the lady persisted in lingering on in the
south to the despair of the Captain, whose leave did
not expire until November. In her ordinary mood
of arch coquetry Mrs. Mallow was trying enough.
Under the influence of a strong attachment from
which legal—or indeed social—sanction was withheld
she became a woman whom a St. Anthony alone could
have managed successfully. There was no character
in the whole range of history or mythology whom
the Captain less resembled than that particular saint.
And whatever tolerance he may have had for the
feminine weaknesses of Mrs. Mallow he lost during a
period in which he employed every argument of per-
suasion and threat to induce compliance with his view
that the sooner " Julia " went to Harrogate and
" hubby " the better for all parties concerned. Rowan
uttered his words of wisdom with the voice of a bully.
Matters came to a head with a stormy scene in the
dining-room at Porchester Terrace, the man shouting
out that he hated the very sight of her baby face, and
then decamping to an unknown destination. After
weeping her eyes out, the deserted lady ricochetted
into a fit of connubial remorse, and out of it to Harrogate.

But Mrs. Mallow had fallen out of the frying-pan
of brutality into the fire of selfishness and hypochon-
dria. She found the husband she had married
propped up in a bath chair, with lackluster eyes, a
shaking hand, and a mind concentrated on his dietary.

The waters of Harrogate acting on a constitution corroded by Eastern suns had turned Ponting-Mallow's thoughts inward. What·to eat and what not to eat were now the supreme facts of his existence. His wife he expected to take the place of nurse, a position for which, had she known it, she had always been designated, even on her wedding day. A potential nurse, to be fed and clothed till the day came for her to sit by his bedside, measure out his doses, stir the fire, and read aloud—due reward and provision being made for her by will—that was what Ponting-Mallow had seen in the white-robed figure, crowned with orange blossoms, meekly awaiting by the altar-steps the service that was to turn her from a free woman into an old man's perquisite. Then London, with its promiscuous hospitality, its endless functions, its willingness to ask no questions so long as it was amused, had kept the young wife in cheerful ignorance. There are plenty of doors in town that will open to a *nez retroussée* and a twenty-one-inch waist, and any number of tables at which a permanent place is kept for such qualifications. In the husband Mrs. Mallow met at the Yorkshire health resort she, for the first time, realized her fate.

Try as she would, Mrs. Mallow could not inure herself to the penance which was inflicted on her. For all his roughness, the Captain was virile, he mingled his insults with caresses, and he went some way toward satisfying the longings of Mrs. Mallow's empty heart. The contrast was too much for the lady. She stayed a fortnight in an atmosphere of bath chairs and dressing gowns, and plunged in a soul-destroying routine of dietetic observance, for an invalid with the soul of a mummy, before dispatching a telegram to

Rowan's club and flying from the intolerable ennui of Ponting and the Spa.

It takes two to make a meeting, however, and the wily soldier was not to be drawn from his retreat by appealing notes or prepaid wires. September waxed and waned, the crops were cut, blinds were drawn up, and still Mrs. Mallow scoured the West End of London by day, and at night sat disconsolate amidst the sheeted furniture of her ill-starred home. But the reliance of the lady on the homing instinct drawing the leisured bachelor back to the metropolis from moor and mountain to replenish his wardrobe, and refill his cartridge-magazine, had its just reward. The Captain was run to earth one morning in the Burlington Arcade, and what I suspect to have been a comedy of dissimulation took place on both sides. Rowan, caught unawares, unconditionally surrendered, apologized for the manner of his abrupt departure, and pleaded deep regrets for the inconvenient illness of an Irish uncle, which had kept him so long from the side of his "Julia." Mrs. Mallow graciously accepted the labored excuses, concealing whatever feelings might have possessed her under a sweet smile. The old relations were resumed with new trappings, and the resorts of autumn fashion once more received the lady and the soldier.

As to the permanence of the affair I can offer no opinion. All I know is that, wherever the final scene is enacted, it will not be in the pages of Steward's journal.

.   .   .   .   .

Haines and I are both agreed that, in the interests of science, George Burn ought to bequeath his brain to the College of Surgeons for dissection and preservation, since nothing else but abnormal cerebral development can account for his vagaries. In July he was convinced that only the instant adoption of Mormonism would save him from the consequences of his temperament. Now, in October, he is all for celibacy and death to Brigham Young. George attributes his changed ideas to "years that bring the philosophic mind," but, for the matter of that, he is only three months older than when he told me at Lord's about Lady Lucy Goring and Kitty Denver, and I notice nothing philosophical about him, save a tendency to moralize, which the sooner he drops the better. No, the reason for George's sudden conversion is the same as that of the couplet:

> When the devil was sick, the devil a monk would be,
> When the devil was well, the devil a monk was he.

'And a week at Henley Hall with Lady Lucy's people, and Kitty Denver also staying there, was enough to cure George forever of so carrying on with two young women that they both fancied him in love with them.

George himself was not inclined to be communicative on the events of that week.

"I was off color in the match," he told us at the club, and no wonder, with the uncertainty as to what every hour might bring forth in the shape of reproaches, recriminations, and even sterner rebukes from the outraged pride of the daughter of a hundred earls on the one hand, and a Transatlantic heiress on the other. With forethought, tact, and good luck, one might manage in town to prevent the rival forces meeting, and save oneself from the fate of a "wishbone" at their hands, but within the circumference of

a country house it would be impossible for any man
so to control fate as to let each lady still continue to
think that she was "the one and only" without her
suspecting the presence of another. George hadn't
managed it, anyhow. When I inquired after Lady
Lucy he turned a heavy eye on me, and said "she
was fairly fit" in a tone that implied she hadn't fitted
in at all.

"Wasn't Miss Denver staying down there too?"
asked Archie Haines, willfully ignoring the fact that
George had himself informed us of her presence not
a quarter of an hour previously.

"I believe she was," replied George, with a singular
absence of interest.

"Believe!" chuckled Haines. "I thought she was
a particular pal of yours."

"I didn't see much of her," George answered
wearily.

"You were with Lady Lucy most of the time, I
suppose?" Haines put his finishing question with a
fair assumption of indifference.

"I didn't see much of her either," George made
reply. "Shut up asking me questions, I'm going to
take forty winks," and he composed himself accordingly.

At the thirty-ninth wink, by my watch, George stole
a peep and found us still staring at him. Haines
shook his head. George sat up wide-awake in an instant.

"You haven't had much of a nap," I said, "and
you want all the rest you can get after the sleepless
nights you've had lately."

George showed no signs of comprehension, so I was
forced to elaborate. "Henley Hall—remorse at hav-

ing treated two nice girls so badly—the smart of recent wounds—you know!"

"Bilge!" George reserves this expressive term for emergencies.

"You'd better give us the true version," I went on; "otherwise the story will be getting about that you were tarred and feathered for constructive bigamy, or for being an accessory before the act."

"The truth is," said George, "that girls read a great deal too much into a man's unstudied actions."

"When they ought to know," added Haines, "that he is only passing the time with them, and doesn't mean half he says and does."

I was beginning to be interested. "What does he say and do?" I inquired.

George shuffled his feet and pretended not to hear. Haines answered my question.

"Tells her how sweet she looks, and that he must have supper and all the extras, and that he's never seen such small hands, and he's so sorry she's angry, but if he hadn't liked her very much he would never have done it, and isn't that the music, and will she be in the Park next morning?"

"Well, if he says all that," I gasped, "he deserves as many wives as Solomon."

Haines stared at George, who was smiling—at his own thoughts, presumably.

"Philanderers, like our friend George"—Haines' voice was very stern—"deserve 'the Death of a Thousand Cuts' inflicted by their friends and acquaintances—the cut direct, the cut by inference, the cut dance—social ostracism, in fact, for a heartless criminal."

"I agree," I chimed in, "but as Society is at present constituted, George gets petted and pampered, and encouraged in his wild and willful ways, and supplied with fresh victims by eager mothers, while a poor fellow like Griffiths, with no spirit, gets 'caught out' the first time."

"That's strange," said George, joining in of a sudden. "What made you mention Griffiths? He's in the club somewhere. He was creeping upstairs as I came in."

Haines summoned a servant. "Our compliments to Major Griffiths," he dictated, "and Mr. Hanbury and myself would be glad if he would join us here."

"It's no use," said George, getting on his feet as the man disappeared. "It will take more than that to get Griffiths to meet us all. I'll go and see what I can do."

Haines and I "looked at each other with a wild surmise."

"It sounds sad," he whispered to me.

"Excruciating," I whispered back. "The saddest thing since Henry VIII died. Hush, here he comes!"

We could just tell that the figure entering the room at that moment was our old friend Griffiths, but how changed from the victor of many a hard-won fight over "snooker-pool"; the warrior whose complexion mocked the rising sun; the man behind "the man behind the gun," and ready to stay there so long as the cherry brandy in the butt lasted; the sportsman at ten stone four, "ready to meet any other sportsman for a purse of ten sovs. and half the gate" at biting an inch off the end of the poker; the Merry Andrew, experienced in giving supper to rising "stars," and seeing shooting ones afterward—how changed! There was no difference that one could lay an immediate finger on, but the whole man had altered somehow, much as though he had shrunk, although that wasn't the explanation, because Griffiths' clothes fitted him far better than in the old days, were neater, more fashionable, and his trousers had a crease—but in some subtle way virtue had gone out of him. The man we had known was dead, and a changeling spirit in possession. This ghost of Griffiths stared at us as though we had been strangers, and Haines and I found no other words of welcome than the conventional "Hope you're well." We could no more have slapped him on the back than we could have offered him a drink.

Fortunately for our good name as bachelors, George had had no misgivings in that direction, for a waiter stepped forward with four whisky-and-sodas on a tray, mixed according to the Major's famous recipe— "two big whiskies and a small soda split, and not quite all the soda, please."

"Here's luck!" said George, raising his glass. Haines and I followed suit. "Here's luck!"

The look of despair on Griffiths' face, as he paused before the tumbler that should have been his, checked our action in mid-air.

"Finish the toast without me, you fellows," the Major said, with painful distinctness and hesitation. "I'll have a limejuice and 'polly' instead. My wife thinks I'm inclined to gout."

We all stared open-mouthed. Inclined to gout! Why, Griffiths had been a martyr to gout for years, but he'd never thought it necessary to take so drastic a step as knocking off his "pegs" for such a trifle. According to the same chain of reasoning, the lion in the Zoo ought to leave off meat and subsist on nuts, because it sometimes gets indigestion from swallowing a shin bone. The thing is simply not worth it.

Haines left his glass untouched, I rubbed my eyes to make certain I wasn't having a nightmare, and George's whisky went down the wrong way, and he collapsed in a paroxysm of coughing. The Major felt that an apology was expected of him.

"Faith says," he began, "that I'm putting on too much weight for my years, and that I shall enjoy life much more with two stone less to carry."

Here Griffiths puffed his chest out to prove the soundness of Mrs. Griffiths' counsel. We three continued to sit there like children at a conjuring entertainment, in eager anticipation of a rabbit and a bowl of goldfish being produced from beneath the performer's waistcoat. To fill up an awkward pause—since no rabbit or goldfish appeared—the Major took a sip at his limejuice horror, and absent-mindedly made a very wry face—absent-mindedly, because it didn't fit in with his rôle of the repentant sinner rejoicing in his salvation.

"I shall hope occasionally to see something of you all now I am back in town," he proceeded, with the aspect of reciting a lesson he had committed to memory. "Faith says——"

But here Haines' patience gave way.

"Confound what your wife says, Griffiths! Judging by the instances you've quoted, she talks utter piffle. The important point is, what do *you* say? Haven't you any opinion of your own now you are married?"

"Temper the wind to the shorn lamb, Archie!" I said. "Don't lay down such a startling doctrine to a newly married man, all at once! We must help him to stand alone gradually. When he has learned to fasten his boots up by himself, we can then teach him how to smoke a cigarette—only one at a time, though, lest the pretty drawing-room curtains smell!"

The Major had sunk into a chair in amazement at the reception accorded to Mrs. Griffiths' wisdom. But George had still to have his say.

"If you come into the club, Major, you've got to behave like a Christian and a gentleman, not like a savage, babbling of limejuice, and banting!"

The Major had not yet learned his salutary lesson. "But Faith——" he began.

"Man cannot live by Faith alone," retorted the merciless George, "and if you try to, you'll be underground by next Christmas. What's the good, my dear fellow, of going to all the expense and trouble of acquiring bad habits, if you're going to 'chuck' them at the orders of a girl who wasn't born when you smoked your first cigar, and who'll wish she never had been by the time you've smoked your last?"

To convince, a point of view has only to be stated emphatically enough. The gloom cleared from the Major's brow, familiar wrinkles deepened around his mouth, the merry crow's-feet reappeared, the unnatural repose vanished in a grin, and before any one realized what had happened a decanter stood by Griffiths' elbow, and he had mixed a potion of which the rich hue gave the blush of Hebe's cheek, five "bisques" and beat it three up and two to play.

In less than no time the Major was confidential as of yore.

"My wife," he informed us, "is too full of theories —wants me to resign the club, because it will unsettle me for home life. Why, I'd resign her first!

Didn't tell her that, though "—and the Major winked
—" said I'd break it off by degrees. Faith's a clever
woman," he went on, nearly at the end of the decanter,
"but she doesn't understand men; very few of 'em do
—think if they coddle us and stroke our hair, we're
going to sit at home every night, but we're not, we're
not!"

The Major set the refrain "We're not!" to a music-
hall tune much in vogue and beat time with his
fingers.

I looked at my watch. "Faith's saying to herself
all sorts of things about your being still out, Major.
Oughtn't you to be going to her?"

"Hi, there!" shouted the husband so addressed to
the smoking-room attendant. "Telephone for four
stalls at Daly's, and tell the steward I am dining at
7.30 with three friends, and want oysters, a brace of
nice partridges, a dish of Pêches Melba, and a Jero-
boam of the Pommery 1900!"

Then the Major looked around for the admiration
he sought, and found it.

"The secret of a happy marriage," said Haines to
me *sotto voce,* as we left the place to dress for the
Major's dinner, "is for the respective spheres of authority of husband and wife to be well defined. Each
should know where to draw the line."

"Just so," I replied. "But what a pity Griffiths
has never learned to draw anything—except corks!"

.   .   .   .   .

Can I overcome my objections to matrimony sufficiently to give up my flat, and the vices which make
life worth living, and clipping the wings of my muse,
put it in a nursery to croon nonsense to a fat podgy
creature with no hair, and a crinkled mouth that blows

bubbles, and says "Goo-goo"? I was beginning to think I could, till Audrey Maitland came to tea here this afternoon, under the chaperonage of Lady Susan Thurston, and had a desperate flirtation with Clive Massey, while I, the host, was neglected. Besides being a gross breach of the laws of hospitality, it was exceedingly thoughtless of Audrey, for although he apes the ways of a man, Massey is only a boy, and to play with a boy's feelings is shameful. Dolly Thurston has certain rights in him which oughtn't to have been ignored as they were, and I blame her for watching impassively while her friend—if Audrey is still her friend—made a barefaced assault on Massey's heart. Lady Susan, too, should have had more sense of what was due to her daughter than to have tolerated the proceedings. And as for Massey, letting himself be made a stalking-horse by an outrageous flirt, so that a fellow-man, who has befriended him like a father, might suffer cruelly by his folly—the less said about his ignoble part the better.

No, I'm not jealous. I have many, many faults, but jealousy is not one of them. I am deeply pained and grieved, that is all, at my misjudgment of all their characters, and I'll never speak to Miss Audrey Maitland again. -Indiscriminate flirting is a social curse that must be stamped out at all costs, and I intend to show my whole-hearted disapproval of the practice by cutting one of the worst offenders—Miss Audrey Maitland—at the first opportunity. Meanwhile, I sent the following letter after her, directly she had left:

"DEAR MISS MAITLAND:

"I'm so glad you could come to tea, and that you

got on so well with Clive Massey.   He's a charming
fellow, and with no fault save that he's unstable in his
affections, and forgets all the old faces when he's attracted by a new one, which is pretty often.   Personally, I prefer old friends best.   But after your conduct
this afternoon, I can't expect you to agree with me.

"In case you may wish to see more of Mr. Massey,
he is up at Christ Church, Oxford.   Telegraphic address: 'Blood.   Peckwater.'   But 'Stage Door, Firefly Theater' will be more likely to find him.

"I am just off around the world!

"Yours very truly,

"G. Hanbury."

. . . I had mapped the whole thing out so beauti-
fully.   Lady Susan was to sit in the big armchair
by the table and preside, Dolly and Massey were to
occupy the sofa near the fireplace, while my writing
chair, reserved for Audrey, was so placed that it could
be left without disturbing the rest of the party, and
Audrey be shown my treasures till we had maneuvered
around to the small settee behind the bookcase, where
she and I were to remain ensconced until Lady Susan
thought "things had gone on long enough."   I had
arranged volumes of prints and photographs handy
so that the chaperon's attention might be occupied if
the conversation flagged.   Dolly and her young man
could be safely left to their own resources.

It may have been a false step on my part to have
gone into the passage to meet my guests, a step due
to my anxiety to greet Audrey suitably, for when I
ought to have been stage-managing the party within,
I was hanging up coats outside.   The first hitch
occurred when Dolly Thurston plumped into the place

appointed for her mother—the minx looked ridiculous in the big chair, with her feet not touching the floor. Then, if you please, Lady Susan must sit down on the sofa by the fire, asking, "Who is coming to share this with me?" I thought I'd never heard such a silly question from a grown-up woman—as though she couldn't perfectly well have sat there by herself. Massey, however, showed no signs of doing the obvious gentlemanly thing, by saying, "I shall be delighted to, Lady Susan." Nothing of the sort; instead, he was hanging over Miss Maitland,—the only person to take the right chair,—chattering to her as though I didn't exist. *I* had to sit by Lady Susan.

When things begin wrong, they generally go on from bad to worse. Dolly poured out the tea disgracefully. One cup was full of tea leaves, the next was too strong to drink, and then, going to the other extreme, she flooded the pot and gave me hot water faintly flavored with Orange Pekoe. Audrey Maitland was in a mischievous mood, laughing at Massey's brainless remarks as though they contained the essence of wit, and then rallying me on my silence. As for Lady Susan, she was as "jumpy" as the Chicago Wheat Pit in a crisis. The cushions didn't suit, the footstool had to be placed at a different angle, she wanted milk instead of cream, and her tea cake had to be changed for a sweet biscuit. It would have given me the utmost pleasure to have smothered her in her own veil, and hid her body in the wainscoting. Her one redeeming feature was that she liked my rooms, and said so.

"This is a charming place of yours, Mr. Hanbury. Do you get through much work here?"

"Mr. Hanbury doesn't do any work," put in Miss

Maitland, before I could reply. " His theatrical correspondence takes up all his time."

An uneasy thought crept into my mind that the girl
might know about the letter I had in my pocket from
Cynthia, asking me to go to the next Covent Garden
ball and save her from an all-night dose of Jimmy
Berners. As Audrey was neither Miss Maskelyne,
nor Miss Cooke, I dismissed the suspicion, for a feeling of annoyance at the cool aspersion on my character.

" Lady Susan," I replied, " I do all my work here.
Knowing nothing of my habits, Miss Maitland thinks
it amusing to invent."

" Manners have changed very much since I was a
girl," Lady Susan remarked. " We were taught in
those days to take men seriously, and we married very
much earlier, in consequence."

Was Lady Susan becoming a humorist? Audrey
Maitland and Dolly broke into shrieks of laughter,
the latter saying, " Mother, you *are* funny!" I confess I saw nothing funny in Lady Susan's statement,
which struck me as extremely sensible.

" That's why American women have to come over
to Europe to find husbands," explained Massey, taking part in the general conversation for the first time.
" They never ' go off ' in New York, because they
' pull fellows' legs so.' "

" ' Pull   fellows'   legs ' ? "   asked   Lady   Susan.
" What dreadful slang is that, Gerald? "

Massey looked abashed—for him.

" Make fun of them, tease them—what Miss Maitland was doing to Hanbury," he explained.

" My dear," said Lady Susan, looking across at
the girl, " I hope you were doing nothing of the sort.

As I am always telling Dolly, 'If you want men to like you, you must humor them!'"

Miss Maitland gave a becoming toss of her head.

"I don't believe any man would respect a woman who showed she had so little self-respect as to descend to flattery to make him like her."

I liked the spirit with which that was said, and the blush accompanying it, but then the girl spoiled the whole effect by withdrawing with Massey to the alcove behind the bookshelf which I had mentally reserved for our two selves, and there carrying on a whispered duologue which entirely destroyed my peace of mind, and led me into inattention toward the remarks of Lady Susan and her daughter. Dolly's equanimity in the situation created by her friend's coquetry, and Massey's neglect, filled me with astonishment. Surely there couldn't be connivance on her part, and myself the victim of a carefully laid plot? I was still occupied in sounding the appalling depths of treachery and ingratitude this idea revealed when Lady Susan prepared to depart. I made no attempt to stop her. Tea parties of more than two are a mistake, and with that number tea is merely a superfluity. My expressions of regret were perfunctory and hypocritical, and I avoided shaking hands with Miss Maitland. I don't like nourishing vipers in my bosom.

The only satisfaction I got over the whole affair was in writing the letter to Miss Maitland, although I don't quite know what to make of the reply I received half an hour ago.

"DEAR MR. HANBURY:

"Your letter was unnecessary, for Mr. Massey had already given me his address. I think you have formed quite a wrong impression of his character, and he will, I am sure, prove as stable a friend as most people.   I don't know what you mean by 'my conduct this afternoon.'   The reference seems to me to be rather impertinent!

"If you are back from your voyage round the world by then, will you come to tea with me next Tuesday?

"Yours sincerely,

"A. MAITLAND."

Really George is right.   The less one has to do with women the better!

.   .   .   .   .

I'm not superstitious, and I've never seen anything in the shape of a ghost, but I'm as certain as I'm sitting here at my desk that it was fate which made me suggest to Archie Haines on Saturday night that we should sup at the Grecian Restaurant instead of Oddi's, as he wanted.   I have hardly been to the Grecian since my 'Varsity days, and the last time I did go our party left without paying for the crockery and glass we had broken while pelting an objectionable individual at the far end of the supper-room with rolls. But we were unlikely to meet people we knew there, and I was afraid of Haines tacking us on to another table if we went to a resort which he and his friends patronized to the extent they did Oddi's.

The gallery of the Grecian, divided up into compartments looking on to the restaurant, allows the occupants to see everything passing below without becoming themselves the subject of observation.   For this reason the place is in great request among a certain section of the cosmopolitan London world, and accordingly Haines and I thought ourselves in luck's way to secure the last box that was vacant, and with it a chance to sup in peace before the unkind licensing law of the land turned us adrift at midnight. Once engaged in the congenial task of sampling the oysters and deviled kidneys which Haines and the waiter in collaboration had set before us, there was plenty to draw our interest in the piquancy of the crowded supper tables, the glow of rose-colored lights, the soft caress of conversation, the undercurrent of passion which throbbed in the air and sent the warm tide of youth flowing the more fiercely through our veins. The men, well groomed and opulent, the women, *en grande toilette,* their necks flashing diamonds, their fingers beringed, floated on a sea of pleasure, the waves of which beat upon us.

Haines and I snapped our fingers at despair, stealing just one hour of careless merriment from the heritage of sorrow and regrets which Time holds in trust for all the sons of men. We surrendered ourselves to the spell that was being woven in smiles and laughter by our fellow-revelers.

"You wouldn't think there was much wrong with the world to look at this," remarked Haines, voicing my own thoughts as he did so. The words had scarcely crossed his lips than, in dramatic contradiction, there came a crash out of the partition at his back.

"Come in," said Haines pleasantly.

A second, and a harder, blow followed.

My companion laid down a spoon with which he had been demolishing a soufflée.

"Confound the fellow, whoever he is, making that shindy!" he said. "If he can't carry his liquor like a gentleman he should stop at home."

And Haines proceeded to hammer back—to no effect, for to the tattoo of blows on the wall was now added a voluble clamor, rising to such a crescendo of sound that the restaurant paused in its several occupations to locate the uproar.

I went to the door, and, looking out, waylaid an agitated waiter.

"What's the matter?" I asked.

"Ze gentleman say 'ees bill is wrong," replied the fellow, all eagerness to explain and justify the controversy of our neighbors. "I nevair make out ze bills wrong, nevair! 'Ee 'as drunk too much. Pauvre madame!" and the garçon threw up his hands in a pantomimic gesture of sympathy.

"There's a woman in it," I explained to Haines as I resumed my seat.

"Can't we do a little prospecting on our own?" he inquired, as he went to the balcony and looked over. Apparently he could, for, craning his head around the corner of the partition, my friend proceeded to give me details of the field of battle while maintaining a strategic position that passed unnoticed by the combatants, so hotly were they engaged.

"A case of Edwin and Angelina," Haines telegraphed back to where I stood, "with all the makings of a rare old row. Edwin, full of wine, is swearing like a trooper that he never ordered 'Cordon Rouge,' and that he'll be hanged if he'll pay for what has been drunk in mistake. Angelina, 'perfect little laidy'—but wishing she hadn't taken a night out with a chap who looks like ending up in Vine Street. Stern manager, black as thunder, and wondering whether he shall call in the police, or chuck the Johnny out himself. Hello, there's the first casualty!"

The crash of breaking glass corroborated Haines.

He swiftly withdrew his head and reappeared at my side.

"I'm going to get out of that," he remarked, "before they start flinging the rest of the table decorations about. Take a look yourself, Hanbury," Haines went on, as though my personal safety could be endangered with impunity, "and see what you diagnose the thing at."

I did as Haines bade me, for with everybody else in the Grecian an interested spectator of the scene, I felt out of it. So, gripping the railing of the balcony, I stretched my head into full view of the affair.

Gracious heavens, what did I see?—Mrs. Ponting-Mallow, with that blackguard captain by his disgraceful behavior turning the limelight on her and her folly! I scrambled back to Haines.

"Well?" he asked.

"I know the woman," I exclaimed, panting with excitement. "She'll go under for good if any scandal comes out."

"What can you do?" queried Haines.

"I don't know," I said, "except tell a cad what I think of him. But I'm going next door all the same."

Haines' only answer was to fit a cigarette into his holder and follow me outside. It would have been useless to stand upon ceremony for an entry into the next compartment, where the devil's own row was proceeding, so we merely thrust our way through the knot of eavesdropping waiters clustered round the door, and marched straight in upon the stage set for the last act of " Mrs. Mallow's Adventure."

We were confronted with a situation that promised to lead up to a *dénouement* of melodramatic intensity.

Captain Rowan was lolling back in his chair, before a table littered with the débris of an expensive meal, both hands thrust into his pockets, his face flushed the deep red of excess, the veins on his temples swollen with anger, his eyes bloodshot. He wore a look of sullen ferocity, and was obviously very drunk. Facing him stood the manager of the Grecian, a massive foreigner in a frock coat, at the end of his endurance, for as we appeared he issued the ultimatum that if Monsieur wouldn't pay his bill and leave quietly the police should be sent for and he would be given in charge. But it was Mrs. Mallow whom I regarded with most solicitude, where she sat crying into a lace handkerchief, her whole body quivering with sobs, a picture of woe and abandonment which would have stirred any chivalry in Rowan's nature had he possessed such a soldierly quality. From the agonized and terror-stricken look she gave as she raised her tearstained face on our entrance, I believe she expected the police to arrive every moment. Then her expression wavered between relief at seeing me, and shame at my discovering her in such a *mise-en-scène*.

"Can I do anything, Mrs. Mallow?" I said. "I heard the broken glass, and thought perhaps an accident had occurred."

The excuse was very lame, but it served to justify my intervention. To such a pitch of excitement were we all wrought that no explanations as to the nature of the predicament in which Mrs. Mallow found herself seemed required. We behaved as though it were the most ordinary thing in the world to meet the wife of a friend supping alone in the Grecian with a man other than her husband, and that man intoxicated into the bargain, and threatened with Vine Street police station by an irate manager.

"I am a friend of this lady," I explained to the latter, who was inclined for a moment to resent an intrusion which might mean reinforcements for his refractory client. But this suspicion was instantly dispelled by the action of the Captain, who, mistaking us for members of the restaurant staff come to assist in his expulsion, rose to his feet, and maintaining an unsteady position by leaning on the table for support, glared at us in tipsy menace.

"I re-refush pay a farthing more," he said in a thick utterance, "if I shay here all nigh'. Wha' you think of thish for a bill?" and he flung the document at my head.

"If it's a question of the bill I'll settle the item in dispute if it will only make you go home," I replied. "There's the lady to think about!"

"Wha' lady?" spluttered Rowan, resuming his seat heavily as his legs suddenly gave way under him. "Wha' lady?"

"The lady you've been dining with, of course. Pull yourself together, man!" And I shook him by the sleeve.

"Lemme go," the Captain exploded. "I don't know wha' you mean."

The shock of this denial dried Mrs. Mallow's tears, and her sobs ceased.

"Are you mad, Stuart?" she asked, in astonishment.

The Captain's expression became more savage, were that possible.

"Hol' your tongue!" he growled. "I've finish-shed with you; never inten' shee you again, whining all sh-time at me. Finish-shed!"

To give dramatic point to his words, Rowan swept his arm along the line of glasses and decanters before him and hurled them to the ground.

The sight of this destruction was too much for the manager, and he advanced furiously on the offender. The storm that all the restaurant was waiting open-mouthed for, men and women clustering at every point of vantage below, seemed about to burst, when Mrs. Ponting-Mallow took command of the stage.

"Leave him to me," she cried, brushing aside the manager, her voice thrilling with anger at the Captain's insult to herself. Then she leaned across the table, her handkerchief clenched in her fist. "How dare you, Captain Rowan? Apologize this very minute!"

At this uprising of the victim the other three of us stood spellbound. Mrs. Mallow was in no mood to be interfered with.

"Will you apologize?" she asked again, standing over the Captain like an avenging fury.

Rowan sat stolidly in his chair, looking at the broken glass, but said never a word.

"Stuart, you're a cur!" hissed the lady. "You've killed every atom of feeling I ever had for you. My deepest shame is that I have ever known you. If I were a man I'd horsewhip you. But you shall remember the rest of your miserable life what my scorn is like," and raising her fist, she leaned across the table and struck Rowan with all her strength, first on one cheek and then on the other. The Captain's head rattled with the blows, as though it had been a drum, and a trickle of blood commenced to flow from a gash made by one of Mrs. Mallow's rings.

With the exception of the livid marks left by the blows, the Captain's face became deathly pale.

"Julia——" he began, sobered by the shock, but Mrs. Mallow checked him.

"Don't dare to utter my name!" she flung at the cowering and degraded man. "Never speak to me again. I've done with you—you are a coward and a brute, who would bully a woman till she turns to bay, and then crawl to her. You've never cared a scrap about my reputation, or my happiness. All you have thought of has been yourself. My being with you here to-night hasn't prevented your making a thorough beast of yourself, although by creating a disgraceful scene you risked exposing me to insult and publicity. You have been anxious to get rid of me ever since you had got everything out of me you wanted. But now you shan't have the chance of throwing me over. I discard you myself forever. I think you're the most contemptible creature I have ever known."

Under the force of this indictment, the Captain literally crumpled up. If he had been an unpleasant sight when we first entered the box, he was worse now with his manhood oozed out of him, his clothes in disarray, his hair tangled and matted, the perspiration streaming from his forehead, his face discolored and bleeding, debauchery and stricken pride combining to produce a spectacle for gods and men to stand aghast at.

The manager's knowledge of human nature told him that he would have no more trouble over the unsettled account, and he withdrew. We were proceeding to do likewise, when a word from Mrs. Ponting-Mallow stayed me.

"I am deeply pained," she said, as soon as we were alone, in exhausted tones that showed the crisis through which she had passed, "that you and your friend should have witnessed such a scene, but I know I can rely absolutely on your discretion."

"Of course," I replied, taking the lady's opera cloak from its peg, as a hint of what o'clock it was. "I shall equally contradict any rumors I may hear."

"Rumors?" and Mrs. Mallow paused in the act of drawing on her cloak.

"Well, people have been talking—perhaps naturally!"

Mrs. Mallow came close to me. It was strange how we both ignored the man in the corner.

"Mr. Hanbury," she asked, "what sort of rumors were they?"

"Well, unpleasant. Charity, you know, begins at home, and usually stays there."

Mrs. Mallow frowned.

"You saw me with that——" she failed to frame a phrase suitable to the object huddled up on the table— "once before. I've been a silly little fool, if not worse. Oh yes, I have," she went on, as I made a feeble gesture of protest. "But I've learned my lesson to-night. I've got a comfortable home, and how many women can say that?"

Mrs. Mallow shuddered—at the idea, possibly, of what she had so nearly lost. She recovered herself with an effort. "Will you take me to a cab, Mr. Hanbury?" she asked.

So I led the lady through the dim restaurant, looking, with its lights extinguished and its laughter fled, like the shameful specter of a once beautiful woman, and saw her into a hansom. What became of Captain Rowan we neither of us cared a rap!

"Home?" I asked, as the cabman waited for directions.

In spite of the evening's experiences Mrs. Mallow smiled.

"Yes, home!" she replied.

After all, a humdrum ending to "Romance" is the best.

" Whoso findeth a wife, findeth a good thing."—Book of Proverbs.

NOVEMBER

Steward tells an old Tale—Cynthia Cochrane says Good-by—Back to Fleet Street—Two in a Fog

WHAT is love?" is a question I have been putting to my friends of late, in a sincere desire for enlightenment, to be so inundated with conflicting definitions as a result that I despair of ever getting at the truth. One would have thought that a complaint which is at least as common as the measles would have been diagnosed correctly by this time, but apparently that is not so, and I am still floundering in a quagmire of doubt. For instance, love according to George Burn is "a sensation of hot water running down one's back." That sounds too much like a shower bath for my tastes.—To my sister Dulcie love is "forgetfulness of self in another's happiness," a beautiful saying, though a hard one—too hard for a selfish man. To Sybil Bellew love means marriage, and marriage means—all that marriage means to "two-and-twenty."—Lady Fullard, to whom I submitted my question in fear and trembling, said that "love is all stuff and nonsense; mutual esteem is the only thing worth having." Somehow that reassured me, because if Lady Fullard had believed in love, I should have preferred to remain a skeptic on the subject. More helpful was Haines' theory that the symptoms of being in love were a willingness to give up week-end shoots and cigars and aversion to musical comedies. But he wound up his lecture with the absurd remark that "the proof of the pudding is in the eating." Of course it is, but, as I told the idiot, "the rot is that if one takes a single spoonful one's got to finish the dish, whether one likes it or not." Some day, perhaps, the ten years' trial trips may come into fashion, but at present the weight of public opinion is in favor of the retention of the old-fashioned matrimony, with its "no jack-pot" and all in the "ante."

I have come back from my Socratic pilgrimage little wiser than I set out. Still it has been worth while, if only as a revelation of my friends' points of view, and for the eliciting from Steward of the following:

"Love was given to Adam to create a new Paradise for himself. Love is Faith, Hope and Charity—Faith in the present, Hope for the future, and Charity for all time."

I had been sitting in front of the fire in his Chancery Lane rooms, while the shadows gathered thickly around, when the journalist, fondly polishing a meerschaum pipe, had delivered himself of that fine aphorism.

"Steward," I said, "you speak with the accent of a lover."

The journalist's face, turned to the glowing hearth, was twisted by a sudden spasm. As I caught the change I marveled why I had regarded my friend as a misogynist, who had never strayed out of Fleet Street, and whose years had been dedicated to "copy" and proof-sheets. More, I realized that I had been singularly incurious as to the details of his past career, apart from its newspaper side. Steward's reticence about himself had not been encouraging to would-be Boswells. It had been only natural to accept the man at his own estimate, and he had been at pains to describe his life as consecrated to literature. It would, indeed, be a bold act to penetrate into the secret places of his heart, and pry behind the veil hung before its Holy of Holies, since Steward, if he invited confidences, never reposed them.

Such were my reflections when the silence enfolding us was of a sudden pierced by the still small voice with which soul speaks to soul, and I became aware that my chance remark had opened some floodgate of memory in the other, and that the roaring of deep waters filled his ears. The shadows which danced on walls and ceiling in a flickering fantasy, and threw even such familiar objects as the fighting cocks on the piano into strange relief, might have been ghosts returned to haunt the living, so plain was the look of anguish Steward wore, and the lines of pain drawn round his mouth. Of a truth I knew in that moment that the past can never die, that what has been will be again, and the things a man has once suffered he must still endure.

As I watched Steward with the absorption one turns on a dying man, his expression softened, his forehead smoothed as under the pressure of a woman's hand, and, still searching the mysterious depths of the coals, he began very softly to recite these poignant verses:

> "La vie est vaine;
>   Un peu d'amour,
> Un peu de haine—
>   Et puis, bonjour! ...."
>
> "La vie est brève;
>   Un peu d'espoir,
> Un peu de rêve,
>   Et puis, bonsoir!"

Steward broke the fixity of his gaze, and commenced

filling his pipe, which, during his reverie, had fallen neglected to the floor.

"Shadows, shadows, that's what we are!" he murmured, half to himself, half to me. "Moths fluttering for a few brief moments round the lamp of life, our most lasting thoughts transitory, our deepest feelings shallow; the beauty of to-day but the skeleton of to-morrow; our separate existences of no more account than the paper boats launched by little boys on the river current, doomed to be overwhelmed in the first eddy they encounter. Why should a man tear out his heart over love, when, like any other mortal passion, it is only a flower to be tended for a little while before it fades?"

"What has come over you?" I asked in astonishment. "You spoke very differently a few moments ago. To love, then, was to create an earthly Paradise."

"Did I say that?" replied Steward in a far-away voice. "I must have been thinking of Elise."

Elise?—The world was coming to an end if Steward could grow sentimental.

A jet of smoke shot from the journalist's mouth as his pipe sprang alight.

"Hanbury!" he said. "Forgive the indiscretion I am about to commit, of talking about myself. But my intuition tells me you have reached the parting of the ways, and that your future depends on the choice you are about to make. Before you finally decide, listen to the words of a man who, to his everlasting sorrow, took the wrong turning."

I felt myself incapable of making any coherent reply. Steward proceeded with his strange candor.

"Everybody is given one chance in this world of

obtaining their heart's desire. I threw away my chance when I lost Elise. No triumphs I may achieve in my profession, no heights of society or fame I can scale, will ever atone for *'il gran rifuto,'* as Dante called it. If the Florentine be right, and there exists a frozen hell for such sinners as have offended against themselves, I shall surely go there. For when I was offered love—so strong that the grave itself could have had no power over it, I spurned it. I only realized what I had lost when She had passed out of my reach forever."

"Did death take her from you?" I asked, with a reverence that befitted the other's tragedy.

"If it had, I should have been spared the remorse that torments me," replied Steward, his face contracting with an agony of recollection. "No, I blame nobody but myself—and Paris," he added, apportioning the guilt with a judicial accuracy.

"Love is the *raison d'être* of Paris," Steward went on, at an apparent tangent of ideas. "The life of a Parisian is a prolonged intrigue, one long affair of gallantry. He thinks of nothing else. Yet a born critic, he is compelled to analyze even a woman's heart; a profound skeptic, he doubts the permanence, or indeed the reality, of love. Having no illusions, he can have no faith. It was my curse that I met Elise in this atmosphere, when I was a special correspondent to the Exhibition."

"But you weren't a Parisian," I interrupted. "So it didn't matter what Parisians thought, or how they behaved."

Steward smiled grimly.

"Paris doesn't let the artistic temperament off as easily as that. By her appeal to one's sense of all

that is beautiful in literature and art, by her rapture
in living for living's sake, by the whispered enticements to Youth that stir in the plane-trees of her
boulevards, and the fountains of her parks and gardens, by her gray stones and hoary traditions, by her
joys and sorrows, Paris speaks to the artist as no other
city. Mother and mistress, she demands the affection
meet for both. I showed my gratitude to her in the
only way I could. I became more Parisian than the
Parisians, discarding my English modes of thought
as completely as though they had never existed. My
mind had always been keen to see through folly
and vice; it now saw through virtue. It was when
thus transformed that one morning in the Bois I
rested on the same seat as Elise, and our delight in
the glorious July weather was so mutual and spon-
taneous that we walked together, the girl becoming
my guest for *déjeûner* at the Cascades."

"What was she?" I asked. "A grisette?"

"She had been a governess in Touraine, and had
returned to Paris to secure another situation. As far
as I could discover she had no parentage worth speaking of. A Captain of Chasseurs had some claim to
be her father, but Elise never could tell me the rights
of the matter. My private belief is that she had
dropped from a nest, and assumed human shape the
moment before I came up, for she had the bright
black eyes of a bird, the same quick movement of the
head, and was vivacity itself. But I never bothered
much about the question. Elise was created to make
others happy, and herself miserable. She had the
amazing intuition of the Parisian for every mood of
her companion, and as she was a dozen women rolled
into one, she could assume a fresh personality to suit

the occasion. She could be obdurate, melting, unapproachable, intimate, witty, provoking, and all in the hour. Her society was stimulating for the reason that one never knew whether her greeting would be an embrace or a repulse, sunny smiles or floods of tears. Take her in one's arms, and she might prove to be a shy wood nymph, or a Bacchanal."

"You loved her, of course!" I interrupted, rather fatuously.

"I never had time to," replied Steward, lighting a fresh pipe, "so occupied was I in studying Elise, invoking the various spirits which possessed her. She was interested in everything, and I gave her the best that was in me to satisfy her craving for information and knowledge. She was a harp on the strings of which I played the most exquisite melodies that ever ravished the souls of a man and a woman. And how I wrote in those days! Heavens, how I wrote while Elise's spell was over me! My articles on the Exhibition were a revelation to London, and the proprietors of the paper doubled my salary. Two stories I found time to do went far to establishing my reputation as a man of letters. My contemporaries were sinking into my train. In my pride I thought I could do without Elise, that it was myself, unaided, who had done these things. But the Artist, Hanbury, can never stand alone. He must receive inspiration from some source, and the higher and purer the source is the better it will be for him."

"But, surely," I said in genuine surprise, "even from your own showing, Elise wasn't conspicuous for virtue?"

Steward's look darkened.

"Don't make the mistake of ignorant people, Hanbury, and apply terms like virtue and sin universally. In England, so long as one keeps the Seventh Commandment, and incidentally attends the Established Church, one may break all the others with impunity. Yet there are countries just as much deserving to be called virtuous as ours, where everybody goes about stark naked, and a woman thinks nothing of six husbands. Elise, like her countryfolk, was no hypocrite. She was a pagan, responsive to every natural instinct, and worshipping the beautiful. The pinnacles of Nôtre Dame, the curve of the Seine of Sèvres, the Petit Trianon, the view over Paris from the Church of the Sacred Heart on Montmartre, the music of *Tristan,* the prose of Pierre Loti and Anatole France, the romances of Dumas and Balzac, the poetry of Hugo and De Musset,—Elise loved them all, with an appreciation that often wrung tears from her. I understood Elise. From me she drew silence, or conversation, attention or indifference, as she had need of them. And because I understood her she loved me. Yet it was more than that. She felt that I required her, that to turn to her for sympathy, companionship, was a craving which took a firmer hold on my nature with each meeting. The divine motherhood flowing from a woman toward a man—precious ointment with which she would anoint his head—the comprehension of the strength and weakness of which he is compounded, impelled Elise to give me all that she had to give. I took it—to learn the greatness of the gift too late."

Steward's masterly analysis of a woman's soul, the subtle inflections of speech with which he etched in the lights and shades of his word-picture, the stress of mind which had led him to the confessional, had

drawn me under the spell which Elise had woven—
to his undoing and hers. My heart beat fast in anticipation of human blindness and error parting what
God had joined; my temples throbbed with a pre-
monition of woe. Steward was stretching me on the
rack of his own agony, gagged by emotion and incapable of uttering a word to break the narrative,
which continued its course.

"Paris looks upon women as playthings, inseparable adjuncts of Man, who is the sun around which
they must revolve—playthings to be discarded and
adopted again at will, petted and deserted by turns.
The *ménage à trois* with which the theaters deal eternally mocks the fidelity of the sex, exalts feminine
treachery into a cult. In this environment Elise's
sacrifice, which should have convinced me of her devotion to myself, merely confirmed my acceptance of
the warped views I heard enunciated on all sides. I
thought Elise without a soul. At the cost of the happiness of both of us she proved to me she possessed
one."

The speaker's voice died away for a moment, and
his face was hidden in his hands. When Steward
resumed it was with an obvious effort.

"With a truly masculine confidence in my power
to retain Elise's affections, I grew casual in my treatment of her, prolonged my absences, frequented the
society of other and less reputable women, proved by
my conduct that I accepted the code of Parisian gallantry without reserve. Success had gone to my head.
Had misfortunes come to me I should have flown,
like a homing pigeon, to Elise's arms, but destiny, to
teach me a lesson, refused to allow a single failure to
cloud my horizon. Then it was that one night return-

ing late to my apartment, I found a letter pinned on to the mantel to catch my eye.   It was Elise's farewell. I still keep it!"

Steward broke the thread of his narrative to go to an inlaid cabinet that stood by the window, open a drawer and extract with much fumbling an envelope, with which he returned to his place.   Drawing the contents forth, the journalist read the following, screening his eyes the while:

" My dearest Friend:

" I say good-by to you with tears that will never cease to flow for the sorrow of our separation.   But it is far better that you should weep for Elise departed, caring for her, perhaps a little, and pitying her much, than that, having her by your side, you should think lightly of her.

"From the happiness that living with you has brought me, I know the sadness which life without you holds, but if, by renouncing you, I can prove to you the sincerity of my love, I renounce you gladly.   For I do love you, with a passion that thinks nothing a sacrifice which can minister to your happiness.   I am leaving you, and with you my heart, so that you may keep the memory of our affection—for you do love me, little though you may suspect it—pure and unstained, a memory unsullied by thoughts of Elise's frailty and your own folly in wasting your talents on a light woman.

" We shall never meet again in this world.   If God is good I may see you hereafter.   My prayers shall win Paradise for us both.

" Farewell, beloved,

" Elise."

The end was reached in faltering accents, but, beyond a slight trembling of the hand which held the paper, Steward repressed all outward expression of grief. Forbearing to profane the moment with speech, I reached over and drew the sheet from my friend's fingers. Written in French in small, precise characters, the letter conjured up a vision of that far-away night in Paris, when the man by my side was made conscious how he had flung away the pearl of great price. The thin sheets of violet-tinted paper, now faded almost white, still exhaled the perfume of the writer, recalling the gracious presence of a good woman. I cast a glance at the man whose life, apparently so full, was so empty, whose career, so enviable, was robbed of the one prize which could make success worth acquiring.

It was a full five minutes before the silence in the room was broken.

"I believe Elise was right," Steward said at last, once more in command of himself. "Her instinct told her I should remain faithful to her forever, and that, while losing me in this world, she would possess me in the next. My heart is a shrine to her memory, wreathed with immortelles. No other woman will ever enter it. But Elise did a greater thing for me by giving me back my faith in her sex. And that is the moral of my long tale, Hanbury. Don't try to analyze women; love them for what they are! Don't pick them to pieces as you would a toy, for you can never put them together again! Destroy a woman's faith in you, and her soul shall cry out against you at the Judgment Seat, and condemn you! If you are a cynic, never let your cynicism extend to Woman. For as it was a woman who brought you into the world, so pray that a woman's consolation may lead you gently out of it!"

I left Steward with Elise's letter clenched in his hand.

Vanity of vanities—all is vanity save the love of a man for a maid, and the love of a maid for a man!

. . .. . '.

Nothing less than the strictest sense of obligation to Cynthia Cochrane would have taken me, after Steward's solemn warning, to Covent Garden Ball on the following Friday. Only the compulsion of strong friendship could have induced so reticent a man as the journalist to impart the secret of his lost Elise with the object of hastening my plunge into matrimony. But by going to a Covent Garden Ball at Cynthia's invitation I was entrusting myself to influences decidedly anti-matrimonial, Cynthia because she was Cynthia, and the Ball because it stood at the opposite end of the scale to marriage.

Covent Garden Ball is the one public function throughout the length and breadth of the United Kingdom to which Mrs. Grundy is refused admittance. If she so much as shows her nose under the façade of the Royal Opera House on such an occasion, she is taken in charge by the constables on duty for causing a nuisance. Last time she appeared at Bow Street she was fined £5 by the presiding magistrate. Therefore, once upon a time I used to be a regular attendant at the fortnightly fêtes, but as cares have accumulated, and my habits grown more regular, I have been less and less, till now it is only imperative necessity which mulcts me of a guinea and half my night's rest.

On the particular evening when Cynthia had com-

manded my presence in order to stave off the ardent
attentions of James Berners, Esq., Solicitor, I had
intended dining quietly at the club, finishing a long-
overdue article on "Kings I have never met," commissioned by *The Penguin,* and looking in at the
Ball about 1 A. M. But George Burn scented mischief
from my mysterious demeanor, drew my destination
from me, and enrolled himself in the expedition. One
can't say "No" to George with any effect, so I con-
sented, and borrowed my entrance money off him as a
forfeit.

As we ascended the staircase from the underground
buffet level to the polished floor laid over what, in the
opera season, is the stalls, we were assailed by the
blare of Dan Godfrey's orchestra, and a rush of warm
scented air from the house, crowded in every part—
even the top gallery, reserved for spectators from the
everyday world, being ringed round with a fringe of
eager faces staring in amazement on the motley throng
below. George and I thrust our way to a conspicuous
position on the partition separating the promenade
from the parquet, with no more mischance than the
upsetting of a buxom lady whose partner was remedy-
ing his ignorance of the waltz steps by a praiseworthy
attempt at an Apache dance which involved seizing
the fair one by the neck at intervals—none of them
very lucid. Freed from this entanglement, we both
surveyed the gay scene with interest.

Most of the ladies present thought that if their
skirts stopped short at the knees they had done enough
in the way of disguise. Of the so-called fancy costumes—a compromise between allegory and realism—I
was inclined to award the palm to a *svelte* blonde
whose petticoat of gauze net trimmed with bivalves,

and headdress of kippers, represented "Caller Her-
rin'," although George was strongly in favor of a
charmer in heliotrope tights slashed with orange,
green and scarlet, her bust draped in a tasseled cloak
of gray *panne*. A great many men one knew seemed
to be enjoying the "light fantastic" after a debauch
of covert shooting and domesticity, and George was
kept busy returning the salutes of both sexes as they
whirled past in revelry.

It is an easier task to discover the proverbial needle
in the haystack than to keep an assignation at Covent
Garden, and I had given up all expectation of finding
Cynthia when, happening to raise my eyes to the
grand tier boxes, I suddenly saw a "mask" seated
by the individual whose ancestors had obviously
crossed the Red Sea with Moses. George had already
gone buccaneering on his own account, so I made my
way with all speed through the mass of spectators to
the box and its occupants.

Cynthia, disguised in a black satin *loup* and a
domino, received me with an enthusiasm not shared
by Jimmy Berners. He had taken the box for himself and Cynthia, and he didn't want to be disturbed.
The disfavor with which he eyed me told me as much.
But disturbed he had to be, and to a distance out of
hearing.

"Berners," I said, ignoring his hostility, "there's
a pretty little woman in black and red by the buffet
on the right of the band asking after you."

"A little woman in black and red?" repeated Berners, his anger forgotten at the pleasant fabrication.
It was the ambition of his life to procure the reputation
of a lady-killer, partly from the abstract delight he
himself would derive from the title, and from the

added worth he imagined it would invest him with in Cynthia Cochrane's eyes.

"Yes," I replied, "a little ripper. I had half a mind to forestall you, you dog! You sly dog!" and I poked Berners in the ribs.

"Quick's the word," I went on, so soon as he had recovered, "before somebody else snaps her up. She was going to the supper-room."

"Did she mention her name?" asked the duped Berners, in a gallant pretense of knowing it all the time.

"'Tell Mr. Berners that Maudie wants him; he'll know.' That was all the message I got."

"Excuse me, Miss Cochrane," apologized Berners, fingering the door handle. "I must just see the lady for a minute."

"If he sees the lady for a second," I said as the door closed on Berners, "he's got better sight than I have."

"Poor Jimmy," said Cynthia Cochrane, who had sat an amused spectator of the comedy. "It's a shame to tease him so. But he really must take lessons in conversation. He's already asked me twice to-night to marry him. I had to tell him I had come here to enjoy myself."

I thought of the duty that had brought me to Covent Garden Ball, and steeled myself for the deed.

"Jimmy's not a bad sort," I remarked, as unconcernedly as I could. "One could do much worse than marry him."

"Do you mean that advice for me, Gerald?"

A frill of lace hid the expression of Cynthia's mouth from me, but I caught a flash of indignant eyes through her mask.

I evaded a direct answer.

"If I were a woman, and thought a man cared for me, I'd let the knowledge weigh down a good many of his disadvantages."

Cynthia turned her head away.

"What nonsense you talk, Gerald! You don't even know the simplest facts about a woman. Why, if we could only control our affections like that, we should certainly be spared all the things that break our hearts."

"I seem to be having as depressing an effect on you as Jimmy," I said, with an effort to be gay, despite the sadness stealing over me at the prospect, very close now, of parting from Cynthia. "Cheer up, there's the March Past beginning!"

A crowd of dancers had congregated on the stage by the band-stand, ready to pass in single file before the judge's box, while the rest of the company, in fancy dress and out, were being marshaled by stewards along a length of rope stretched down the ballroom, to keep a wide passage open, order being further guaranteed by the presence of an inspector of police and two constables. The band struck up a ragtime, and the competitors for the various prizes offered by the management started to display themselves and their costumes by sidling and pirouetting down the line of spectators, to the accompaniment of cries of encouragement or derision, according as the popular verdict wavered. Ever and again a storm of cheering greeted a stage favorite, or a dress of unusual originality of design, studded with electric lights, while the crowd behind kept up a succession of antics, varying from a display of high-kicking to a "ring a ring o' roses" which ended in the participants collapsing in a struggling heap. I felt as though I should like to join the fun, instead of moping in a box over what had been, and could be no longer.

All of a sudden I became aware that Cynthia had removed her mask, and, instead of watching the mad scene, was intent on studying my face.

" Do you care for her very much?" she said at last.

" Indeed I do," I replied, surprised out of the secret I had planned to reveal in quite a different way.

" I guessed as much, Gerald," Cynthia said, in a low voice. " I haven't had a line from you for a month, so I asked you here to-night to find out what was the matter. Your manner gave you away straight off. Well, it's good-by this time!"

" I suppose it is," I muttered. My idea had been to bring our friendship to an end on the ground of her future, but this seemed to be reversing the process. I felt remarkably uncomfortable. But if I expected any reproaches I was spared them.

" The very best luck to you," said Cynthia. " You'll ask me to the wedding, won't you? You needn't be frightened; I shan't come."

" You're going ahead too fast," I replied, with a deep relief. " I haven't got to the engagement yet. But, of course, if there's a wedding, I shall want you to come, and feel deeply hurt at your absence."

Cynthia shook her head sadly.

" Of course, if I came to the wedding you'd be charming to me, and the more so because I shouldn't be ' in the picture.' But you'd wonder to yourself, ' Why has she come?' and your fashionable friends would stare and say, ' An actress; what shocking bad taste of her to turn up,' and the fat would be in the fire about your bachelor days before the honeymoon had properly begun.   I don't want to come to the wedding."

And drawing out her handkerchief, Cynthia dabbed her eyes with it.   I felt uncommonly like following suit.   It would never do if Jimmy Berners came back and found us both in tears.

"Dear Cynthia," I said, leaning forward to where the girl sat with her face hidden by her hands, "don't spoil it all by making me feel I've behaved like a brute.   Things are much better as they have turned out, for I should only have destroyed your career. You've got a big one, you know you have!"

"Yes, there's always my career."   Cynthia's voice shook with suppressed emotion.   "But a career to a woman isn't the same satisfying thing it is to a man. With her it is never independent of a home and a husband.   She wants some one she loves to share it with."

Overcome by her emotion, Cynthia stopped.   A knock came at the door of the box.   I delayed a second in raising the latch, and put my face close to Cynthia's.

"Cynthia," I whispered.   "You've shown me what a good woman is.   I'll never, never forget you."

Then I gave her the last embrace of our long friendship.

When Jimmy Berners entered a moment later he found her departing.

"Any luck with Maudie?" I asked, more to turn attention from Cynthia than anything else.

"You got that all wrong," said Berners.   "Her name was Grace," and he sat down with a proprietary air.

For his own sake I hope that Jimmy Berners didn't

propose to Cynthia Cochrane for a third time that night.

.   .   .   .   .

The unconventional strain in my blood has triumphed, and I have gone back to Fleet Street. Instead of the club and its luxury of exclusiveness, drawing-rooms and country houses, I once more frequent the Cock, the Cheshire Cheese, and Wine Office Court. The freemasonry of the journalistic world of pressmen, war correspondents, critics, reviewers, authors and dramatists, has succeeded that of Society, with its sportsmen, idlers, and womankind. To me

> The world's great age begins anew,
> The golden years return.

From the moment I accepted a position in connection with the *Evening Star's* new magazine and literary page, my old habits and mode of living have slipped from me as though they had never been. My fate no longer hangs on the cut of a coat or the folds of a scarf, but on quickness of brain and sureness of judgment. A servant of the public, with a roving commission to keep it supplied three times a week with the brightest of bright articles, I am immersed in the fascination of the task. When I am in search of a subject to deal with, nothing escapes my observation. The hanging sign of a beauty-specialist at once suggests a course of treatment, and "A Wrinkle Doctor at Work" astonishes the metropolis three days later. Another time it is "The Morals of the Music Hall," a week's pilgrimage from the "Met" to the Pavilion, and an animated correspondence in the *Evening Star* started by myself under the pseudonym of "A Frequenter of the Halls," and the limelight turned on Page 3 and its contents.

Half the charm of journalism is the sense of power it gives. Not only have one's words a quarter of a million readers, but one has the *entrée* everywhere, and a sight of the chief performers on the world's stage with the paint off—as they really are, and not as fame presents them. The Actor-Manager drops the Olympian manner and, over a cigar in his dressing-room, talks affably on the need for a National theater, and "Should Bernard Shaw be canonized or cremated?" The Cabinet Minister gives his private, as distinct from his published, views on "My Colleagues, and what I think of them"; the dancer of the moment describes in her motor brougham "Heads, crowned and otherwise, I have turned in my career." The journalist is in contact with the new ideas of the age, sustained through the wear and tear of his profession, by the pleasing sense that he knows more than his neighbors.

The successful journalist has to combine the qualities of an ambassador, a detective, and a man of letters. He must be urbane, indomitable, able to extract the secrets of other people without divulging his own, prepared to bluff every one from his news editor to the village policeman, never giving up a mission till he has a column of news, or been sandbagged by the victims of his pertinacity and zeal. He must have no qualms as to his fitness for any task allotted him, whether it be the unraveling of a crime which has baffled the police, and the securing, single-handed, of a desperate ruffian, the interviewing of a Countess in the middle of the night, or the description of a cross-Channel swim during the gale of the century.

Carefully removing the paper guards to his cuffs, cramming into his pocket, in case of emergencies, the remains of the buttered toast he has been eating, and smoothing his tangled hair with a broken comb before two inches of cracked glass, the Pressman receives last instructions from his news editor, and plunges forth into the fray. Arriving on the scene of his assignment, he is confronted with obstacle after obstacle set in the way of his procuring the information he wants, and which he has to surmount by his own initiative and resource. To ply reluctant folk with a string of questions, to be ready with the soft answer that turns away wrath, to climb in at the window when the door is closed, to mistake the servant's "No" for the master's "Yes," to goad ignorant people into intelligence, and coax silent ones into speech, to scatter largesse in the hope of recouping it from the cashier, to write good and vivacious English after six hours' hard labor—these do not comprise the equipment of Napoleon, but of a working journalist.

At present I am engaged on a series headed "If London became French," forecasting an impossible future to the Entente Cordiale. The *Evening Star* artists are preparing a picture of Regent Street lined with cafés and kiosks, and sketching our public men à la Française, with pince-nez, beards, and the Celtic fringe, while I am supplying the letterpress, describing how Chelsea turns into a Latin Quarter, the Royal Academicians commit suicide in a body because of the raising of the national ideals of Art, the London County Council steamers pay at last, fights are the order of the day in the House of Commons, and a Bal Tabarin usurps the Albert Hall. In addition, the opinions of various prominent personages are being

canvassed, so that one day's number may be devoted
to a symposium of their views on the results, beneficial
or otherwise, of such a surprising change.   I have
been at great pains to make this last feature as complete as possible, and in many cases have interviewed
the celebrities myself.

It strikes me as extraordinary how some great folk
resent being asked to talk for publication.   In this
age of advertisement the attentions of the Press should
be encouraged rather than repelled, for it is a demon-
strable fact that few reputations can stand without
the newspapers.   Yet I had to write to the Duchess
of Surbiton twice, and then call at eleven one morning
in order, when I finally did reach her presence, to be
met with the statement from her Grace that the only
thing we could with advantage copy the French in
was their cooking.   This brusque and discourteous
comment is going into print in this form:

Her Grace of Surbiton spared our representative a
few minutes from her busy morning of arranging
social engagements and seeing to the books (for the
Duchess is a model housewife and keeps Surbiton
House in " apple-pie " order) to discuss the subject of
our article.

" How well I remember," she said, toying the while
with a tiny spaniel that lay in her ample lap, " those
dear, delightful times in Paris when I was a girl! "—
here the ducal bosom heaved with regret for the days
that were gone—" the omelette aux fines herbes, the
ragoûts, the volaille suprême, the salads, the sauces,
in fact the whole cuisine of La Belle France.   There
were chefs in those days, but now——! "

The gracious lady shrugged her shoulders (if a

Duchess can have anything so common as shoulders)
with one of the expressive gestures caught from the
Paris of her youth.

"We have nothing like the cooking in England,"
went on her Grace. "If I had my way every Polytechnic" (who will say that our Aristocracy is un-
educated?) "every Board school, would include cook-
ery in their curriculum." The Duchess safely
negotiated the treacherous word, and turned to our
representative. "I'm afraid I can say nothing more.
Surbiton" (the dear Duke Ed.) "doesn't like the
papers, since they encourage Socialism. Ah! I see my
Secretary is waiting for me. Good-morning!"

With a kindly smile the visitor is dismissed, to carry
away with him the impression of a great lady, stamped
with the caste of Vere de Vere, but interested in other
modes of thought than her own, and carrying her
years as lightly as her lineage bears the centuries.

There are coals of fire heaped on her Grace's
toupée! The readers of the *Evening Star* are not
going to be deprived of the news which is their due
if the enterprise of the staff can secure it.

But I can trace to another source than the charm of
active work in Fleet Street the change which has come
over my outlook upon my old environment, making the
round of club and restaurant, of scandal and sport,
belong to a shadowland, peopled with phantoms, un-
concerned with the real issues of humanity, and only
toying with life. It is true that I had become suddenly filled with a vast amazement that I ever expected
anything of that existence save ennui, since the interests were so portentiously trivial, the ambitions so
warped, and truer still that Miss Audrey Maitland has

effected my mental transformation. I am getting older and wiser because she has effectually destroyed my interest in every other woman, and it is an interest in women which keeps a man young. Don Juan lives to a green old age. It is only when the Don Juan in us is "scotched" by marriage that we begin to show gray at the temples. And that I have said good-by not only to my former frivolous days, but also to Cynthia Cochrane, is proof positive to me that the pitcher has gone to the well for the last time.

·   ·   ·   ·   ·

It was rash starting out in the fog. I knew it was. But Lady Susan Thurston had made such a point of my dining with them that night that it was obligatory on me to keep the engagement if I could. For two days we had lived in a city of Dreadful Night, traffic almost at a standstill, link-boys driving a roaring trade by conducting pedestrians from pavement to pavement, the radiance of the town departed in gloom and mystery. I had expected every moment to receive a message announcing that the function had been postponed, but as none came I made the perilous journey from Jermyn Street to Lowndes Square on foot under the hour, although in crossing Hyde Park Corner I went astray in the lines of crawling cabs and vehicles for ten minutes, till a man with a lantern came to my rescue and steered me into safety by St. George's Hospital for two shillings. How Miss Maitland reached the house I don't know, but the determination in her character, which at other times leads her to rebuke my shortcomings, brought her from the neighborhood of Portland Place by a circuitous tour of the Tubes. The rest of the guests failed, and the gaps at the dinner table, Mr. Thurston's cough like

a fog horn, and the inappropriate choice of pea soup
to commence the meal with, ruined the festive side of
the evening. The atmospheric conditions did me one
good turn. They sent me back as escort to Audrey
Maitland.

"Mr. Hanbury," said Lady Susan, about ten
o'clock, when my uneasy movements proclaimed the
strain of the forced merrymaking upon me, "you
will have to see Miss Maitland home. I strongly dis-
approve of young people driving about together late
at night, but my sense of duty as chaperon must give
way to considerations of personal safety."

It was not my place to offer any objections, so I
closed with the proposal on the spot.

When Miss Maitland and myself, cloaked and
coated, opened the hall door, we looked into a wall
of vapor hiding even the curb, and faintly resonant
with the muffled sounds of an unseen world. It
seemed hopeless to grope our way through the somber
pall of fog, and the girl would have accepted the improvised couch which the hostess made haste to offer,
had not a "four-wheeler" chosen that moment for
colliding with the lamp-post opposite, despite the fact
that the cabman was guiding his horse by the reins,
swearing profusely to notify all others of his progress.

"Hi, cab!" I shouted.

The man, showing as a gray shadow at a distance of
a few feet, looked every way to locate his would-be
fare, even turning his face upward in case an apparition might appear from the direction of the roofs. A
London fog so changes the accustomed order of things
that nothing is undreamed of in Horatio's philosophy.

Taking my bearings Nor'-East by Sou'-West, lat.

43°, long. 10°, I marched from Lady Susan's doorstep to the distressed cabby.

"All right," I exclaimed cheerfully, "you're in Lowndes Square. If you go straight on for another ten yards you will be in the area of Number 70. Can you take me to Portland Place—half a sovereign an hour, and something hot when you get there?"

"S'elp me, guv'nor, I cawn't do it," replied the fellow. "I've been round this Square like a bloomin' squirrel in a cage for the past three-quarters of an hour, and I'm nearly off my chump."

"Be a sportsman!" I urged in desperation. "I've got to take a young lady home, and if you get us there somehow I'll ask you to the wedding."

Humor won where argument would conspicuously have failed. The man winked, drew his cab out of the lamp-post, and turned the horse's head toward the direction in which I indicated that Knightsbridge lay. Hastening back to the house, I rescued Audrey Maitland from the suggestions and sympathy with which she was being overwhelmed, and we began our journey through the fog, which engulfed us in an abomination of desolation once we were out of sight of the pavement. Proceeding at a slow crawl, we reached the main thoroughfare by the French Embassy, crossed it without collision, by dint of much shouting from our guardian cabman, and, assured that by hugging the curb we could not go astray, I relinquished my vigil at the window and turned to my companion in distress.

"It's an awful night," I began feebly.

"Why did we ever start?" asked the girl. "We shall never get home. I wish I'd accepted Lady Susan's invitation to stay with them."

At all costs Audrey's spirits had to be kept up.

"Never say die. We shall be all right."

"You are very cheerful."

"Of course I am; I'm with you."

The girl drew away into her corner of the cab.

"Please don't say those sort of things. Do be sensible and try to realize our danger!"

"I realize *my* danger." I put all the emphasis I could on the pronoun. "I'm in deadly peril, I know."

"Oh!" shuddered Audrey as a huge black mass loomed up at the window on her side, and drove her to seek the protection of my fur coat. How I blessed the van, which avoided colliding with us by a hand's breadth.

I felt myself growing light-headed.

"Let us die together, at any rate," and as I spoke I slipped my arm through hers. Providentially, the shaft of another cab struck us full astern, and instead of releasing herself, the girl pressed my arm for security. I patted the only hand I could secure, to convey additional comfort to her. "We're as right as rain," I went on, with a confidence I didn't feel.

"Shall we soon be there?" asked Audrey, ignoring anything unusual in our relationship.

"In a very few minutes now."

As I spoke the cab came to a dead stop.

While our conversation had lasted we had passed through a period of violent commotion, during which many voices had joined in a cacophony of sound, dim figures had sprung up out of the mist, and had been lost again, collisions been suddenly threatened, and then as suddenly been averted by magical disappearance of the obstacle—a Walpurgis Night of Brocken specters and phantasmagoria. But now, of a sudden, we were wrapped in a silence that could be felt, the clinging mantle of fog hanging round us in damp folds, not a footfall, not a movement of life to penetrate the chill shroud in which we had been prematurely buried.

Smothering my misgivings, I took out my watch.

" Why, we've only been thirty-five minutes," I said. " I call that an excellent journey in weather like this. I suppose he's ringing the bell."

The door creaked open, and the driver stuck his head in.

" I dunno where we are," he muttered, with heavy intensity, suggestive of the view that he had given up all hopes of ever seeing his family again, and was resigned to slow starvation on the spot. In later, and less foggy times, his skeleton would be found to bring the tragedy of his fate to light.

I got out with all haste. If Audrey wanted a good cry to relieve her feelings, falsely buoyed up by my ill-timed confidence and pleasantries, let her have it while my back was turned. I drew the cabman aside and consulted. He had, it appeared, followed the line of the curb past what he thought was Park Lane until, thrust out from its friendly pilotage by a hansom abandoned as derelict by the driver, he had never been able to regain the pavement, and in desperation had followed a covered van down the center of the roadway, encouraged to do so by the apparent sureness of judgment which was controlling its destinies. Then of a sudden it had stopped, and our charioteer, drawing level, had discovered on its box a bewildered individual fresh woke from sleep. But the most puzzling feature to the cabman was the non-appearance of the slope of Piccadilly. Faith may be able to remove mountains, but it hadn't been able in his case to prevent the removal of the hill in Piccadilly.

In emergencies he who hesitates is lost.

" I've got it," I said, with calm decision. " We are on the top of the hill looking toward the Circus. Go quickly to the right, and when you come to the Park railings call out."

The man vanished, walking gingerly as though he expected snakes to materialize from the wood pavement. In a few moments I heard his shout, " There's a row of bloomin' 'ouses."

" Confound it!" I said when he came back, guided by my cries. " You must have turned right around, and be taking us back to Lowndes Square. The park is on our left. I'll find it in a brace of shakes."

All I did, however, was to find another row of houses. Had we all died in our sleep and become ghosts, condemned to an endless quest in a foggy Purgatory for a phantom Portland Place? Surely we hadn't been such sinners! Then a stroke of luck happened. A person, solid-looking enough to dispel all fears that I was disembodied, who was advancing by means of clutching on the area railings of each house in turn, ran into me. I hugged my bruise and greeted him.

" Hello, where are you? "

" Well," he replied, " I left Grosvenor Square twenty minutes ago, and I ought to be in North Audley Street by now."

How on earth had our cab taken the intricate turnings requisite to land us there? It always seems to me a difficult route to steer in daylight, through the narrow, winding passage from Park Lane.

" Are you quite sure? "

I put this further question to my savior, but he had started on another area and was swallowed up in blackness. With difficulty I regained the cab and revealed the truth to the cabby. His blank amazement was refreshing, but he had other news for me.

"Pore young laidy," and he jerked a finger toward the cab. "Taking it very much to 'eart. She thinks you've gone forever. No weddin', no nuffin'," and he dashed an imaginary tear to the ground.

"Nonsense," I replied sharply. "We're not going to be married."

"Not going to be married!"—and the cabman slapped his chest. "Why, I'd never of come this blasted journey if I 'adn't thought I was doing a kind turn to a pair o' 'spoons'!"

"What's the man saying?"

Why Audrey Maitland chose that particular moment to interrupt the *tête-à-tête* between the cabman and myself passes my comprehension. It was uncanny to a degree.

"The fog's got into his head," I stammered. "He was telling me that his sister was going to be married, and he intended giving her two spoons."

My interruption was ignored.

"What did you say?" the girl asked the cabby imperiously.

The man shuffled his feet, an irritating habit, but that didn't justify the severe tone Audrey Maitland addressed him in.

"Did that gentleman say we were going to be married, and induce you to take us as fares in consequence? Did he say that?"

Audrey had been listening all the time, the deceitful creature! My blood boiled with anger, and several other feelings I shan't specify, and carried me out of my usual timid self.

"Yes!" I exclaimed, "I said all that, and I'd say it again if necessary. I *am* going to marry you. Get back into the cab this instant, or you won't survive to marry anybody. And you," I said to the cabby, paralyzed at the turn given to the situation, "take us where the devil you like. But if you get into another mess, you must find your way out yourself. Don't bother me!" And I climbed back into the cab, which had suddenly become the most desirable spot on earth. I registered a sudden vow to pass the rest of my days in four-wheelers.

"Audrey!"

Not a sound escaped from the girl, hidden in her corner. Very gently I took her hand, which lay impassive in mine.

"Audrey, I told the truth to the cabman. I love you.. I am going to marry you. Will you marry me?"

There came the soft pressure of her fingers on mine. That was the only answer I got, but it was sufficient!

I *believe* we reached Portland Place about midnight, and I *know* I gave the cabman a five-pound note. "The rest is silence."

DECEMBER

"The poppied sleep, the end of all."—SWINBURNE.

DECEMBER

Hanbury v. Hanbury, Rev. Sturgis intervening—The Plight of a Fiancé—A Bachelor Deceased

MY engagement to Audrey Maitland, the public announcement of which appeared in the *Morning Post* less than a week after the events in the fog, has been welcomed nowhere more heartily than in my own family. The bachelor career of an only son gives rise to apprehensions which are entertained in lesser degree where the male olive branches grow thicker, and I learned from my father's confidences how deeply concerned my parents had been lest I should bring an unsuitable bride to receive their blessing.

"All anxiety is laid at rest now, Gerald," my father said as we sat together settling ways and means during a week-end I had stolen from Fleet Street. "But I must confess we had grave misgivings as to your possible choice of a wife."

"My dear father," was my reply, "it is the parents' fault when a son marries a barmaid, and a daughter elopes with her riding-master. The society of the opposite sex is a necessity for healthy youth, and if girls and boys can't meet possible suitors of their own rank in life at home, they will cultivate impossible ones outside it. For all the young women mother has made any efforts to invite here, I might have died celibate."

"Yes, your mother is difficult, I know. She says she finds everybody unsuitable when she comes to make their acquaintance."

" But that's no excuse, sir, for having nobody down here. Look at Dulcie. Is she going to marry the curate, for as far as I can make out he's the only man ever about the place?"

If I had wished to draw a red-herring across the trail of my own affairs I couldn't have done better than drag in the curate.

"Should you call Dulcie impressionable?" asked my father, with apparent irrelevance.

"Well, as she's my sister, she probably is," I retorted. " I thought she took a fancy to George Burn at Easter, but then taking a fancy to George is like taking a share in a foreign lottery. There are so many competitors that the chance of drawing the prize is one in ten thousand."

"Why is it," mused my father, still pursuing the devious line of thought he had started on, " that though the clergy occupy such a privileged position, and play the chief part in the most important crises of life, one never welcomes them as prospective members of one's own household with any enthusiasm? You would have broken my heart, Gerald, if you had wanted to enter the Church."

"Fortunately, sir," I replied, "I preferred giving orders to taking them. What's the 'padre' here like? I didn't see much of him when I was down here last."

My parent rubbed his chin.

"The Rev. Mr. Sturgis is a regular curate," he said, with apt description.. "Your sister's got the woman's notion that to marry a clergyman is a mission."

"So it is, submission! What makes you think the matter is serious?"

"Dulcie attends the early morning Celebration, she

reads the Parish Magazine, and she thinks he sings quite nicely, when she must know he's never in tune."

I gave a groan. "She's as good as engaged, sir. Can't anything be done?"

"Your sister looks up to you, Gerald," said my father, "because of your friendship with Mr. Steward. If you should say something it might have an effect. It's very hard that these domestic worries should come on top of the agricultural depression."

I agreed, and with that our conversation "returned to its muttons." My father, desirous that the marriage should take place as soon after the New Year as possible, made such handsome provision for Audrey and myself that the financial side of the question was settled there and then.

My own satisfaction was considerably modified by the suspicion sown in my mind that my only sister might be about to endow me with a clerical brother-in-law. Without doubt Dulcie is impressionable, and lacking the worldly wisdom to counteract her impulses. How often do those sudden attachments formed for a partner at a county ball, or the mysterious masked soloist on the sands, survive the discovery that the parent is "something in the city," or that the adored one's handwriting resembles the perambulations of a spider which has fallen into the inkpot and is trying to dry itself? That is to say, the budding affections wither away in the case of a well-balanced person, but with Dulcie the prudent course would savor of cowardice, and she would feel all the more attracted to the individual placed on the wrong side of such social gulfs. But I didn't see what I could do, nor how I could lead up to so delicate a subject without giving the show away.

When I am undecided I am wont to trust to the inspiration of the moment, and on this occasion it came on Sunday afternoon, when Dulcie was doing needlework, and I was reaping a miscellaneous harvest from the bookshelf. It was in Dr. Johnson's criticism of Pope, in his *Lives of the Poets,* that I came upon the following passage:

" The freaks, and humors, and spleen, and vanity of women, as they embroil families in discord, and fill houses with disquiet, do more to obstruct the happiness of life in a year than the ambition of the clergy in many centuries."

I gave a hoarse chuckle at the Doctor's mellow wisdom.

Dulcie looked up. "What's the matter?" she asked.

"Listen to this!" I said, and read the passage.

Dulcie tossed her head. "An ill-tempered, spiteful old man!"

"You've got to live as long as the Doctor to see the truth of it," I remarked. "He couples women and clergymen as the disturbing elements in life. Women and clergymen," I repeated sagely.

"Gerald!" Dulcie's voice sounded sharply. "Has father or mother been saying anything to you?"

I assumed my "village idiot" expression.

"No. Why, what do you mean?"

"Nothing," said Dulcie, bending quickly over her work, but not quick enough to hide her rising color from me.

I pretended complete ignorance of my sister's confusion, and went on with my homily.

"The ambition of the clergy—I wish they had more, or, rather, one that took a different form than that of having twice as many children as they possess 'hundreds' a year. No clergyman should marry until he is an archdeacon, and as for curates, matrimony on their part ought to be a penal offense, entailing the loss of civil rights for seven years."

"What are civil rights?" asked Dulcie, not in the least interested, but anxious to stave off further denunciation of the "Cloth."

"The right to give up one's place in a public conveyance to a woman and strap-hang; the right to jump up from a comfortable chair to open the door for her; the right to accept personal discomfort as though it were pleasure in order to conform to a medieval code of chivalry. But to return to curates——"

Dulcie gave a start. So she'd thought, had she, that she was to be spared any more wounds in her tenderest feelings? When I undertake a commission I invariably execute it.

"The only one of my contemporaries at Oxford who became a curate," I rolled out, "died from injuries he received at the hands of a landowner whose daughter he was courting against her parents' will, after a three-quarters of an hour's sermon, on a day, too, when the ice in the park bore for the first time that winter. The coroner's jury returned a verdict of 'Natural death,' and very natural it was under the circumstances. No, curates are outside the pale of human tolerance and charity!"

"Gerald," said Dulcie, "I quite agree with you. I haven't heard that point of view put so clearly before! How well you express yourself!" and she sighed with regret for all those rosy visions of a future in a vicar-

age which my logic and eloquence had destroyed forever. Nevermore, she felt, could she be comfortable
in the company of a man the faults of whose calling
had been so strikingly revealed to her. To show her
gratitude to me for tearing the scales from her eyes,
Dulcie put down her needlework and, crossing the
room, perched herself on the arm of my chair, put one
arm around my neck, and began stroking my hair.
"Dear little sister," I thought. "If only I could
help to make you as happy as I am."

"Gerald," said Dulcie in her sweetest tones, "I am
so glad you are going to marry Audrey. She's a perfect darling! But I shall miss you dreadfully. I
didn't realize before how much a kind brother, like
you have always been, meant to a girl. You are so
clever, and see through things so quickly, that I can't
think what I shall do without your advice."

I was thoroughly touched. Gratitude of any kind
is rare, and between members of the same family
phenomenally so. Dulcie had done me the justice to
recognize the disinterestedness of my counsel, and
some reparation was undoubtedly due from myself to
the little girl at my side. As I had pulled down one
plan of her own, I must help to build another in its
place.

"I shall miss you, too, Dulcie," I said. "I've tried
to be a good brother to you, and if I have sometimes
been rather 'down' on you, it's only because I've
taken such interest in you. But if ever you want any
help come to me. I'll do anything to make you
happy."

Dulcie bent down and kissed me.

"Would you really do anything for me, Gerald?"
she whispered. "For I do want your help now."

I made a rapid mental calculation. After all, Dulcie deserved a return for so bravely throwing over her curate, on whom her thoughts, I am sure, had been set before I spoke to her. It was probably some trivial service she had in mind, magnified by her feminine lack of proportion. Her faith in me had been so touching that I could rely on her asking me nothing I couldn't readily grant.

"Yes; I will do anything for you."

"Promise me on your word of honor that you will never go back on your word, but will always stand by me!"

If it had been a man who had tried to extract this solemn pledge from me I should have been suspicious, but women love these dramatic touches.

"All right, Dulcie. I promise on my word of honor to stand by you. What is it?"

Dulcie drew my cheek close to hers. "Gerald, I'm secretly engaged to Mr. Sturgis. I'm so glad you're going to help me to marry him."

It is a rule of mine never to swear before ladies, but I broke it six times in as many seconds, before leaping to my feet in a towering rage.

"Dulcie, you deceitful little hypocrite! you abandoned little wretch! How dare you make me promise a thing like that? I'll never, never, never trust you again, or believe a word you say!"

Dulcie burst into tears, and buried her head in the cushions. I looked into the glass to straighten my tie, grinding my teeth to keep my temper up to fighting pitch, and drown the noise of Dulcie's sobs. Crying is a most unfair weapon to fight with. However much a man may be in the right, tears make him feel a brute, in spite of himself. I stood on the hearthrug,

like a convicted criminal, when all the while I was
championing the cause of Truth and Decency against
my sister's attacks upon those sacred principles in our
domestic and civic life.

"For heaven's sake, Dulcie, don't cry like that," I
exclaimed in desperation, "or I shall shriek aloud.
You've behaved very badly to me, but I won't go back
on my word, although I ought to. You've played
it low down upon a trusting brother, but if you'll stop
that noise and promise to do nothing rash,—registrar's
office, for example,—I'll see what I can do. There
now!"

My sister changed gears, turned off the radiator,
and ceased to exceed the speed limit. In a few moments she was drying her eyes, and turning up her
tearstained cheek to be kissed. But as I kissed it I
wasn't thinking of Dulcie, but of myself, and how I
had been outwitted by a girl in her teens. So much
for masculine vainglory!

.   .   .   .   .

The only one of my friends to whom I am not an
object of chaff and commiseration is young Massey,
and his sedulous inquiries as to the conditions of an
engagement, and the sensations engendered by it,
show that he takes far too intelligent and lively an
interest in it for his two and twenty years. The great
problem before him is the choice of a career, not a
wife, and if I were Lady Susan Thurston, which, thank
God, I'm not, I'd forbid Clive Massey to see anything
of Dolly until he could call with a check for £100
and say, "I've earned it." But with this not very
bright exception I am made to feel by George and
Archie Haines and the rest that I have betrayed the
citadel of my sex, and handed over the keys to the

enemy. I am stopped, too, from airing a contrary view by the quoting against me of my own dicta, uttered six months ago, and which have been preserved by oral tradition owing to their spontaneity and wit. I am a jester strangled with his own toby.

In one's salad days one knows, really, very little about women, for the light side of the lantern is always turned on one. With a more intimate experience of the sex the crudity of a bachelor's notions gets toned down. The disgusting selfishness of the unmarried man appals me now that I have risen to loftier heights of sacrifice, but I see it is useless to convince hardened skeptics of the type of George Burn as to the reformation to be effected in their characters by getting engaged to what is described as " a nice girl." To any right-minded bachelor all girls are nice, and discrimination only sets in when the fact of his engagement makes it an act of disloyalty to his fiancée to think otherwise. Some day George will be in the same plight, and then he will come to me for advice, and get the stiffest lecture on his past career he has ever had. When that is done I shall be ready to give him tips, and the first one, printed in the heaviest type, and framed to hang over his bed so as to drive home its message, will be, "Have as short an engagement as possible."

The engagement is a strain for both the "high contracting parties," to quote a phrase from the preamble of treaties which takes my fancy, since the couple are in much the same state of excitement as that which fills children in the theater before the curtain has risen. Audrey is a sensible girl, and she does her best to assuage the miseries of my position, but she can't alleviate the sufferings of being "bear-led" around her

relatives and made to show my paces, or of the surfeit
of one person's society which an engagement involves.
I'm sure it's a great mistake for engaged couples to
spend all their time together. To get to know each
other too well leaves nothing to occupy those long,
long evenings, after baby has been put to bed, and
before the last post has brought its sheaf of household
bills. Then, surely, is the time to explore the depths
of a wife's character, and, by skillful inquiry into
parental antecedents, to discover whether that tendency
to hysteria at the breakfast table, which does so much
to make home seem like home, comes from the aunt
who gained "honorable mention" in the class for
goiters at the Hydrocephalic Congress, or the uncle
who became an involuntary parricide by aiming with
a coal-hammer at the blue rat he saw (and corroborated the fact on oath in the subsequent criminal proceedings) running over his father's bald head. To
postpone such research work till after the nuptial knot
has been irrevocably tied adds to that unexpectedness
which is the chief charm of marriage.

Far and away the worst ordeal is the personally con-
ducted tour through her family circle which the bride-
elect inflicts on the bridegroom-to-be. Nearly every
night I am the honored guest of one branch or another of the Maitland family, and suffer the same
pangs as seized me when I underwent viva voce
examinations in the University of Oxford, painfully
aware of my own limitations and the overwhelming
odds against me. Most of Audrey's relatives act upon
the assumption that she isn't fit to choose a husband
for herself, and that therefore it is their duty to make
her realize how unworthy is the object of her choice.
The questions they address to me prove that *Lodge's*

County Families has been searched in the hopes of finding a blot upon the Hanbury escutcheon, and in default of damning evidence there, I must be made to reveal personal shortcomings. I don't know that I don't prefer this attitude to the one adopted by those ladies who fall upon my neck and welcome me into their circle with embraces. I can stand being cut, but not kissed.

I must make a very poor figure in the eyes of the uncles, aunts, cousins and personal friends who are invited to inspect the new recruit at dinner. I enter the room crowded with strange faces, as well hidden behind Audrey's skirts as I can contrive. A silence falls upon the groups, which have been chatting animatedly till we arrive to stop the conversation, so that our gestures may be studied, the exact angle of my handshake and bow noted. Trembling in every limb, I am introduced to General Sir George and Lady Maitland, Mrs. Maitland, Mr. and Mrs. Arthur Maitland, Miss Maitland, Mr. Humphrey Maitland, the Misses Clodagh and Grace Maitland, and expected to remember the identity of each upon any subsequent occasion I address them. I meet the uncle whose bump of philo-progenitiveness stands out like a volcanic crater, and who initiates me into all the family scandals of the last two generations. I take into dinner a maiden aunt whom I form an instant aversion for because her idea of breaking the ice is to suggest that I shall volunteer assistance to her *crèche* in Whitechapel. On my other side is a lady who knows some distant cousins of mine, and expects me to supply their biographies while I am struggling with a tough pheasant as full of lead as a 9.7 gun. I explain that I am no relation to the Hanburys of Crane Court, that my father hasn't married twice and mortgaged his estate up to the hilt, and that I am older than I look. I listen to statements that Audrey isn't an heiress, but that her mother was a Mold, one of the old Molds of Worcestershire. I drink sour claret and smoke green cigars—all for love of Audrey. Can devotion go further?

The presents are a more satisfactory side to an engagement, and with my wedding fixed for early in January, they have already begun to oust my books from the table to the floor, and to litter my rooms with straw and tissue paper. One of the first to arrive was a dispatch box from Mrs. Bellew, a handsome present considering her frustrated hopes for Sybil.

"We are so glad," Mrs. Bellew wrote, "that you have at last settled to marry, and such a charming girl as we hear Miss Maitland is. Sybil thinks she has met her, but can remember nothing about her. I am afraid we shan't get to the wedding, as we are thinking of going to St. Moritz after Christmas." Mrs. Bellew needn't have qualified her generosity in that way!

The Thurstons have sent a bridge table, and an invitation to Rosshire next autumn for the pair of us. Griffiths' contribution is a liqueur set—"The married man's best friend," as he described it in the covering note. From Lady Fullard came an electro-plated butter dish, which I had the presence of mind to change at once for a cigarette case. I don't want a butter dish ornamented with an embossed head of King Edward upon my breakfast table.

I was much puzzled as to the donor of a finely bound set of Browning's works, till I found a sheet of paper slipped in to mark the poem "Any Wife to Any Husband," and containing one line:

" May you be as happy as I mean to be.
.   " JULIA PONTING-MALLOW."

So that escapade with Rowan has brought good in
its train, since it has taught Mrs. Mallow contentment
with her lot.

But it was not until a parcel arrived addressed in
Cynthia Cochrane's handwriting, that I suddenly realized I had all the while been wondering whether I
should hear again from her. I undid the coverings
hastily, to find a miniature set in a plain gold circlet,
with my monogram on the back. The likeness was
remarkable, done with a daintiness that reproduced the
beauty of Cynthia so vividly that all the tumultuous
memories of the past rushed back again. A letter accompanied the gift:

" DEAR GERALD:

" I am sending you a memento of our friendship as
a message of good luck. Still think of me as a friend
who wishes you well, whatever happens. As you told
me, I have my career, and careers have a way of not
going with happiness. You are one of the lucky people who have found how to combine both. Jimmy
Berners is, at last, beginning to realize that I shan't
like him any the less if I don't see so much of him.
Who knows but that importunity and persistence may
not win the day over romance?

" Good-by, Gerald; you can be a hard man to a
woman. Show your wife the soft side of your nature
sometimes.

                               " CYNTHIA."

A husband and wife, they say, should have no

secrets from each other. 'All the same, I shan't show Audrey that letter.

.   .   .   .   .

My race is run, and I am ready to stand before the altar of St. George's, Hanover Square, and swear away my single-blessedness with an "I will" in which the spectator may detect a cheerful or a mournful note, as he pleases, for I have spent the last New Year's Eve of my bachelor life with my three greatest friends, Frank Steward, Archie Haines, and George Burn, and I am sitting, solitary, before the dead ashes on the hearth, with an empty pipe between my teeth.

At first I had contemplated gathering some twenty acquaintances around me for the last solemn rite of drinking "no heel-taps" to my wedded future, but, uncertain as to how far I could control my feelings when the moment came for "Ave atque Vale," I did not wish to parade my sorrow before folk who might be unsympathetic. I therefore limited my hospitality to the three men I knew I could trust never to reveal any weakness I might display, for New Year's Eve is a celebration I always find affecting. To strike a moral balance sheet, and reckon the profit or loss of the past twelve months, is a responsible undertaking. Even a saint must expect to find a few items, which no sophistry can explain away, to cause a twinge of conscience, although as time goes on one's sense of proportion tends to adjust itself. The facts which seem to require expiation at twenty, merely evoke a tolerant smile at thirty. The mortal sins of our youth are the peccadilloes of our middle age. If George, for instance, wore a hair shirt for every indiscretion he had committed in the year, he would appear as bulky as an Eskimo in winter plumage. The philosopher, rather, spends New Year's Eve in self-satisfied recollection of the failings of the past, and in pleasurable anticipation of those to be indulged in the future. And it was in some such mood that Haines and George arrived in Jermyn Street to partake of my farewell supper, for they showed no sense of their coming loss, and indulged in ill-timed jibes at my expense. Steward, too, whom I relied upon to tune the proceedings to the key of doleful reminiscence in which I wished the scene to be played, encouraged the others in their badinage, by telling me to " cheer up " and not be " as morbid as a mute at a funeral " when I commented on their bad taste.

I had no appetite when we four sat down to dinner, but that didn't excuse George snatching my oysters, in order, as he said, "to accustom Hanbury to the frugal fare of married life."

"I know," I said, "that marriage means giving up many of the luxuries to which one is accustomed, but oysters aren't luxuries, they are necessities." Whereupon I recovered the "succulent shellfish" (*vide* Little Willy's Natural History) by main force, and left George lamenting.

"I always thought you were going to get off scot-free, Hanbury," remarked Haines, when we were well under way with the soup.

"You needn't talk as though I had been convicted of some crime," I retorted, nettled.

"We shall hear of Haines going off next," said Steward.

"There'll be no fuss about it, anyhow, when I do," Haines replied.

"No, that will come afterward," I interrupted. We had assembled to talk about myself, not of what

Haines would or would not do in a remote contingency. The excitement of seeing George help himself to whitebait with a fork came to my aid, and by the time the meal had resumed its smooth progress, I was in possession of the House.

"Marriage is not the separation from old interests and friends that it is assumed to be. The wise man makes the best of both worlds."

"Yes, my friend," said Steward, "but don't end up, like Mahomet's coffin, halfway between heaven and earth. In a few weeks you are going to marry a charming girl. Thank God for it, and don't let any one of us to-night say anything to belittle your good fortune. Here's to your happiness and hers!" and although it was nowhere near the period of the evening for toasts, Steward raised his glass to mine, and we drained our bumpers as one man.

I felt deeply grateful to the speaker, not only for his sentiments, but also for the harmony he spread over the party. George and Haines ceased to tease their host, and the host himself threw off the shades of regret which had begun to close over him and entered on a strain of cheerful recollection which set every one recalling the adventures they had had together, and forecasting the others they would share. Steward excelled himself as a raconteur and a wit, while the courses advanced and the wine circulated, till the mirage of an existence without a care or a sorrow floated before the mind's eye of each member of the party. Upon this flow of words and thought Haines' proposal of my health intervened, to which I suitably responded and brought the speech-making officially to a close, when George, who had shown signs of preoccupation for the past five minutes, jumped to his feet and, laboring under strong excitement, gave the unconventional toast of "Lost Opportunities."

George on the hustings was George in a new rôle, but, carried away upon a wave of emotion, he made his oratorical bow with credit.

"Opportunity," said George, "makes the thief, but lost opportunity marks the coward, the man who can write 'Fain would I rise, but that I fear to fall.' The host of the evening"—I bowed in astonishment as to what was coming next—"is losing the greatest of all opportunities, the free life of the bachelor. If I"— George struck his shirt front—"lose an opportunity— I forbear to mention what opportunities—I can retrieve it. Not so Mr. Gerald Hanbury! Henceforward he is not his own master. 'Vae Victis.' To him, as to the wounded gladiator in the Coliseum, the thumbs of the spectators have been turned down, and he must die."

George drew his handkerchief out and mopped his eyes. Really he was acting a part very well, and a part I should have applauded him in once.

"Marriage," he repeated, "involves the loss of the greatest of all opportunities," and, proceeding, he drew a highly colored picture of what he thought marriage was—a kind of inferno of discomfort, in which the screams of teething children mingled with the lurid blasphemies of drunken domestics. Then, against this grotesque travesty of the truth, George set up a rose-red fantasy and styled it bachelorhood, devoting a purple patch of rhetoric to a mythical monstrosity he called "the happy bachelor."

"This," said George, "was our host, Gerald Hanbury. He is no more. To-night we stand by his open grave, and drop into it a sprig of rosemary—for remembrance!" Here the speaker resumed his seat "amidst the thunder of the captains and the shouting."

Steward instantly stood up.

"I rise to respond on behalf of the dead man," he began. "The late Gerald Hanbury, bachelor, could he speak for himself, would say that in marrying he was seizing the greatest opportunity of his life. He has fought gallantly in the foeman's ranks till overwhelmed. As he lies in his warrior's grave he deserves the reverence, and not the scorn, of men. What are the opportunities he loses by committing the noble sacrifice of 'hara-kiri'?" asked Steward, and went on to enumerate a grim catalogue—the opportunity for self-indulgence, for intrigue, for all the pleasant vices George had hugged to himself with such unction. The "happy bachelor" was stripped of the finery George had wrapped him in, and shown to be a thing of shreds and patches.

"The married man," proceeded the journalist, "rises Phœnix-like from his bachelor self—bright and burnished. And looking into the tomb where the dead creature lies, he addresses it thus: 'While breath was in you I lived the life you bade me, caring nothing for the great moments of life, passing my days in a fairyland of toys and trinkets, never raising my eyes to the riches and realities of the splendid world. I regret nothing, however, for out of the child I was has grown the man I am. Pass away into the limbo where discarded relics and beliefs lie.' Lo and behold, the corpse crumbles into dust and is gone."

Steward waved his hand at George and Haines with a magician's pass. "Vanish, phantoms, you are disembodied spirits compared with our resurrected host. He has been down into the dark places of the earth to find his Proserpine, and he stands now in the light of a sun you cannot see. For, if he has lost the opportunity of bachelorhood, he has found himself!"

"A very good effort," said George irreverently, "but what's it all worth?"

"As much as yours," retorted Steward, following my example and moving away from the table to the armchairs, and as George wasn't prepared to put an immediate price on his own philosophy, the matter dropped. There we sat in a ring talking as only men bound by ties of intimate friendship can talk, while the Old Year died and the New Year was born, and hour after hour struck from the tower of the neighboring church. It was past three o'clock when Haines dragged us apart, and the final leave-taking began. We should meet again, but never as fancy-free. The shadow of "The Sex" would be over us. Haines, George, Steward—each in turn gripped my hand, and, as they struggled into their coats, gave expression to the affectionate regard they had for me. But I listened in distracted silence, as though their farewells came from a great distance, and from beings of a different creation—finding no words to fit the tragedy. Not till they had gone, and were falling noisily down the darkened stairs, did I wake to a realization of the parting. In that bitter moment I nearly ran after them, saying, "I am coming with you, don't leave me." But I controlled myself to clutch the mantelpiece in a despair that defied consolation.

Suddenly a thought struck me. I would make a bonfire of Vanities rivaling Savonarola's in Florence, so gathering from my drawers and shelves the miscellaneous spoils of years, I heaped them in the fender and set them alight. There were at least three hundred dance programmes, dating back to the Commemoration balls of my early manhood, three locks of hair of varying shades, collected out of bravado rather than devotion—all the same I felt a pang as they were consumed; several signed photographs, marking as many daydreams, one, I am ashamed to say, of a barmaid in the Lakes, the trophy of as wet a week as only Lakeland can show; a lady's shoe, minus a heel, its white satin surface lost beneath a coating of dust; a fat packet, tied up with a bootlace, of a correspondence that was only checked by parental intervention, and in pursuit of which I displayed more sincerity than ever I have shown since; and a vagrant mass of ribbons and bows, spangled hair ornaments and cotillon favors—in short, the complete arsenal of a man of sentiment.

As the funeral pyre of my romantic self blazed, I dived at random into the letters to catch a fleeting glimpse of that far-away idyll. But the reading left me cold. I could not recapture the fragrance of the rose leaves, and the passion of the writer struck no answering chord in me. In petulance I threw the bundle on the flames, whence, in a brief time, it vanished up the chimney. I never saw an *affaire du cœur* so easily and expeditiously disposed of.

Jealously was that conflagration guarded until not a relic of my bachelor self remained. I was resolved to keep that memory untouched by matrimony. Audrey has neither part nor parcel in the man I have been. The Future is hers, not the Past. That belongs to me alone.